Travels with Charlie: A Modern Search for America

Sol Smith

© 2014 by Sol R. Smith

All rights reserved. No part of this publication may be reproduced or transmitted in any form or by any means, electronic or mechanical, including photocopying, recording, or by any information storage and retrieval system, without permission in writing from Brave New Genre, Inc. or Sol R. Smith. Reviewers are welcome, of course, to quote brief passages.

Library of Congress Control Number: 2013953668

Smith, Sol R
Travels with Charlie/Sol R Smith
ISBN 978-0-9887737-3-8

1. Novel—Fiction 2. Memoir—Fiction
3. Travel—Fiction 4. America—Fiction
5. Texas—Fiction 6. Highways--Fiction
7. 21st Century America--Fiction

This is a work of fiction. Names, characters, places and incidents are either the product of the author's imagination or are used fictitiously. Any resemblance of any character to actual persons, living or dead, organizations or government or foreign government entities, or locales is entirely coincidental. The publisher does not assume any responsibility for author or third-party websites, their content or opinions expressed thereon.

TO THE REAL CHARLIE

Just three states to go!

Author's Note:

This is me, and it's not me. The lines are blurred. I thought that was a fun idea, blurring the lines. Traveling is amazing, it opens your eyes to the world. But it also opens your eyes to your eyes—you see the world as you see it and not as anyone else does. You are the center of your universe, until you travel. Then it unravels.

This is a tall-tale. This is hyperbole.

But it is also a love note. A love not to my wife and a love note to the country and culture that brought us together.

-Will Stronghold

Introduction

I saw an accident on the Interstate in New Mexico that changed everything.

I was 18, taking my turn at the wheel as my family drove from California to Texas for the millionth time. It was early; the sun had come up an hour or before and the desert of New Mexico was delicately lit around us. Looking ahead, driving around 85mph, I noticed that something on the road was dreadfully wrong, but I couldn't quite tell what. Before I had any idea what was happening, The car in front of me had slammed head-on into an oncoming car in a tremendous collision. We pulled over to see if there was anything we could do about it. And there wasn't. I narrowly avoided a killing my entire family.

My dad and I stood in the road for two hours and watched four people die, some slower than others, unable to do anything about it. When the medics arrived and we drove away, I had seen more gore than I had ever wanted to. The thought of driving made me sick to my stomach, and I swore off life on the road. Heading out the door and taking to the asphalt seas to go across the country was rolling the dice and I didn't want anything to do with it.

Then, of course, there was a girl. And that changed everything again. All kinds of previous certainties I held about life dissolved. She was quite certain that for our honeymoon, she wanted to drive cross country and find a new place to live.

"You act like it was my idea," Charlotte says as I type. "Like I just popped out of nowhere with this plan for your life—that you should drop what you were doing and chauffer me about the continent."

"It feels that way, sometimes," I tell her. "But you're right. We unfolded ideas together through whispers in the dark. Like a Ouija board, I feel like you were pulling and you, no doubt, feel like I was nudging them."

"Don't get all literary here. I'm just saying that to blame me for uprooting you from your contentment isn't really cool. People might read this."

"Hmm," I think as I type. "I don't know how much credit you should actually get for it. But the fact is, I *was* uprooted. That couldn't be undone."

"Just move it along," she waves at me like a stormtrooper who hasn't found the proper droids. "I'll try not to intrude on your writing time."

I was profoundly unemployed at the time we were engaged, which I found comforting. Here was a girl who didn't care that I hadn't had a job in the entire time that we had known each other. She didn't care that on our second date both my cards were declined and she had to pay. She didn't freak out when she came over to my apartment and saw that I had nowhere to sit in the living room but a broken lawn chair, that my bedroom was a walled-in balcony, or that I had to share a shower with three other people down the hall. All my money at the time, including the money for the ring, came from student loans. It was well that she didn't care, because years later, with a high-paying job, I have no more discretionary income than I did back then. And our couch is so lame, it may as well be a broken lawn chair.

Honestly, I don't know what she saw in me. I don't think that she knew either. I somehow slipped under her radar. I'm not sure that she knew how interested I was. She didn't evaluate our relationship, just went with the flow. For me, however, it was an absolute conquest from day one.

It's a story of love at first sight, but, honestly, it wasn't so romantic as all that. Unemployed as I was, I would hang out all summer with a friend of mine who was a teacher on summer vacation. We would rent crappy movies, get Chinese food, and hang out at coffee shops until her boyfriend was off of work, then the three of us would usually hit a bar for happy hour. We went to a Starbucks in downtown Fresno to visit a friend of hers who worked there. I gave a shallow protest to the endeavor, wanting to stay far away from corporate coffee. In the end, she promised that we would just stop in for a moment, say hi to her friend, and then move on to a more credible coffee shop, where the coffee wasn't as expensive or as good.

Charlie rolls her eyes here, "*You* wanted to stay away from corporate coffee? *You?*"

"Yes, I did. I wanted to go to Stanislaus Street Coffee."

"How many times have you been to Stanislaus Street?"

"It was going to be the first time."

"Don't act all alternative," she says. "Every single Starbucks barista in Fresno knew you. You were a regular at at least three different stores when I met you."

"I was turning over a new leaf," I tell her, as I type. "For real. I was done. Happenstance brought me in that day."

There Charlie was, working the register. When I saw her, a voice in my head said, "Well, shit. There she is. How in the world am I going to end up marrying this girl?" And my friend couldn't have been more surprised when I swaggered up and started ordering coffees and snacks. From that moment on, I was waking up early, getting to the Starbucks when it opened at 5, having coffee, reading books, and striking up the occasional conversation with the girl I knew I would marry.

There is a lot of excitement in those early stages of dating. It's easy to let these things slide into a graveyard for memories, but it is this graveyard that I rob for the sake of art. I can't explain what it's like to be a virile young man to the uninitiated, but a lot to do with meeting girls and being forced—by evolution—to picture their boobs.

"Oh, God," Charlie says.

Now, this doesn't happen with every set of boobs you meet, but most get at least a passing imaginary effigy made of them, even if mostly unintentional. The girls who you fall in love with, however, get the full on treatment. Those boobs are pictured in different lighting arrangements, in various stages of undress, different angles, and a contextual map of a diversity of reasons a girl gets undressed is thoroughly explored. If every young man were a wizard, the manifestation of boobs would be endless and welcome, the world over.

  I thought about Charlie a lot. Any time she wasn't at work and I wasn't visiting her, I was thinking of her. I pictured her face; I saw her smile; and her boobs were brought to visual glory through the cooperation of every possible neuron available. And when the time came that I actually saw the bra (which, at the time, didn't match the panties—a possibility I had never considered in all my coming of age!) come off, the rapture of imagination and reality met with glory and fanfare. I can't say that I pictured them accurately, but there was such a grand sense of destiny ringing through the night as my imagination died in the face of the real things. It is a moment blazed into my mind forever and that comes to life still every time the girl takes a bra off in front of me.

  "You are so romantic," Charlie says. "Undressing my boobs in the first chapter."

  "I can think of no better way to show, succinctly, the surprise and excitement of such a conquest being successful. I mean, it was just *so* exciting. Here I had seen them in my mind so often and then *boom*, there they were. Like meeting a cartoon character, or something."

  "Maybe it's cute," she says. "What's weird is how oblivious I was to the whole thing. Here you were picturing my nakedness and there I was just eating my cereal in the morning and making my bed and going to work. I had no idea you were interested. I just thought you were nice and that we had a good time. Next thing I knew, we were kissing."

"You didn't *hate* it, though."

"No, it was nice. It felt right, even if I wasn't looking for it. And even with all that kissing and with my boobs and everything, I was still so surprised when you wanted to get married."

Dude, Go For It!

I gave her the ring at Disneyland. To this day, it is the most expensive thing I have ever paid for in cash[1]. Every dime of it came from financial aid. It was a traditional surprise engagement made all the more surprising by the fact that it happened only 4 months after we met. She thought she was opening a present that I had bought for her at the park, but was tricked instead into a wedding proposal. I was just sure she was going to say, "I'll have to think about it." Who in their right mind would just accept such an offer, spur of the moment? One minute you're sitting there, minding your own business, then the person next to you says, "Hey, change your whole life and hang out with me every single day from now on." I really think that she should have taken some time. But she didn't; she went for it.

In all the world of consumerism, Disneyland is my favorite feature. Charlie had spent the day there holding out her hand, stretching her fingers, and gazing at the little ring. I was still shocked that she was cool with it. The first ride we went on after becoming betrothed was, of course, Pirates of the Caribbean. When we got to the front of the line, we requested—as we often do—to wait until we can sit in the back of a boat.

---

[1] My card had been declined and frozen. I got a phone call explaining that my card was stolen and that the thief was trying to buy jewelry with it. Maybe, in the modern age, instead of asking the father for permission to propose, you ought to ask your bank.

The drop is better in the back, and you don't get clouded by the inane words of the other passengers sneaking up to your ears from behind. The dude in the striped pirate costume waving people onto boats told us to step aside and then promptly sent another couple onto the back of the next boat. Charlie and I didn't try real hard to mask our childish outrage, and Stripy Pirate turned to us and said, "I'm giving you your own boat. Would you *rather* be in the back?" Our cups of gratefulness spilled over.

    We climbed into the next boat, sitting dead center in the 8 rows, and watched the little gates close behind us. The passengers craned their necks over the gates to see why the boat was leaving so emptily. A black guy wearing sunglasses in the artificial nighttime of the loading area looked at us and said, in all excitement, "Your own boat? Dude, *go for it!*" I gave him a thumbs-up and on we rolled. It was a strong affirmation to me — I was doing the right thing.

    I have since heard that the cast of Pirates enjoys putting predictably amorous couples in their own ride so they can watch the ensuing sex on the thermal cameras[2]. Had I but known that it was smiled at instead of frowned upon, I'd be telling you now about how awesome it is doing your brand-new fiancé surrounded by the skeletons of pirates. This was a once in a lifetime chance, after all, and instead of going for it, I blew it. It's so overwhelmingly disappointing that we didn't consummate the engagement there among the robots,

---

[2] I find this reasonably believable. The ride is exceptionally long and slow paced. The pirates working there can space the boats out as they like, giving the illusion of privacy to an enamored couple, as they did for us.

that I don't even have the heart to tell you about how awesome the kissing was³.

Over the next few weeks, Charlotte amassed a right collection of bridal magazines. Mostly, these magazines are filled with models sporting the most recent and expensive gowns. But, like any teenager with a playboy, Charlie pretended to read the articles and not just gawk at the pretty ladies. The articles were about wedding etiquette, decorating ideas, and budgeting. The budgeting articles were my favorite only because their cognitive dissonance was so transparent. They would tell you about how to save money on your wedding, and then tell you how much you save by cutting your guest list to 500, or how destination weddings can save money by only flying a group of 50 to Hawaii for your modest ceremony. The idea, I'm sure, was to make you think, "Gee, here I was going to invite only a hundred or so people and serve light snacks, but I'm being a real cheap wad. I need to save some face here and book Yo-Yo Ma to play at the wedding shower. I'll call a wedding planner and ask how we can siphon our income for the rest of our lives into the wedding industry."

Do you realize that the average wedding in this country costs just under $20,000? That is an amazing price to tell your friends and family that you promise that you love this person and will choose none other. Seems like a mass email would do the trick⁴. We're

---

³ If this is ever made into a movie, I'll have us do it in the script.
⁴ These were the days before Facebook and Twitter, mind you. While MySpace technically existed, we would be fooling ourselves to act like it was ever

talking about some amazing costs. Over $500 for a cake? $400 for a guy to play records? Not to mention the thousand dollars for a one-time use dress. This is a hell of an industry and even if you don't want to buy into it, you can't escape every aspect of it.

By far the best part of the bridal magazine is the advertisements. In particular, one advertisement. While the term "The Poconos" was familiar to my ears, I didn't really know where it was or, perhaps, what it was. But apparently somewhere in the Pocono Mountains there resides a resort that specializes in the honeymoon. They have perfected the marriage of romantic feelings with carnal pleasure through the invention of the exclusive 7-foot Champagne Glass Whirlpool Bath-for-Two. The image that just ran through your mind—as improbable as it was—is exactly what this full-page ad has pasted all over it. A couple sitting in a large champagne glass with bubbles swirling around them. Why it is at all desirable to sit in a champagne glass, I'm not sure. It's not like you can get out and admire the 7-foot height while you try to maintain an erection in a hot tub. Every time Charlie flipped through a new magazine, she would come to this ad and we would laugh. To this day I'm not sure who would dare such indulgence.

As time marched forward from Disneyland engagement day to planned wedding day 18 months later (a full four and a half times longer than we had known each other before getting engaged), I was

---

popular enough to house nuptials. But one does have to wonder: has the first Facebook wedding occurred?

introduced to the strangely constructed world of wedding planning. Charlie's parents, who refused to help her fill out a FAFSA when she wanted to go to college, busted out a pre-made folder of wedding do-dads and cost-calculations in order to get the show on the road. Credit cards were applied for and location scouting started. The efficiency and determination made me feel like I was in a Bronte novel. Either Bronte.

Charlotte and I moved to Monterey for my first teaching gig, part-timing at CSU Monterey Bay where Charlie started going to school. She was just beyond the age of the traditional student, having spent several years building a career at Starbucks. While we didn't meet there and in fact moved there together already engaged, it was a certain fancy of mine to consider the situation from different angles. She was sleeping with a professor, after all, and I was sleeping with a student. And everyone knew it. This is a sexy situation and forbidden in most instances of its occurrence throughout the country. We were insulated by the power of a ring and disclosure, but there was still something delightfully naughty about it[5].

Living in Monterey was amazing. It's built on a peninsula, has mild temperatures, and smells like the ocean constantly (in both good and bad ways). There was so much to do there compared to Fresno. One of the coolest things to do is whale watching. From time to

---

[5] We actually had to work pretty hard to get titillated by this. It was hard to think of me as a professor, for one, and for another, the idea of actually sleeping with a student is creepy at best. Still, efforts were put forth.

time, you get close enough to touch these mammoth creatures (even though you're supposed to stay 100 yards away). It's scary when you apply thought to it, but there really are no Moby Dickesque whale attacks, like one would assume. It's almost a shame, how safe it is, really. Living in Monterey was so amazing, that we just assumed we'd be there for the rest of our lives.

But Monterey, like most places on the California coast, ended up being too expensive for us. The California State University system was experiencing a hiring freeze on all full-time employment. Over two thirds of our pay was going towards our employee housing on the former Ft. Ord. They were fine digs, but an equivalent in rent almost anywhere else in the country would have scored us a three or four bedroom house. Credit cards and Charlie's financial aid filled in a lot of holes in our budget, but we just couldn't see staying there long-term. It just wasn't possible for us to live without amassing massive amounts of debt in a place as luxurious as Monterey[6].

The decision we came to led us to our little adventure in question. Many, many times since leaving Monterey, we have questioned the rationale. Couldn't I have found more work? Couldn't we have waited for the hiring freeze to end, which would probably have synced up with the proof that I was a master educator? In our four cities and six houses since that time in Monterey, we have wondered about the wisdom of

---

[6]Spoiler Alert—turns out it doesn't matter where we live or how much we make. We can rack up debt anywhere.

leaving such a place. On boring Sunday afternoons in Whereverweare, Whicheverstate, we dream about the times that we spent sitting on the rocks on the shore of the Pacific, eating homemade sandwiches and listening to the waves and the gulls.

We decided to leave Monterey. There was no future there, we decided, and we were probably right. We amassed more in debt many months than I made in pay. We begged for help from our parents every few weeks. We had to find a new place that we could stand, where we could make it on a professor's beginning salary. We had to move.

But where?

I had lived in Texas when I was younger, but Charlie was a born and bred Californian. We really didn't know enough about the rest of the country to just set out on our own and make a living somewhere. When we searched the internet for teaching jobs, we could never picture Tennessee, or Michigan, or Montana, and those were the kinds of places that were hiring. So Charlie, displaying a massive amount of enthusiasm, walked home from class one day in the rain with a bright idea.

"We'll sell everything, buy a car, and our honeymoon can be searching for a place to live across the country."

A Return to Chastity

Summer vacation came along before the wedding did. We had about 5 weeks between leaving Monterey and making public vows. We would each live with our own parents and actively date. It was such a delightful little idea. We had lived in sin for a year and had grown accustomed to each other in such a way that we wanted to make the wedding night a bit more special. We would renew our own virginities in the weeks leading up to the wedding. Really, how brilliant is that?

Only it didn't work out to be very brilliant. For one, a bride's days leading to the wedding become stressful and horrid. For the groom, there isn't a lot to worry about once the tux has been rented. More nights than we could have guessed, Charlie would have a hard day and invite me over to stay the night—no sex allowed. Subsequently, we discovered the pleasures of grown adults having forbidden sex in their parents' house. We weren't naughty teenagers—we were both sort of square—but now we had a chance to act the part.

We spent our days getting ready for the honeymoon. We had been borrowing a car from my parents for the time that we were living in Monterey. The car was my mom's old Accord, with a license plate that paid tribute to the Rolling Stones. Only, since it was shortened quite a bit, consonants pushing vowels away to allow space for the palm tree design, everyone thought that we were big fans of the author R.L. Stine. While I don't have anything against the guy, it was a pain in the ass to get out of the car at Target and have the guy next to us say, "You like Goosebumps, do ya?" all the time.

My grandma supplied us with a generous wedding gift. She wanted us to start off on the right foot, so she gave us $5,000 towards the purchase of a new car. Only thing is, we didn't have any little kitty to add that money to, so that money alone would have to cover the entire ride.

The car we picked was a white 2001 Honda CRV. It had been in a head-on collision and looked like it. The front was all mashed, exposing the engine. The driver's side door was torn to bits and the airbag hung limply out of the steering wheel. The passenger door was missing entirely and all four tires were flat. Whoever had been riding in the car was either dead or a lucky son of a bitch. Our mechanic, who bought the car at auction especially for us, assured us that fixing cars that were in head-ons was much easier than it looked. It was impossible, he told us, to fix cars that had been hit in the front from the side because alignment would forever be an unrealized dream of the vehicle. We bought the car in February and paid many visits to our mechanic in the interim to see how things were going.

It was always the same. The car was sitting at the body shop in terrible shape without a single modification. I would call him on the phone and he would tell me how great things were going. Almost all the parts were collected that needed to be replaced (mostly from other junkers) and it would always sound almost ready. Then we'd make the drive to Fresno to deal with some wedding issue or another, pay the car a visit, and see the same old wreck in the same old condition sitting in the rain. It looked the same in February as it did in May, just weeks before the wedding. Now, towards the end of things, it seemed like the car would never be finished in time for our trip.

The CR-V had plenty of room for all of our worldly possessions, if it was ever fixed. The only thing we'd leave behind would be Blitzen, our white German Sheppard. He would stay at my parent's house for the duration of the trip and patiently await collection before we moved to wherever we were moving to. Everything else would be liquidated or, in the case of a few items, kept in my parents' garage. The wedding gifts would be kept in Charlie's parents' house.

Our plan was pretty loose. We had a goal in mind, Plainfield, Vermont by July 8th, in time for my graduation from graduate school. On the way there, we would drive through the south, visiting states that we thought had jobs to offer and a cheap cost of living and rumors of good food. On the way home, we would go through the north, looking at the states that interested us up there, though our expectations of food were a might lower. We would keep the costs low by spending an ample amount of camping and spending time with friends and relatives who were willing to put up with us. It would be a six week trip, altogether, and something that neither of us had ever done. But first, the car had to be fixed. And before that, we had to get married.

Men and women tend to have different cultural expectations of weddings. These expectations are based on the biological tendencies for independence in males and inclusion in females. They are perpetuated through the media in the form of old TV shows, commercials, and peers.

For men, a wedding is supposed to be some kind of an ending; an ending of the carefree bachelor lifestyle. Men have years to understand themselves, discover themselves, and sow their wild oats. Men are supposed to enjoy the life of predatory sex and excitement, constantly jockeying for position within their social class to be an alpha male. For men to be a man, only the affirmations of the peers will make it so. There are no big physical changes that make it obvious that manhood has been achieved. For a woman, there's this whole thing with, you know, freshness, and cycles, and breezes and shit[7]. But a guy sees his mirror in his peers. Prowess and power make him a man. Giving up the easy lifestyle of free love isn't exactly the most hardcore thing a guy can do.

For women, a wedding is a beginning. They've spent their lives readying themselves for this commitment. They've seen the effects of gentle winds and moon cycles and the ebb and flow of the tide and

---

[7] And riding horses on the beach while wearing tennis skirts and all that.

they know they're a woman. The pleasures of womanhood include the affirmation of a man, the public respect of a man dedicating his life to hers. This inclusion verifies their worthiness and opens the curtains on a life being built by a loving couple.

Of course, they're both wrong.

It's not an ending of anything. The ending of the bachelor life happens that first moment when the guy realizes that his male friends don't have everything he needs. It happens when he realizes that there's nothing exciting about personal accomplishments without someone to whisper them to. It happens when he moves off to college and just can't see debasing himself for bragging rights. He works hard on his subjects, music and writing, perhaps, but finds little fulfillment in them by themselves. Even this, he realizes, is empty without someone to share it with. It happens when the guy wants someone to talk to, to speak of dreams, to be with. This happens years before he meets the right girl. The end has started years before he ever saw it coming.

It's not a beginning, either. It starts when the girl first steps away from her family to pursue her own dreams. She wants to ride horses, but her family thinks it's a waste of time or money. It happens when she gets that job at Starbucks to support herself. She runs out of time for the horses, filled with new responsibilities. She gets a promotion, makes a little more money and gets that first apartment. That apartment opens doors to the possibility of settlement, of building on things, constructing a life. The direction her life is going leads naturally to a husband, long before the right guy has been met.

So what is a wedding, if not a beginning and not an ending?

It's a recognition. It's a moment where you pause to reflect. You notice that things aren't the same as they used to be, that they're heading in a new direction. You notice that these two rely on each other as much as they rely on themselves and they rely on others less and less. They want to change their worlds, move things into place for their own lives, build on things. To make it anything other than that is to not respect the power that it represents. To make it a start is to not respect all that has come. To make it an ending is to not respect the vast changes and constructions to come.

It was those last few days, though, when the pressure cooker started heating up. Our pastor, a lady who married Charlie's parents, decided that she couldn't read the poem that we picked out for our ceremony. She couldn't read it because she "couldn't make it sound right." We didn't believe her. We felt it was for religious reasons. It wasn't a religious poem. It was Chinese, as a matter of fact, and gave a nice depiction of the Tao and how this marriage was in accordance of it. This, we think, offended her god to some extent.

The next day she contacted us and told us that she couldn't do the wedding because she had "this eye thing." Apparently this eye infection of hers made her participation impossible. This is about one week before the wedding, mind you. But not to worry! She had a sister named Patty (hurray for Patty) who could probably do it.

We met Patty at a Chubby's Diner in town. One of those 50's throwbacks, offering modern food at modern prices but with the names changed to match musicians and actors who were big in the 50's. She was sitting at the round booth in the corner and we helped ourselves to seats kind of sort of next to her. Patty looked exactly like her sister. Exactly. Had I not known better—and maybe I didn't—I would have thought she was the other pastor exactly, but in slight disguise. Like she grows out her ample witch hair a little longer so that she can properly read unreligious poems at weddings, or something. As if the reading of unreligious poetry is a form of super power that requires a disguise in the form of longer witch hair and a slightly slimmer figure.

It truly escapes me if we ordered anything to eat or not. Surely we had drinks, but I'm not certain if we ate. Patty, however, ate. She ordered wet fries. If you are like me, of my generation or disposition, a shadowy question mark just appeared above your head. You ask me what wet fries are? I will tell you. Do not go to Chubby's and order your own, no! That would be a mistake. I'll tell you already. Wet fries are French fries covered in brown gravy. Read that last part slowly, like *brooowwwwn graaaavyyyy* to get the full effect, like a record suddenly slowing down to accidentally emphasize the perfect passage in a sentence. Or like The Big Bopper has decided to tell you what they are, and he throws in his own personal touch *pro bono*. "Wet fries are French fries covered in *brrroowwwwn graaaavyyyyy*." Like that.

Patty agreed to marry us. Though her life, as it turned out, was in complication as well. She was divorced and moving and living with friends at the time before moving somewhere else on a more permanent level. Why this was our business was not, at first, clear to me. But as a muddy pond sits still and becomes clear, so would this situation; her predicament would eventually relate very directly to my own position in the universe. But I wouldn't know it until we were in Gallup, New Mexico some weeks later.

With the pastor issue fixed, we moved on with our lives. We had a pastor, a DJ (a friend of Charlie's former step-dad), and the food picked. The dress was going to be delivered a couple days before the wedding and reservations were made at the Piccadilly Hotel for all out of town guests. Things were just swimming along through their own momentum in my mind.

Not in poor Charlotte's.

While I was chilling out by the pool, relentlessly welcoming out of town guests, Charlie was dealing with headache after headache. A couple nights before the wedding, I decided to go out with a friend of mine, just the two of us, to a bar in the Tower District to talk about things past and future and generally have a reflective time. At that same moment, Charlie was getting her hair done by a friend of hers with the intent of the style being what she would wear for the wedding. It was a bit exciting, I suppose, a bit extreme of a style, but nothing out of line. She had it done and excitedly drove to her dad and step-mom's house. She opened the door and saw the smile on her step-mom's face turn to an obvious look of concern while moving a camera away from her eyes and into a camera bag. "No," her step-mom said.

And poor Charlotte was crushed. *Crushed.*

Before

The night before the wedding, Charlotte and I had a long planned last date as an unmarried couple. We wanted it to be us and only us, and we wanted to just have a low-key chill-out kind of night. We ate at a Mexican food place called Toledo's that we had liked plenty. But on this occasion and this occasion only, everything was bad. The food was bad, our table was bad, and our service would've been better if the waiter had actively tried to shoot us. The people next to us—a youngish married couple with three kids — were fidgety and stressful to be around. They brought two or three bags worth of toys, activity books, and videogames to distract their kids so that they could eat their chalupas without impediment. We bragged about it being the day before our wedding and they looked at us with a consoling sort of regret. "Ahh, yeah, being married is great," the husband said. "But wait to have kids, okay?"

"Wait!" the wife chimed in. "There's plenty of time, don't be in a rush!"

They sickened me a good deal because their kids were right there and I wasn't about to take any advice thrown around by two people who were such unaccomplished parents. It would be like if, after trying to run a mile and failing, as I was likely to do, I turned to someone else and said, "Don't try and run a marathon. You suck at it and it will make your life terrible." I see no reason to saddle others with my ineptitude the way they did to us. I hope that as we speak one of their kids has just won a pony in a school carnival, forcing the parents to make sweeping changes in their lives to accommodate this picky pony of theirs.

I think that after the dinner we consoled ourselves with ice cream or TCBY or something.

"I can't remember if that happened or not," Charlie says, reading the draft. "Besides, no one knows what TCBY is anymore. This book is dating itself."

It rings a bell, but I don't have pictures developed of us delighting in fudge-covered scoops with the date "6-7-03" printed down in the corner or anything like that. But that might have been the case either way. And yeah, that dates the book. Or the events in the book, at any rate. But that's how this kind of book works, right? It takes place in time.

"That's fine," Charlie says. "It's just, I can't stand it when a movie feels dated."

"What if it's a period piece?"

Charlie rolls her eyes. "This book is not a period piece. But I get , okay? We had TCBY or we didn't. That's where we were. Carry on."

After whatever amusement there was, I drove Charlie back to her parent's house. It was on the way there that she broke down.

If you've ever seen a canyon carved by a river, you understand in a very visceral way the effect erosion can have in this world. With enough patience and persistence, a trinkly little creek can wash a mountain to

25

the ocean. Such was the power of stress in Charlie's life. It was the night before the wedding and Charlie had suddenly become a cavity of human emotion. If she had torn her own skin off and stood there all muscle and skeleton, I would have been no more disturbed than to see her as I did. Just to think she was perched just hours before a day of such delightful magnitude—the day girls dress up for before they even know what it's all about—and she had to crumble into debris such as she did.

She had an existential crisis, is what happened. All of this fuss, all of this noise, all of it about her, but somehow she was forgotten in it all. "No one," she sobbed, "has even asked me how I *feel*."

"Okay," I offered. "How do you feel?"

"That's not the point!"

Charlotte is a woman of the strongest constitution. She has eyes of steel and, aside from sinking Jack in *Titanic,* had never been moved to tears by anything I had ever seen. Quite probably, this was the first time I had ever seen her cry. And it might be the last time I saw her cry while unpregnant[8].

I did what I could. I spoke to her calmly and rationally. Then I changed game plans. She was showing me this unreal side of vulnerability. I started telling her about how I felt about her. I told her about the first time I walked into that Starbucks and saw her working there, how I had known without a doubt that we would be married. About how I wasn't giddy or frightened, but

---

[8] It was one of the last times—in the grand scheme of things—that she *was* unpregnant.

calm about it. I told her about how I had pictured her later that night, naked. Her small boobs looking up at me in my mind, her shy face turned away. Here I walked the line between perverse and humorous. This is a fine line to walk when your fiancé is crying the night before your wedding. But I took to it and pressed it on a bit. Once it looked like she wasn't going to laugh or jump me, I returned to a more serious note.

We were parked in the most ridiculous spot in all of Fresno. It was a parking lot outside of what used to be a Hollywood Video. We were facing a busy street and our car was illuminated by the orange fog-penetrating lights of the parking lot. I saw her face lit by this light, streaming with tears, eyes wide and hopeful. My hands were wrapped up in hers; a tangle of fingers on her thigh.

I told her about how relieved I was when I learned that she wasn't dating anyone. I told her about how I had just logically figured I would have to steal her away from some poor shithead. I told her about the way she looked when she smiled, sweeping the floors of the coffee shop and how I marveled at how happy she was. I told her about the night when we first kissed. We had been sitting on the back patio of her little apartment under a string of little Christmas lights. She was going inside and I was expected to walk myself home. She stood at her door and announced that she was going to unplug the lights. "Don't be scared," she said. The instant it was dark, her lips pressed against mine, then parted. I was not scared, I told her. I told her about how

I ran home, whooping and hollering at four in the morning, amazed that I had done it. I can still taste that kiss, even now, and feel it.

She softened, at some point. We kissed and kissed some more. She acquiesced to going home, getting rest, and getting a move on the next day. She pressed me to come in to her house, but I didn't. We needed to both go home and get rest. I didn't want to accidentally see her dress. I didn't want to sleep with her the night before the wedding and wake up, sneaking down the hall as the sun rose over the mountains, and run into her dad who—certainly—had no idea that his daughter had ever been with a man after 10:30pm before. I kissed her goodnight for the last time as separate entities.

I got home to find my parents sitting out on the patio talking to their old friends from Texas. I went to my dad's 200-disc CD changer and shuffled it around until I found the "My Fair Lady" soundtrack. I found the song I was looking for and came out onto the patio while a cockney drunk sang, "I'm getting married in the morning" on the outdoor speakers. They marveled, believing the song to have been selected at random by an omniscient shuffle program. I let them go on believing it for a while, just for the fuck of it.

The next morning, my brother, our friend Justus, and I headed up into the Sierras again to a bed and breakfast where Charlie and I would spend the first two nights of our marriage. We wanted to check-in since it would be so late before we got there and to drop off our bags, some food, and that pointless bottle of wine, which my brother had to show me how to open. It was a lavish little place and I had reserved the cottage—a standalone room with a hot tub, double shower, and lots of space for tomfoolery. Charlie dropped off her bag earlier that day while I hid in the back of the house to avoid bad luck or karma or something.

On the way up the hill, we stopped at a McDonald's for breakfast, it was made all the more regrettable by the addition of a new breakfast item—the McGriddle. A sausage, egg, and cheese sandwich with a pancake bun complete with little pockets of baked-in syrup. I steered clear, knowing that I didn't want it coming up on me on the dance floor. Justus, however, bravely indulged for posterity's sake[9].

The rest of the day was one of those dreadful waiting days. You figure what time you have to be there, what time you have to leave, and then you start endlessly thinking, "Hmm, should I start getting ready now? What about in 30 minutes?" over and over and over again. It's a total nightmare. The house was hot, the leftovers were cold, and I just wanted the anxiety to subside.

I arrived at the venue in full dress, along with the gentlemen who would serve as my groomsmen. My brother, a dauntingly tall fellow, was excited when I told

---

[9]To my amazement, these many years later, the McGriddle is a constant in the McD's pantheon.

him that the original role of the groomsmen was to protect the couple long enough for them to marry. This was back in the day when weddings by capture were the number one way to get hitched. You'd steal a girl that struck your fancy, perform a heavily armed wedding, and then escape with her for one moon cycle—long enough, hopefully, to render a baby. All the while, you'd enjoy mead, an alcoholic drink made of honey. Hence, the "honey-moon." My brother hoped in vain that he and the other gentlemen would face the challenge of protecting us and Justus spoke up to volunteer to drive up to the cottage and wait outside the door to serve the role of holding up the bloodied sheets to prove consummation. Both were disappointed.

Sealed

Fresno, California averages 35 days a year over 100 degrees. That will surprise anyone who lives in Fresno, as by the end of August, no one can remember the last tolerable day. Many Julys in Fresno house 31 days over 90 and every few years, July scores 31 days over 100. Fresno also has an average of over 300 days of sunshine a year. Sometimes, in the middle of July, if you look up into the sky and see a whisp of cloud floating along, you wonder what's wrong. In the dead of summer, the world looks over exposed and washed out. Sunglasses aren't an option but a requirement. To say that summers in Fresno are bright and hot is a rather plain way of not lying.

  Why anyone would have the idea to have an outdoor wedding in Fresno during the summer is beyond me. When I found out that our wedding was planned for early June, it was January. A few days later, I learned that my fiancé and her step-mom were talking about the June on the following year. I'm not sure why I didn't speak up. I'm not sure, looking back now, how none of us were aware of how rude it would be to invite a hundred people to sit in the sunlight on a hot day while my fiancé and I promised things to each other in formal attire. And while I didn't hear anyone complain about the weather, it was probably because it was so obviously intolerable at 110 degrees. With all the details that demanded attention, I'm not sure why weather didn't factor more into the decision.

Despite the heat, the wedding was exactly what it was supposed to be. I won't go strongly into the details, the white dress or the families in attendance, or the particulars of the vows, or the texture of the cake. But it was all quite well and additionally legal, so we ended up officially married.

During the reception, a boat offered free rides around the lake. As the sun set and right after the first dance (Paul McCartney's "Let me Roll It"), Charlie and I snuck off to have a private trip around the lake. By the time we were half way through the ride, darkness was nearly total. The heat in Fresno, being perfectly dry, subsides totally when the sun goes down. A cool evening breeze swept across the lake, and my bride and I held each other enrapt by the beauty of a moment away from the wedding party and finally very nearly alone. The logical next step—doing it savagely out on the barge—was avoided only because the young lad driving the boat would not shut up for a second about all the kinds of fish one can catch. Had he just shut up and had the class to stand on the other end of the boat, you'd be considerably more titillated than you are now. And he'd have had a story to tell in his own damn book.

When things started to wind down, Charlotte and I went to the dressing room and changed into civilian clothing.

"God, and we didn't even do it then, either," Charlie says.

"No, the bridesmaids were running around in there."

"Not a single person had the decency to let us have sex wherever we wanted. We should get a do-over."

Once we were out of our constrictive clothing and into more civil apparel, the length and intensity of the day hit us. We were tired. Absolutely whipped. We said our goodbyes and rushed off to start our lives together, this time legitimately.

We drove off and stopped at a gas station to get some drinks for our drive up the hill. The cashier was a girl of about our age and she was on the phone. She covered the mouth-piece and said to us, her only customers, "Do you mind if I cuss?" We told her to be our guest and she tore into the poor dude on the other end of the phone. "Now listen here, you shit-face-motherfucker, I'll fuck your shit up!"

Indeed, the magical spell of the wedding was broken. Without our fancy clothes we were just a married couple not above hearing such vulgarity.

Jesus Shit

Our cottage was just up the hill from Oakhurst, about half way to Yosemite from Fresno. It was just past the foothills and just into the honest timber. There's a point in the Sierras where one stops smelling the dried brush of the foothills and starts to smell the pines through the thinner air. It's a wonderful moment where you just feel free and cleaned, somehow.

We passed the Bed and Breakfast first, then turned around and made the proper turn down the long gravel drive and around the main building to the cottage out behind. We got in, all chipper and refreshed.

The hot tub called to us terribly. It wasn't 7-feet tall, it wasn't nearly champagne glass-shaped, but it was a whirlpool-bath-for-two. And it was surrounded by mirrors, which is fun. We had to fill it and, of course, break our first rule of the hotel and adorn it with candles. When I checked in earlier, one of the co-owners was cleaning the room. She told me that candles were not allowed and I said, "What about just these candles?" and I held up an armful of them.

I think she was just trying to be non-confrontational and she said, "Oh, well, I guess if you just light them." I told her that was what I was planning to do with them in the first place. "Well," she said, "our problem is just candle wax, really. Don't get candle wax around." She motioned towards the bed and I thought her a bit fruity. It didn't occur to me until just now that she might have expected us to be doing something deviate and delectable with candle wax on skin or something. Hmm.

We lit the candles and started filling the bath. I stood in the middle of the tub, all naked, and started perusing the control buttons for no real reason. Charlie was doing something or other in the bathroom proper when it happened. My hand hovered over a button— *hovered*, I tell you—and the jets turned on. They sounded like machine gun fire, bursting round after round from every direction. Only the water wasn't high enough to stop the firing jets from hitting *me* from every direction and from my skin, bouncing off like light through a prism all around the room. The candle lights went out instantly and I caught a view of candle wax splashing on the mirrors just before all went reasonably dark.

"Oh Jesus Shit," I yelled, thinking I had communicated to Charlie to bring towels.

"What?" yelled a naked bride, coming into the room. "Turn it off, for God's sake!"

"I can't figure it out!" My hands fumbled over the buttons, pressing mightily. The water continued its heavy handing pummeling and Charlie ran off to find towels.

Finally I achieved a delicate enough touch to turn it off. Turns out the button was made for a hovering hand for whatever fancy reason and not an actual push. Charlie used up every towel in the room trying to mop up the water. "Well," she said in a tone just short of grumpy. "I don't know if we should still get in. We don't have any towels." I wouldn't hear of it and I insisted on bathing.

Nothing particularly sexy happened in the bath, which was somewhat of a surprise to me. I long had a dream of mixing bathing with doing Charlie. She didn't really see the point and my insistence that there was no point was not good enough to warrant the extra detail of any shower or bath. There was no wine because I had forgotten to get it out of the fridge and I didn't remember my brother's instructions on how to open it anyway.

Tired, exhausted, wiped out, we headed for bed. We drip dried and used a single unsullied hand towel to dry ourselves. We were happy and drained, barley able to keep our eyes opened as we went to bed. We were almost too tired to have sex. Almost. We had to, and of course that's always worthwhile, but it wasn't exactly notable, after all the buildup. It wasn't bad, or anything, just mandatory. It had to be done and done before we fell asleep atop one another. And I'm telling you, that was one of the most emotionally intense days I've ever had, and one of the longest, too. But what had to be done had to be done, and my new wife had to be done.

To the detriment of our honor, Justus wasn't around to display the sheets afterward.

"That's vulgar," Charlie says, looking up from the manuscript. "You should take that out. It's not even funny. Just disgusting." She looks at it again. "Plus, you're making me into some kind of a prude. Like I'm the editor sitting over your shoulder, criticizing what you're writing and that somehow having it in there absolves you of writing the very thing you felt guilty about writing.

"Plus, this is really meta."

I Vow not to Kill my Wife

Our grand plan was to stay in the room for the entire two days. The reasoning was because: a) we wanted to enjoy each other's company without any outside influence; and b) we had spent a shit-load of money on the room and didn't want to waste another dime. But now our room was a mess that needed to be cleaned, professionally. Having scraped all the candle wax we could off, we still needed new towels and a mop. Also, cooking breakfast for ourselves sucks and we had already heartily slept through the complimentary one.

We drove into Oakhurst looking for a place to eat and came across a little diner that looked something like a broken down Denny's. It was on the main road and had pictures of fried eggs on the windows, so there was a winner.

We sat in a booth near a window and quickly discovered the lax care that had been given to one side of the booth as opposed to the other. No matter! My chivalrous instincts told me to sit in the shitty seat and an exchange was negotiated. I ordered biscuits and gravy and Charlie had poached eggs on toast. The food was tolerable. For as long as I could remember, I had a vision of the most perfect biscuits and gravy in the world. It was an idealistic vision, based more on fantasy than experience. These, alas, did not quite measure up.

Another thing that didn't measure up was the service. If the waitress had cussed her boyfriend out on the phone while taking our order, I would have at least been happy about the symmetry of the experience. A theme would have been established for Will and Charlie, the married couple. For the second time in just a few days, the possibility of not tipping was touched on. Could we do that? Was that really an option? What were the ramifications of acting like a happily satisfied customer and then, in essence, spitting in the waitress' face? Well, maybe just stepping on her toe.

We hadn't yet wasted enough time. We needed that room clean, like real clean. And we couldn't even be sure if it had been touched yet. So after breakfast, we headed up towards Yosemite and turned off to visit the Sugar Pine Railroad.

The Sugar Pine was a logging railroad used from the start of the 20th Century until the dawn of the Depression. They had massive wood burning locomotives that would haul lumber by the ton from cutting points to processing mills. Now the Sugar Pine is restored to its former glory and hauls passengers by the ton on a four mile trip through the wilderness. The Shay locomotives take things at a slow pace, especially up hills, and the whole experience lasts about an hour and a half or so. Half way through, passengers stop to look around a little wooded area and take pictures of and that kind of thing.

We got to the railroad just moments after the train left. We actually saw the behemoth spewing out steam and escaping the station. The thought crossed my mind to run and jump aboard and ride the rail like a true hobo. And it would have been cheaper, too. At $17 a person. But time had to be wasted, and usually when time gets wasted, so does money. We bought tickets and ambled about the station looking at postcards and trinkets.

On the train ride proper, Charlotte and I could not keep our eyes off of our hands. Next to Charlie's engagement ring, an old friend to her now, was a new little band with sparkly tiny diamonds peeking through. And on my hand was a white gold band with some kind of hammered texturing. We both wore white gold, finding it somewhat less gaudy than the yellow variety. Early in our dating relationship Charlie had made some off-handed remark about how she doesn't wear yellow gold. She may have even hinted that she wanted a white gold engagement ring—I wouldn't put it beyond her, such was her infatuation with this handsome young man. I chuckled a bit, I remember, and pointed out that I would never be able to afford such luxurious items as white gold.

I think that I was thinking about black pearls, to be honest. I don't rightly know if I had ever heard "white gold" spoken before and I figured it must have been the more expensive variety for certain. Basically, any time a concept is new to me, I consider it beyond my reach.

"Thank god for student loans, huh?" My wife says, completing the above passage. Yes, indeed; thank God for student loans.

Just in case the other passengers didn't notice us admiring our new hand decorations, we kept remarking about how strange our condition was. Today was our first day to be married. Yesterday we weren't and then we were, and now we are. It was assumed to be a continuous condition from now on and it was already here. How lovely and exciting. It seemed only fair that innocent bystanders should take note; really it was the least they could do.

When we weren't rapt with amazement at our own beautiful adornments and our own unique disposition, we took in the splendor of the trees around us. The smell of the Sierras, to me, is unmatched by any other place I've been in the outdoors. There is a unique scent to it, a mix of the trees, brush and soil that just says "you're not on the valley floor anymore, aren't you grateful?" The pines surrounding the Sugar Pine are interspersed with my favorite variety of tree available, the redwood. Prominent among the trees in the area, rather obviously, is also the sugar pine. The sugar pine is a gracefully tall tree with pine cones shaped, more or less, like arrow heads pointing down. There is a Native American creation myth in which a god drops a sugar pine cone from a tree and the seeds plant to become the first man. This is a happy myth to me. I like the idea of being made out of a dropped pinecone somewhat more than I like the idea of being made out of mud and spit, as other creation myths would have you believe.

Our train stopped at the half-way point and we got out to amble around with all the German tourists. We offered to take a picture for a lame group of people trying their luck at setting their camera on a table and running over to join the group before the timer went off. We took their picture, and then gave them our camera to take ours. We bragged off-handedly that we had just been married the day before. They responded with an "oh!" much like you'd respond to a child who said that their birthday was in three and a half weeks. We got it. We were being overly excited. Too bad for them.

We returned to our hotel room, several dollars the poorer, had sex and a nap, in that order.

When we woke up, I quickly realized that having dinner in the hotel room was out of the question. We needed waiting and service and food cooked to order. We needed fuss.

Dinner that evening was at a place near Bass Lake that we always wanted to try. I had prime rib, which is generally something I don't have due to cost and extravagance. Refusing to let cost prohibit me (it was about as much as that train ticket, after all) and in the hearty mood for extravagance, I indulged merrily. Our view of the lake was sullied only by the people sitting near our table. The worst thing that can happen to a casual diner is to be sat near a microphone.

For years my family had called those people in restaurants and other public places who wouldn't shut up "microphones". Often, especially in places like Houston, they are more aptly called blow-hards. But the microphone distinction implies a few things about your annoying neighbor:

1) They know everything. If they run into a situation or topic where they don't know everything, they will within an instant convince themselves that they have learned everything about it out of pure necessity.

2) They are loud. Like supernaturally so. Their voice has a mysterious quality that lets the air carry it better than other voices or sounds are carried. They don't even have to raise their voice to be heard across a street or across a dining room.

3) They dominate the conversation. It goes without saying that their friends listen to every word they say and have given up on ever adding to a conversation. But furthermore, they dominate *your* conversation. You didn't invite them to your table, you didn't take them on your camping trip, you didn't pay their ticket to the top of the Eiffel Tower, yet you and your actual friends cannot carry on your own conversation because you're so wrapped up in theirs. The fucks.

4) Despite all of the above (especially despite number one), they are ignorant. They know nothing, in actuality, about anything. Or they know only the common facts that even your demented,though generous, grandmother knows but they present their knowledge as somehow special, unique and exciting.

There is not much worse than getting sat near a microphone in a fancy restaurant[10]. They lecture their friends on the wine selection, then branch off into the subject of vineyards they have visited. It just so happens that they visited the very best one on the best possible day and no one knew it would be the best day because the weather man predicted rain, but those clouds burnedn off by 11 and left a slight ocean breeze that made the day pleasant and wonderful and the best wine experts ventured out into the field to see if there was anyone worth imparting knowledge to and it just so happened he was there and the expert knew, just by looking at him, that this was the man to tell the secret to their vintage to and he happens to know exactly which bottle to buy and it's not the most expensive, no, that's a sham, but it's the second or third most expensive, that's right, this one right here, that's the one made of grapes that he himself picked and expertly ground and his form and mastery were just the envy of the day out there in

---

[10]This is, however, the most common way to experience a microphone in the wild.

the wine country. Fuck! I didn't marry this guy! I didn't want to hear him or talk to him!

I asked the waiter over and whispered in his ear. I asked if it was possible for my prime rib to be taken from this man, this microphone. If he could slip under the table with a carving knife, lop off an ample cut of beef, prepare it medium-rare and let me dine upon it in full view of the microphone himself. Then, upon completing my dinner, when the man finally notices that a considerable hunk of his midsection is missing, I will laugh a satisfied yet understated laugh behind my napkin, never letting him in on the secret.

"No, sir," the waiter said. "We use only grade-A beef." I wanted to not tip him, but he had a point.

We stopped for ice cream in Oakhurst and then buckled down for an evening of chillaxing. I had a book to read, *Fierce Invalids Home from Hot Climates* by Tom Robbins. Charlie had read it with great enthusiasm a few weeks earlier and I started it in the sitting area of our wedding cottage. I didn't get very far, though, because for whatever reason, the TV came on and there was a special investigative report. It was about the Laci Peterson tragedy.

At this point in history, it wasn't known, like for certain, that Scott Peterson had killed his pregnant wife. But John Q. Public had it figured out and the entertainment media was presuming him guilty for sure. Like many, if not most Americans, we couldn't take our eyes off of the train wreck that this news story was. We watched and discussed the program for its entire two hour length.

For whatever reason, the news media usually catches on to one type of a story or another for a year or so at a time. I think they are usually surprised by how a story of, say, a kidnapping takes off and sells papers, ad time, whatever. So once that kidnapping gets old, or God help us, solved, they find another kidnapping to go on. For a year or so, everyone will be up in arms about how blond toddlers are being kidnapped without knowing that the media has just picked the blond toddler story because it proved so successful in the first instance. At any point, there are over 100,000 actively missing people in the country, so they can easily fill the shoes of an old story with a formulaically identical one, like a Hollywood producer. They ignore the other ones because there are more missing persons out there than there are reporters. Thus there appears to be just enough news to fill a newspaper every day.

That year, the Laci Peterson year, killing your pregnant spouse became the big story. When details about the Peterson story fizzled, they'd find a guy who stabbed his wife in Nevada or a fellow who drowned his wife in New Jersey to try and keep up with their expected ad revenue. This prompted, some many months later, a strange conversation between Charlie and her grandmother that I just happened to witness.

We were sitting in a restaurant with Charlie's grandmother while on a visit back to California. We had moved away that year and I had recently impregnated

Charlie with my very own offspring, like some sort of invading alien race[11]. We sat on one side of the table with Grandma Pauline on the other. Charlie was happily pregnant, eating a hearty breakfast, her very favorite thing when pregnant with our first daughter. The Peterson case had recently had a break-through so it was in the news again. Charlie talked about how happy she was to be having this baby and Grandma Pauline shot a dose of reality across her bow that she just couldn't believe.

"Watch out. William, here, could kill you."

"Grandma," said my wife. "Will is not going to kill me."

"You never know. You're pregnant and even he can't be sure."

"I'm sure, Grandma Pauline. I wouldn't kill my wife and unborn child. I promise," I interjected.

"I'm just saying. You never can tell."

I don't think that it fazed Charlie much, except to point out the obvious deficiencies in her grandmother's condition. After all, if she really thought I was going to kill her, wouldn't she have waited until I was in the bathroom to bring it up? And for the record, to this day, I haven't killed her. I've never even wanted to for very long.

---

[11] This is something I'm totally capable of doing. I'm really amazing.

The Increasing Emptiness

The car continued to present an issue. We had a fanciful notion that we would drive away from our wedding in our newly rebuilt car. Instead, there was one delay after another. There was this delay, that delay, the door didn't get shipped from the factory on time, the body shop used the wrong radiator, the alignment wasn't right, the CHP regulations weren't met, and on and on. We were getting really frustrated.

We tried to push the car to the back of our minds as we continued to plan for the honeymoon as if it were not an issue. During the final planning stage, the no-man's land between our wedding and our honeymoon, we bounced back and forth between my parent's house and Charlie's parent's house. We would spend a few nights at one until we felt that we were taking up too much space, then head over to the other parents' place. Sometimes it had entirely to do with who was having what for dinner. We stopped short of asking for menus at the start of the week, but we did know our parent's eating habits and were pretty well able to predict what was going on.

We found a happy little short-cut between my parent's house and Charlie's. It involved going down a road parallel to a railroad track. Clouding the landscape between the road and the railroad were industrial shipping places of various description. One of them, for whatever reason, made and shipped huge cement tubes. The tubes were a multitude of sizes, the circumferences (that's $2\pi r$, to you) would vary from the size of a human head to the size of a house. The lengths would be anywhere from between a few feet to several tens of feet long. We passed this place several times a day, depending on the competing menus, and always managed to talk about it. It is the sure sign of a happily married couple that they can be married for as long as a week and still be able to make and enjoy idle chit-chat about huge cement tubes. It is a sure sign of the boring terrain that huge cement tubes would constitute a conversational option while driving across town. Charlotte confessed at passing, just as twilight was setting in, "Every time I see those, I imagine us having sex in them."

This serves as a very strong example of how we saw the world as a huge sexual play-pretty at the time. "We can do it in the tube after we do it in the shower," I said.

"Umm, no," Charlie said. "Showers are for getting clean. We might take one after the tube-sex, but it won't at all be a sexy shower. It'll be a completely functional shower with washing."

Pain in the ass.

On one of those nights passing from my folks to Charlie's folks, my parents followed. They came over to watch the opening of the gifts. Opening wedding gifts is a totally unique experience in the world of gift-unwrapping. And I have to say that I totally don't dig it.

Despite the thousands of dollars that people spent on us, opening the gifts was more like a pain in the ass and less like a joyous occasion. The main reason for this is because we asked for everything so specifically. We sat down with people and/or computers at various stores and coordinated the specification of gifting ourselves through our loved ones. In many ways, it was less like writing a letter to Santa and more like writing a prescription for different levels of financial commitment to our unification. One could buy us anything from the few dollar silverware set to the hundred dollar tent, to the many hundreds of dollar fancy mirror.

We would open a gift and go something like, "Oh, hey, the knives. Hmm. Are these the ones we registered for? I thought it had a sharpener. I can't imagine I would have picked a set without a sharpener, you know?" Totally boring.

As much as registering for the gifts spoiled the fun, the only thing worse was when people ordered off the menu, so to speak. A plastic pie plate? Lame. A ceramic lighthouse with working waterfall? Why the hell would you buy that for someone? It just didn't make sense.

"God, you're calling people out here. Our family and friends," Charlie says.

"If they wanted me to say nice things about them in my book 10 years later, then they should have given us nice things back then."

"It's happening again," Charlie says. "You sure are defensive of your writing, you know that? Every time I talk in this book, I end up getting set straight by you. Just what is my function here? You're traveling with me, right? That's the idea of the book. I'm not the antagonist. Maybe I can make a really good point once in a while or I can be funny, too, or something."

"Noted," I say.

"This doesn't count. I get to be right again later," Charlie says.

"Yes, noted."

We stashed the gifts, now opened, into an extra bedroom in Charlie's parent's house. We tried to make them seem unobtrusive so that we wouldn't incur resentment of any kind. Once Charlie's brother had left a set of golf clubs in the corner of the garage and they ended up being put into our car after we visited for a weekend, even though they knew that neither of us had ever golfed. "*We* don't want them," her step-mom said. To my knowledge, those golf clubs are now hidden in the corner of *my* parent's garage. So leaving our presents in the back bedroom for the five weeks of our honeymoon was bordering on the daring.

And I don't mean to paint Charlie's parents as the crazy ones. Or at least not as the only crazy ones. The night after the present opening, my mom called crying. I was the first of her four kids to get married and apparently, watching me open gifts was just too much for her. She was afraid we wouldn't talk, that I didn't care, that the world would fall apart.

I just couldn't wait until it was time to leave on our honeymoon. I just needed to be away[12].

A Car

Why do things always take until the last minute? It's a question I've pondered since I was very little. Why is it that in movies and TV shows, whenever there is an hour glass involved, the final grain of sand slips down the neck right as the hero bursts down the door? Why is it that the home team scores the final point as the buzzer goes off? The true love always races in and speaks his objection at the sham wedding just as the preacher grants this final chance. So why is it that the powers of good need every possible second allotted in order to make good possible in the world?

I ask this question because I really want to know why we had to wait until 5pm on the day we planned to leave in order to have our car ready. It's not fair. If I live to be a thousand years old, I will never forget the stress that it put me through. Charlie and I were at the store, grumpy as could be, shopping for our last minute travel items when my mom's cell phone rang (she was letting me borrow it) and the mechanic told us the car was ready. It was one of those things that you waited so long for that you didn't even give a shit anymore; it wasn't exciting, it wasn't a relief, it was just about goddamn time.

We picked up the car and took it back to my parent's house. The damn thing looked new. I don't

---

[12] Moms are full of self-fulfilling prophecies.

mean that it looked like a used car that was in fine condition, but it looked like it had just rolled off of the factory on the top of Mt. Fuji, or wherever Hondas are made. It was shiny and polished, and it even smelled like new car inside. I don't know if I'd go so far as to say that it was worth the wait, but it was almost certainly worth the price.

We loaded it with all the things we were going to take with us. We each had a bag of clothes, our tent all wrapped up in its bag, cooking utensils and a small gas stove, food, extra blankets, a cardboard box filled with camping supplies like matches, a hatchet, flashlights, and the like, and also the papers and files that I needed for graduation in a locked suitcase. With all that stuff, we didn't have a lot of extra room for hitch-hikers we might consider picking up.

Excited and impatient, we ignored my dad's suggestion to drive around the rest of the day to make sure the car was okay. We ignored the idea that 5pm was too late to get started on such an ambitious road trip. We didn't want to spend another single night with our folks[13]. In our minds, we had been gone for days; it was time for our bodies to keep up.

So even though it was late, we needed to get a start. Our marriage was aging, after all, and we didn't want to miss our honeymoon altogether. We figured we could get to Tehachapi or, at the very least, Bakersfield. With the car packed to its gills, we got the hell out of Fresno. Charlie was so excited to have the car and

---

[13] Especially when we learned that both households were having leftovers.

insistent that she was going to "drive at least half way to Vermont." It was a kind of wild ambition that she held on to for at least an hour and a half of the trip. I was fine with it, even though I could easily have been counted among those dudes who laugh inwardly (and sometimes outwardly) at guys who ride shotgun while a girl drives. I recognize the silly patriarchal attitude of that position, but still it was a reality of mine that I thought I might be the tiniest bit castrated by sitting in the passenger seat, letting my wife—of all people—rule the road in our Honda.

Charlie took the wheel handily and we backed out of my parents' driveway. I thought for the first of a million times how silly it was that we were going to make our little wheels roll, covering a yard and a half of pavement, over and over again until we were staring at the opposite coast of the entire continent. What a day.

Dying of a Jack Kerouac Obsession

We first heard "the sound" somewhere around Visalia, about an hour into our thousand hour trip. It was a quick flutter-flapping, like a bird that lost its mind and was trying to hover behind your ear. It would come and go, come and go. No matter, I thought, these things have a way of working themselves out. The car is fine. It must be fine. Just *smell* the damn thing!

The sun was setting when we got to Bakersfield. We stopped and ate at a Wendy's on California Avenue, just one exit up from where we would depart from highway 99. Wendy's used to have these table tops that were supposed to look like old newspapers from the turn of the 20th Century. They had these ads for old washing machines and hats and girdles. It was fun to sit down and look at all the ads and check out the absurdly low prices for all the advertised items. It was endlessly engaging to peruse the variety of men's hats that I could have for a dollar-fifty. The tables aren't this way anymore. I don't know why they changed it. Why does every single place have to become the same thing all the time? Why did the market researchers at Wendy's have to come back to the board and say, "Burger King is outselling us, and it's because we're thinking outside the box too much. Our table tops are upsetting people by making them realize they're not at any other of a dozen homogeneous fast-food joints. It's totally fucked-up.

Make the décor more regular if you want to ever sell another square burger in your lives."? For that matter, why the hell are their burgers still square? I mean, I know for a fact by now that square doesn't taste any better than round. One could build a case for the opposite, if shape is the main distinguishing feature in the difference of a cupcake and a cardboard box, for example.

From Bakersfield, we took highway 58, the Stockdale Highway, up into the Tehachapi Mountains. This is the same road one takes when headed from the valley to Las Vegas. All along the way are little towns that one would hardly think of as "Californian." Old boom towns from gold rushes and silver rushes and perhaps the world's only boron rush pepper the sides of the highway. I had been through these towns dozens of times and so had Charlie, but it was our first time doing it together. Just think of how memorable it was for us to see the "World's Largest Thermometer" in Baker, California for the first time as a married couple! Sheer romance.

We ditched out on our silly ideas of stopping in Bakersfield or Tehachapi. We decided to press on to Needles, the actual armpit of California. We stopped for a snack at the Barstow Station, a tourist stop aimed at those going between LA and Las Vegas.

Barstow Station was primarily a McDonalds, but it was attached to a little gift shop and food court which happened to be closed at 10pm. The McDonalds is pretty fun, as far as those places go. You order your food and then go sit in an old train car where you eat the food that will later make you sick. The train cars were narrow, forcing large families to split up into little rows of twos and threes. This was especially exciting for me as a kid, feeling like a big man sitting without his parents at the same table eating Chicken McNuggets. This night we wouldn't be hanging around the dining cars much, but just going to the bathroom and grabbing a couple of soft-serve cones for the road.

Near the bathrooms is a large map on the wall. It's a map of the United Stated, complete with three-dimensional topography. I remembered the first time I had ever looked at that map, 20 years earlier. My family was moving to California from Texas, and my brother and I stood in front of it while my dad showed us how far we had come and how far we had to go. At the time, we had come so far and had so little more to go. The map was such a relief to run your fingers over and know you were almost there.

Now, we had barely moved on the map. Five hours from home, we still had thousands upon thousands of miles left before us. I traced our projected path, along I-40, up to Grand Canyon, over through Albuquerque and into Texas. South into the interior of the state, then up through Arkansas to Memphis; from there, east to Virginia, Washington, D.C. and then north through Philadelphia and New York to Connecticut and finally Vermont; over through Montreal, south through Toronto, slightly east to Niagara Falls; back into the states through Detroit, south to Chicago, north to

Minneapolis, and east to Mt. Rushmore; farther east to Portland, then south all the way back to Fresno.

And then what? With the trip over, we would have nowhere to live. In fact, it occurred to me, we had nowhere to live right *then*. Our furniture was piled in the garage of our old apartment where my sisters now lived in Monterey, our presents were piled up in a bedroom at Charlie's parent's house, and everything else was with us. In fact, for all practical reasons, at this point in our lives, we lived in Barstow Station. Our home was the closest building to our car, or, actually, in our car. It was all sort of sad. Here we were with nowhere to be for almost three weeks. No one would miss us for that long if we drove off into the Canyon at sunrise. And then, only the people at my school would wonder where we were. Our families wouldn't notice we were gone for at least five weeks. We wanted to be alone, and we got it. Alone in this huge, huge country.

My god, people die in car accidents, you know. They die just going to the grocery store and here I was driving across the country with the expectation of survival. The settlers used to make a life-or-death trip across the desert we were headed across. They used to die on the plains, they used to die crossing the Mississippi, they used to get dysentery and bury their own on the side of the passage and trade clothes for oxen and bring extra axils in case one broke—I had played Oregon Trail as a child, I knew what to expect. Was this really such a good idea, or did this whole trip reek of hubris? Was I just an arrogant fuck who would disappear into the American interior, forcing Robert Stack to come back out of retirement to host a special episode of *Unsolved Mysteries* to ultimately pose the question, "What was this jackass doing floating around the country like a nomad? Did he die of a Jack Kerouac obsession? Why did he drag his wife to her death as well, burying her body in Oklahoma after she died of dysentery?" All of a sudden, my stomach was in knots. No doubt, Robert Stack had a difficult night of it as well.

"Check this out," I said. "We've come less than a finger on this map and we have like two entire legs to go."

"Isn't it great?"

"I just mean, look! The money, the miles, the hours and hours alone; is it too much?"

Her face was bright, cheery, the emotionally negative image of her face from the night before the wedding. "It's not too much. It could never be enough."

"What about Robert Stack?"

"Irrelevant. We're together and alone and we can go on any one of these roads, see any one of these mountains, and while we're there, seeing that sunrise or that skyline or that beach, we'll be home." She reached out and took my hand.

When she's happy or sad, she's infectious; her attitude helped me tremendously. Well, I guess the soft serve helped me a little, too.

No Room for Breakfast in Kingman

From when you get to Barstow until God-Knows-Where[14], you are harried by Route 66 signs. Gift shops, Route 66 gas stations, road signs, exit here for Historic Route 66! Honestly, I never knew what the hoopla was. So people used to use the road. So it's known as the "Main Street of America." So there are songs and TV shows about it. BFD. It's a road, and a pretty boring road, that winds along I-40. I don't mean to be a disrespectful jerk-ass, or anything, but I'm telling you if you take I-40 for any more than 5 miles, you will be sick to death of Route 66. Maybe it gets all pretty in Missouri or something, but from Barstow to Needles, you feel like cutting yourself just for fun. Or slamming into a Route 66 sign on your way down a gulch at top speed. And it's no picnic later on past Flagstaff, either. Blech.

It was late when we drove into Needles. Needles, by the way, is one of the worst spots on Earth. If you come over the ridge and descend into the city during daylight hours, you better be ready to feel some heat. It's as if the sun itself has teamed up with ancient gods of fire and made their own little pleasure garden. There's an airplane graveyard, and that's entertaining for a second, but it never drowns out the heat. You could literally scoop up a jar of air there, take it to the Arctic, and melt a glacier. I know you can do that because it's

---

[14] And He knows that it's Chicago.

done all the time. It's kind of like frying an egg on the sidewalk for travelers who are passing through Needles and the Arctic. I'm sure there are videos on YouTube. I think I even did it once.

As we came into Needles, it was dark. And yet. Even in the dark the place looked like a bad idea. The lights came up over the hill and as we got closer, I saw that a good deal of the light we were seeing wasn't manmade electrical regular light, but a raging fire on the north side of town. I mean, the place is depressing enough when things are fine and dandy. You could pave the sidewalks with kids skipping along eating ice cream and singing lullabies and that place would still be creepy[15]. But Needles, sporting a raging fire lighting up the night sky? No good. Charlie was sleeping, I was sleepy, but I decided to take the advice of shepherds I had once known; I got the flock out of there.

We pressed on until almost two in the morning. I couldn't believe that even leaving at five in the afternoon, I had made it as far as my family used to make it on the first day driving to visit relatives in Texas. I made it all the way to Kingman, Arizona. Day one and we had reached our first new state of the trip. Day one and the Mohave Desert was behind us. Now we just had to find a place to stay.

We found a motel in Kingman. The Desert Pirate Arms on Andy Divine Blvd, and it looked like a giant barn with rooms dug into it. It was on the clean side of the filthometer, so that was good. They also gave me

---

[15] Fine, Charlie, fine! That would make it creepier.

something like ten bucks off because I pointed out that we were there just a few hours before we really had to check-out. While I don't think that I carried Charlie into the room physically, my arms were too full of bags, I did carry her into the room in spirit by bugging and taunting until she zombied into the building and crashed out on the bed.

I made another trip back to the car to get our shower case. Since we were planning to camp a lot, we made a little waterproof shower case to bring into the various bathing situations that one finds themselves in while camping. I came back into the room and saw that Charlie hadn't budged a muscle, and I paused to admire the beauty of her crashed-out form. What's this? Gripped in her little hand and pressed under her little head was what appeared to be a pillow that she had brought from home. Let's see, green pillow case, perfect thickness, not too floppy, not too firm…Yep. She brought *my* pillow from home. And by the looks of the situation, she didn't bring the pillow—my most perfect pillow ever—for my benefit. I thought to myself that she was taking this "mine is yours" business of marriage a little too literally.

Coolly, I tried to pry it out from under my wife's sleeping skull. Hotly, she grabbed it back, lifted her undead head and blurted something about how she brought it for her, stop waking her up. I used a pillow *Pirate* provided, not for free, as part of the nominal fee for staying there. My pillow was limp and squishy, not unlike sleeping with your head on a plastic baggy of lunch meat. Head firmly on the meat-bag, I closed my little eyes and drifted away, dreaming bad dreams about Needles.

I looked forward mightily to breakfast. I didn't get enough sleep, had a big day ahead, and was just jonesing to dig into the free breakfast at the Comfort Inn. And it is because of this free breakfast that I can safely recommend that you not stay at the Desert Pirate Arms on Andy Divine in Kingman, Arizona.

What they had for us was not breakfast. They had toast. Not even toast, but a loaf of bread and a single toaster. To go on your toasted bread, there were jars of jelly sitting haphazardly around the counter. There was also, if you should wish, a box of Corn Flakes that you could pour into a Styrofoam bowl and a carton of milk that had been out on the counter all morning. Honestly, I've had breakfasts in Great Britain that were better than that.

"You can be pretentious, you know," Charlie says. "Breakfast in Great Britain? Sounds decadent, not all cruddy like that breakfast we had that day."

"Great Britain is tacky. Especially for breakfast."

"Calling Great Britain tacky is the most pretentious thing you've done today. And it's almost midnight."

An incongruous number of workers stood around the breakfast room. Maybe they were supposed to be doing other things, but they just stood—all four of them—behind this little counter thing and talked about what they were going to have for breakfast. One of them was headed to the McDonalds down the street and picking up McThings for them to eat. This breakfast was so piss-poor that even the workers manning the breakfast counter area would rather pay money than burn their own toast and discover the limitation of expiration dates on milk cartons. I didn't blame them.

"Charlie, they have the right idea," I said. "Let's head out. Kingman actually has a Whataburger[16]. What's more," I told her, "The Whataburger is *next door* to an In-N-Out! The world is our oyster!" As far as I know, Kingman is the one place in the world that has the Texas favorite family-owned burger joint, Whataburger, next to the California favorite family-owned burger joint, In-N-Out. It's like a little diorama of my life, being a Texafornian myself. But Charlie was hardened.

"This is free. We need the money for the trip. Remember how big the map was last night?"

I sulked through the rest of my toast. I stared out the little window in the breakfast room that opened out to, not the outside, but an indoor pool area. The same indoor pool, I'm sure, that was the centerpiece of their advertising on the billboards. Only there was no water in the pool, but fans. Big industrial fans that blew big industrial air at the newly painted surface of the pool. I wasn't planning on going for a swim, but since it was no longer available to me, nothing seemed like a better idea.

---

[16] Sadly, this is no longer true. There is no place for a Texan in Kingman any longer.

Plus, I was pissed and I wanted to make everyone miserable. A baby fit.

My plan was to strip down to my boxers, throw open the door, and jump into the empty pool. Then I would procure a magnificent lawsuit that would bring the entire hospitality industry to its knees. Before I even got to step one of my plan, however, I saw a sign placed haphazardly on the door. "Wet Paint" it warned. I figured that was probably a well-researched way for the hotel to keep claim of a pool and save themselves from being sued. "Your Honor," the corporate lawyer would say. "What man in his right mind would jump into a pool that had wet paint? It wasn't the empty pool that hurt Mr. Stronghold, but his own foolhardy lack of fear of getting paint on himself. Besides, do you realize that he planned to take his wife all over the country and avoid dysentery all the while? Hubris, Your Honor, is the mark of this man." No. I ate my toast and pouted.

Charlie didn't like her meal any better, but enjoyed it a hundred times more. No doubt it was the comfortable pillowing her head got the night before that led her to such a happy morning.

Cooter

Just outside of Kingman is a dry riverbed liberally labeled "Rattlesnake Wash." This little wash had long been a sort of milestone for my family on trips to Texas. The reason is, I suppose, because it is so terribly in the middle of nowhere and there is nothing around it, as result. As far back as I could remember, on those yearly trips one of my parents would announce it, having not announced anything for a long time. And it would always piss us off.

It would piss us off for several reasons. For one, we often would try and sleep to pass the endless time on those trips. And the announcement was always made with such urgency that it would wake us and for no reason; there was nothing around but a dry riverbed in the rearview. It was announced both going out of California and heading back in. It became a sort of sign post of just how shitty passing the time on the trip actually was. A gentle reminder that you hadn't been on road long enough to be anywhere interesting and you were going to be on it much longer before you saw anything worth mentioning again.

While most kids I knew had little summer vacation spots that were desirable, I did not. Some kids would go off to camp for a few weeks; some kids would have families with houses on the coast or cabins in the mountains; to this day, I know people my own age who say things like, "Yeah, I practically grew up in that little mountain cabin on Lake Tahoe. There was always so much to see and do. Hell, while my parents were off gambling on the Nevada side, I lost my virginity *seven times* to carefree vacationing teens such as myself." The fuckers.

I grew up on I-40 between Barstow and Amarillo. Every time we had enough time off of school and grandparents willing to help with costs, my family would pile into the unairconditioned van and hit the road. Sometimes, in college, when I couldn't sleep, I would close my eyes and try and remember that drive moment by moment. The scary thing is, I actually could do it. I could count the exits, see the little rocks tumbled off the hills and onto the road, the Joshua trees reaching for the heavens, the signs for gift shops selling moccasins.

And here I was, triumphantly on my honeymoon, passing Rattlesnake Wash. And the total crap thing about it all was, I was loving it. I was loving the familiarity of it all, the comfort of retracing childhood steps, but with a girl I could legally and morally defile later that night. A childhood memory turned into an adult pleasure. It was exactly like if I were to sit down and watch a pornographic version of *The Chipmunk Adventure*, except not nearly as disgusting as that metaphor just came out.

We were very glad to have gotten all the way to Kingman the night before. We wanted to get into Flagstaff and buy us a CD player for the car. Oh, what a joy it would be! The car we bought (complete with periodic helicopter sound) had only an FM radio. And I can't stand the radio. The night before, as Charlotte was sleeping, I was driving through the Tehachapis with my headlights making the darkness around us yellow, trying to find a station to listen to. I pressed scan several times and all it found was a fuzzy station playing some kind of tribal chanting.

It wasn't that I was averse to tribal chanting, mind you, it was that I was scared of it. What kind of dark as hell mountain range was I driving through that the only demanded music was tribal chants? Were they war chants? Did they tell, through savage code, the whereabouts of trespassing cars driving through the area (Yes, I was well aware that the music was prerecorded. I just figured that they could have been written by very knowing medicine men centuries earlier)? All the while I could only see yellow blackness ahead of me and hear fuzzy tribal calls for my own blood.

Yes, a CD player was called for. It was no longer a question of *if* but of *when*. And that was no longer a question of *sooner or later* but of *how much sooner*. We had this little vision of driving into Flagstaff and pulling into a Good Guys or Circuit City or Best Buy, picking out a one hundred dollar job and having it installed for free.

When you get into Williams, Arizona, you start seeing signs that tell you to exit there for the Grand Canyon. There are little motels peppering the exits that are all named different combinations of "Grand Canyon" and "Lodge." The thing they don't tell you is that every exit from the far west side of Williams to the far eastern side of Flagstaff calls for you to "exit now for Grand Canyon". Yes, as far as craters in the ground go, the Grand Canyon has a rather selfish size, but the spot where people visit is surprisingly modest. And besides, it's a good 50 miles north of I-40, anyway, so it's a lot of hubbub for nothing, like if you were traveling north on I-15 out of LA and a sign said "Exit I-40 for Washington, D.C.!" and there was a picture of the White House.

We pulled off on a promising looking exit in Flagstaff, hoping to stumble into the comfortable bosom of a big box electronic store. We drove around with little direction, following the I-40 business route, "Historic Route 66" to you. It winded along town and finally back onto the interstate. No sign of a Best Buy. All of my experiences in Flagstaff prior to this had been happy ones. Charlotte and I both remembered the Flagstaff of our childhoods being a quiet, calm place with a slight breeze in the air and sunlight softened through the branches of high reaching pines. It had always been on my list for places to live, and, for this instant at least, I *was* living there. But for whatever reason, it wasn't the nice, quiet place that I remembered, but instead a hot little town bustling with traffic and noise. I don't think it had everything to do with the frustration of not finding a suitable store, but it must have had something to do with that.

Stopping for gas, I caught the attention of a bright-looking local man who assured me we'd find no such store for hundreds of miles. "There's a guy who will cut you a great deal on a CD player just down the way," he said.

"Is it a legal deal?"

"He owns a store."

"A legal one?"

"Yes. They're all new, if that's what you mean."

In Fresno, at least, the only guys who would cut you a deal on a CD player were the same guys who cut yours out of your car the night before. This was a welcome situation because you could then at least get the CD that they stole inside the player back.

We drove "down the way" and found the little stereo shop he was talking about. We walked in and saw that every square foot of the place had multiple walls with installed stereo systems. Behind the counter was a pile of unorganized used equipment that seemed to have pushed the attendant out of his place altogether. We saw a man talking to another man, pointing veraciously at different model stereo systems mounted on the wall. We couldn't make out everything he was saying, but he seemed to say the word "demographic" a lot. If I had to guess, and I did, I would say that his name was Cooter. But, as it turned out, he was *our* Cooter.

"Can I help you?" He yelped as much as asked.

"We're just looking around," I responded. If there's one thing I hate about shopping, it's talking to people. I was sort of hoping we could just pay for a model without making eye-contact and install it ourselves. It's beyond my technological capacity, but nevertheless. We were looking at a sharp looking JVC stereo. It had the dual advantage of being both affordable and flashy, so it drew our eyes very near.

"No, no, nope," Cooter said. "You can't buy that one. Those are for the 16-24 demographic. They want something loud and flashy but with no features or sound quality. That's the wrong demographic for you two."

I didn't tell him that my wife and I were, in fact, both 16-24 because I didn't want to be treated like what he obviously felt was a child. Besides, "no features" made it sound like I was being ripped off.

Charlotte was on top of things. She pointed out a Pioneer that looked more mature and responsible, like our demographic. Apparently, though, our demographic likes to spend fifty bucks more per stereo.

"Now, that's a pretty good one," he said. "About $200 fully installed."

"Cool," I said. "We'll take it."

"No, no, nope," said Cooter. "I have to *sell* it to ya'." Cooter turned into a showman right in front of our eyes. He hoped around and his voice took on the tone of an auctioneer or a rapper, listing off the qualities that made this little Pioneer *our* little Pioneer. Cooter's face took on a shine and a brilliance not unlike our own sun's. He listed qualities that only true market-professionals are generally allowed to know, listing the extremes to which this CD player was superior to many others in his shop; more wattage per dollar and all of that. It featured the ability to scan for the strongest six stations in the area and give you temporary presets of those stations while you were driving through.

My God, I thought, it *is* in our demographic! "I probably wouldn't have been listening to the pow-wow last night with this sucker," I said, drawing undue attention from Charlie and Cooter.

Cooter took our keys and started his installation project while Charlie and I wandered around the shopping center for what felt like three or four days. When we got back to pick up our car, we noticed something different about it. Where we used to have this useful little cubby under the useless little stereo, it had now been replaced. It had been replaced by another, far inferior cubby.

"The stereo just didn't want to fit in your old carriage," Cooter said. "There's a 12 dollar charge for that one. But it's a little neater."

Neat, indeed. What used to be a spacious rectangular module was now an oval about a tenth of the size.

"It's cute," Cooter said. As far as I can tell, he was trying to use the Jedi mind trick on us. "The ladies like it." Was he suggesting, as I thought he was, that the new cubby was, in fact, vagina shaped?

It worked fine as a cubby, as long as you didn't mind whatever it was you put into it sliding to the back where even the most narrow of fingers could never reach it again.

We waved goodbye to our little Cooter as we exited the parking lot. He stood there, cigarette drooping from his lips, with a big, doofy smile on his face, no doubt because he was going to sell our much better old cubby for a huge stinking profit to the next person who came in with a vagina-shaped cubby.

Grand Canyon and the Fate of Microphone #1

There're a few things you should know when heading north out of Flagstaff toward Grand Canyon:
1) It's called "Grand Canyon." It is not called "the grand canyon," which would be a geographical description. While it is a canyon, and a grand one at that, that description could fit a great many other canyons as well. But if you would like to call it by name, do.
2) It's a much longer drive than it appears to be on the map. You will no doubt look at the map, calculate the mileage, and figure on 30 minutes or so outside of Flagstaff. You will be sorely sorry when the winding road takes you three times that.
3) It takes you so much longer that you might make the mistake of falling for the trick of the various campsites along the way, figuring them to be close enough to stop. The one that will try and trick you the most is the Bedrock Campground — a Flintstone's themed camp ground that sits comfortably behind a wall with dino heads sticking up from the other side. Had we but

stopped there, I'm sure that this book would be a bit more interesting, one way or the other.

4) Whatever you think you know about how you will feel when you see Grand Canyon for the first time, throw it out. If you thought being born was a trip, this will blow your mind.

This was my second time visiting the world's most spectacular place. This was also Charlie's second time. It had been a few years for either of us. And even the second time around, my mind was blown. You come up over a hill, or you turn a corner, or you stop your car next to a bunch of trees and run through to the clearing ahead, and it's like the whole world opens up to you.

You, in fact, don't really have a good idea of what size the world is until you stand on the rim of Grand Canyon. You can sit on a boat in the middle of the ocean and see water in every direction. You could sit in some sort of escape pod in the middle of space and see the vastness of the universe. But neither of those sights would show you much the way of size; there's nothing to compare to endless ocean or space. But Grand Canyon gives you a view in all directions complete with references of scale.

I recently read a pretty startling example of just how big Grand Canyon is. You could put the biggest city in the USA down on the floor of the canyon and still be thousands of feet above the tallest buildings. You could look down on the ant-like city and not even hear a single noise, it would be so far away. I almost wish that someone very omnipotent would do something like that some day, just for a little while, so I could see it in action and have the thrill of a thousand lifetimes.

It's big. Very big. The biggest thing that could possibly fit in the human imagination. And you might think, "So what, jackass, just because something is big doesn't mean that it's worth looking at for hours on end." But, truly, it is. The greatest sculptures in the world cannot compare with the mastery of this canyon. The greatest paintings and songs can't touch it. I would go so far as to say, you could put all the great works of art together in one place at one time, complete with all of the artists and composers and performers and give me the choice between going there and going to Grand Canyon (and I can only do one of them one time in my life, you see) and I would pick Grand Canyon. I would rather see Grand Canyon than walk on Mars. The only sight that has ever compared is of my own kids being born. That said, Grand Canyon is the only sight that can sit in the company of seeing my kids be born.

Enough of this. I cannot convince you any better than that. And yet you still sit there, reading this book and not planning your trip. I will give you a moment now. Go talk to your loved ones about the prospect of going to Grand Canyon now. Then go there. I will wait for you before I start the story back up again.

(Go to Canyon. Come back)

Now that you understand what I'm talking about, we can proceed as peers, and I no longer have to talk down to you. I will, however, say this: I told you so.

We had made reservations at the canyon a few weeks before. They were the only reservations that we had made for the trip aside from the hotel in Vermont where we would stay for my graduation. We were petrified of the idea that the camp sites would all be taken and we wouldn't get a thorough chance to commune with the canyon.

At the small ranger station, I gave my name and told them that I would like to check in. Just in case they didn't make a proper note of it when I called in, I told them that we were on our honeymoon. "I've got that right here," the doofy old guy said. "You're going to be in the honeymoon suite."

The site was not, as it turns out, the honeymoon suite. I was being made fun of. Mocked. It was a regular site. And the regular sites had a distinct lack of privacy and a distinct wealth of huge ravens hopping about waiting for you to go to sleep so they can eat your liver. The ravens were in on the joke, so far as I could tell, ready to pounce upon and eat our food, furthering our site's status even more from that of Honeymoon Suite.

But the ravens, and half of the campground, got more than they bargained for that day. They got a little show called, "Newlyweds Set Up Their Tent." It wasn't an especially complicated tent to set up, in all honesty. It was a simple enough tent, for sure. We didn't fumble too much with the support beams or the rainfly or any of that nonsense. But the ground was more or less a thin layer of silt above solid rock. The task of driving a tent stake into the ground was just about like driving a papier-mâché toothpick through the armor of a tank, except not as cool because you were nowhere near a tank.

As mature adults, recently married and setting up where we were going to sleep on their honeymoon, you'd think we would have worked well together to solve the problem. Instead, however, we fought. Whatever I tried to do, it just wasn't right. Every place I dragged our tent, over the whole of the Honeymoon Suite, I couldn't find a place that would welcome the five sided thing with open arms and soft-yet-sturdy soil to drive a tent stake into. I thought about tying rope to the places in the tent for the stake and then stringing the stakes to the tent that way. The idea was readily abandoned when I realized that we had no rope and I had no patience.

Charlotte explained, in great detail, just what kind of half-assed job I was doing. I snipped back at her for micromanaging me. The ravens gathered to watch us argue and by the time the tent was actually set-up, there was an audience of nearly 100,000 ravens, some holding little signs with my face on them and others holding little signs or wearing T-shirts with Charlie's portrait all over them. They settled contentedly before a team of well-dressed divorce lawyer ravens, papers drafted and waiting our signatures.

"Will, pull this side over there and put the stake in."

"It won't go in the ground here, Charlie! It's like loose dirt on top of rock."

"There are ants over here, something like a thousand of them every square inch. We can't move it this way."

"Charlotte, that's why I thought we should set it up over *there*."

"Don't do that. Don't say my name like that, *William*."

"Like what?"

"Like my name that you don't usually call me unless we're fighting. And you didn't know about these ants so that's *not* the reason you thought we should put the tent over there near the spider webs."

We stood there staring at each other as the tent sat half limp all over the ground. The damn structure had something like a hundred sides and angles—nothing like a regular square tent like you see on old TV shows. We took some deep breaths and looked around the bird-infested grounds. Seeing the hubbub we had caused, and not being proud that we had disturbed nature in a National Park to the point of law-practicing birds, we finally finished the tent project by anchoring it from the inside with a particularly heavy bag of luggage. We shooed the aviary away and went on with our little lives.

We spent the rest of the day admiring the canyon. Standing on the cliff, far above the floor, one feels a sense of grandeur that cannot be matched. It's been said before and it's very true, once you're at the edge of the canyon, you get quiet. Only a whisper seems appropriate in the presence of something so imposing.

There are those, however, who are not self-aware enough to understand this, and they bellow into their cell phones and crack jokes and generally horse around. Luckily, the canyon is large enough that you can just slip away, farther down the side and pay no attention to the sacrilegious. One guy sticks out in my mind. He was walking along when his phone rang and he brought it quickly to his ear. "Yeah," he said as to confirm the suspicion of the caller that was indeed there. "We're at the Grand Canyon right now. Yeah, it's pretty sick." We slinked away, disgusted at a genetic pool that could supply such an unremarkable understatement about a place so magnificent.

To be fair to the above dude, he was merely expressing his own ignorance and inexpressiveness. Often times we forget that our feelings or descriptions about the great and wonderful things in the world reflect on ourselves and not the other way around. If you, for example, tell me that Bach was a terrible composer, you have done nothing to harm Bach or his reputation; you have simply exposed your own foolishness to everyone in earshot. It doesn't matter if you like Bach He is many times more immortal than your opinions of him and his abilities in music were beyond your own. You may as well have told oxygen to suck it. So if someone describes Grand Canyon as pretty sick, they have shown their full capacity of thought, feeling, and expression, and Grand Canyon goes on and on being much more than pretty sick for those who get the message.

Expressing your own shortcomings is one thing. But broadcasting a half-assed expression of knowledge is quite another. And I have come to find out that this is something that a great many people like to do in wonderful places where people gather to embrace the infinite. God damn Microphones. Wherever you are, if there is someone who foolishly believes himself to be an expert on something he knows just a little about, you will find a Microphone. Such was the case on our first night at Grand Canyon, sitting on the edge, watching the moonrise.

What could be more romantic than two newlyweds, arms surrounding each other, bathed in starlight and a full moon, watching the alien landscape of Grand Canyon at night? We sat in awe as the moon peaked over the edge, miles and miles off. This should now be a quiet moment, reserved in our minds for later reflection. But instead, a Microphone from behind us yelled for all to hear, "Exactly where I thought it would rise."

There were about a dozen of us in all who had decided to watch the full moon rise from one of the best lookout points along the southern rim. This Microphone of ours had a camera set up and pointing at the perfect spot. Really, there was no need to brag, no need to break the concentration of the heart upon the landscape. His picture snapped, he could have left our company in peace and quiet. But it was as if he thought himself deserving of a medal from our small congress for such a great achievement. He patted himself on the back a little more. "Last night it wasn't quite full, and it rose slightly to the right. I thought that it would have shifted over a few degrees and indeed it did!" I stifled the urge to hush him violently with a fist.

In the ensuing minutes, as the moonlight touched new spires of rock, illuminated different avenues of the Earth below, I was rapt. Or at least I would have been if the Microphone had stopped his oratory on astronomy. "Ahh, there is Polaris, which many people mistakenly call the North Star. In a few thousand years, it won't even be the North Star anymore. It has a more proper name" and on and on.

A child, peering over the edge, saw the faint glow of lights down in the canyon. I, and many of my fellow spectators, knew these lights to be Phantom Ranch. The little rustic resort is one of the most popular destinations in the National Parks system. Hikers, rafters, and mule riders can stay there over night as long as they book their reservation years in advance. I want to stay there very badly myself but have never had the forethought for such things. It looks like a splendid place to pass the time and see the canyon from the other side. As the boy pointed this sight out, the Microphone explained away these lights most foolishly. "That's simply the reflection of our flashlights on the river below."

Silence followed.

"No," I said, though in my own imagination. "No, it's not. The river is 4,600 feet below us at this point."

"So?" The Microphone would have said. "Light travels that many feet in a second or so."

"Okay, stop. Just stop, okay dude? Because you're off. You're way off. A few of us have flashlights, sure, but a river can't reflect such a small bulb at this distance. We don't carry laser flashlights, now do we? I didn't think so. The lights dissipate much more quickly than that. That's Phantom Ranch down there, and if you knew a damn thing about the ground you're standing on, you'd know it and you'd shut the hell up and let us all enjoy our moment with the canyon."

"No," he'd say. "Watch while I flicker my flashlight down there and the light, in turn, flickers from below." And as he reached for his flashlight, I—and a few other hearty travelers—grab the man, hoist him over the edge and give him the Eleven-Second Tour of the canyon, sending him hurtling to the bottom-floor. And just before his light is extinguished on the rough ground below, we hear him yell, "You were right! There is a ranch down here!"

Atonement achieved, we rested well that night, feeling a small part of a much greater whole.

"God, I wish that were true," Charlie says, looking up from the manuscript.

"What? If I had murdered the guy and ended up in prison?"

"Not that much true. I don't wish it was *all the way* true. But the spirit of it. Like, if once in a while we had some kind of recourse, you know? Just once in a while."

83

The Fate of Microphone #2

There's a lot to do at Grand Canyon. There's a lot to take in. While Charlie and I had trouble keeping out of the general store—we forgot to bring camping chairs, marshmallows, firewood, matches, socks, and a few other items, deficiencies all discovered and addressed at different occasions—I can safely recommend that you not visit the Visitor's Center. To get to the Visitor's Center, you have to ride a little tram. This tram is rather convenient, as it goes along several miles of the canyon, stopping at different places, should your feet get tired. But once safely located at the Visitor's Center, you find yourself in a large plaza with nothing to do. Honestly, who wants to watch a movie about Grand Canyon while you're standing right next to it? Pictures never do it justice. The bathrooms at the center were at least serviceable, but not much else was.

Charlotte and I decided to take a little hike. Just a couple weeks before, as we scrambled to get things together for our trip, we decided that we needed some new shoes. Our decision coincided, as a matter of fact, with the viewing of an ad in the newspaper. The ad was for Big Five Sporting Goods and they were liquidating their supply of Doc Martins. While Docs had been cool ever since I was in the 7th grade, I had never actually owned a pair. Hundred dollar shoes didn't really factor into my family of four kids, nor Charlie's family of five, when there were discount stores where functional twenty-five dollar shoes could be purchased. But this liquidation sale leveled the playing field for this young couple and we headed out to buy.

And now was the time. Now was the time to don the Docs and break them in good and proper along the rim of Grand Canyon. It was only going to be a three mile hike, or so, not down to the floor or anything as we didn't have the supplies to make such a trip and didn't want to visit the general store again. We took the tram to a distant look-out spot and set off for adventure.

It didn't last, folks.

I can't explain, nor can I pass up the chance to tell you, how heart-achingly beautiful it was. Every new angle and every new shade of light and darkness renders a more stunning image that you want to lock away in your mind and in your bones to draw on later when you're back in the regular world. We took little pathways and shortcuts coming closer to the edge than a reasonable person should have done, and it was all done in good fun. There was even a moment when—all alone at last—I took it upon myself to break the sacred silence of the canyon and yell as loud as I could just to hear the canyon yell back in my voice. Thrilling.

But our feet were bleeding. They were sore and bleeding and blistering before the first mile was up. These Doc Martin boots had—no doubt—been sitting in the back of the Big Five for years, the leather not being worked, and had turned into torture devices. There was a moment—a none too short one at that—when we considered taking them off and walking barefooted over every rattlesnake nest on the rim to get back to our campsite. But finally, reason conquered ambition and we flagged down a tram and headed back to the main village, defeated. Defeeted?[17]

That night we nursed our sorrows over steak at the Arizona House, the only sit-down restaurant that overlooks the canyon. We made friends, waiting to be seated there, talking with other tourists who couldn't wait to combine the pleasures of steak with canyon-seeing. And while my strange little Southwest Caesar Salad left much to be desired, my entre delivered. For a few solid moments, I shared the most beautiful view in the world—the sun setting over Grand Canyon, my beautiful wife, and my lovely mistress—a medium-rare prime rib with a dollop of horseradish sauce. Then, as the moment passed, so did the meal and my wife found herself the sole object of my attentions once again.

S'more making is an art, it turns out. And my dear bride had mastered it. Back at camp she really showed her stuff by constructing a s'more making system. The graham crackers were laid on the grill above the fire, but not directly over it, with a couple squares of Hershey's dark chocolate on every other one. As the crackers toasted and the chocolate melted, Charlie performed miracles of stick-finding and marshmallow positioning. While she prefers her marshmallows

---

[17] Sorry. That's bad. Like irresponsibly bad. Maybe an editor will take it out and protect my dignity.

slightly charred, she can get a golden brown toast without batting an eye, if you ask her. The end result is a blissful explosion of taste, texture, and decadence that no one appreciates more than Charlotte herself.

"Look at that!" she would exclaim excitedly. "A perfect char!" Indeed the whole of the s'more making process was narrated and appreciated by the chef herself. It was cute and endearing. She was animated while eating them, as well, offering different insights about the tradition as a whole. "I hate it when someone calls them 'some mores.' Just say *smore* like you mean it. They're not 'some mores' no matter what stupid name they used to be called." Campfire, s'mores, and digesting beef were just what my aching feet were begging for.

On our last morning, we decided to visit that great hole in the ground one last time. We were glad that we did because as we were viewing, a huge bird flew over head. Like really freaking big. The California Condor has a wingspan of over 10 feet and was brought back from the brink of extinction at Grand Canyon, just recently being reintroduced to the wild. They each have a nest and a clearly defined territory where the others dare not hunt. And we learned all of that from a lady wearing a Niagara Falls sweatshirt, a huge visor, and those gigantic cataract sunglasses. Yes, indeed, a Microphone decided to bless us with her knowledge while we were trying to enjoy such a rare and wonderful bird. So annoyed was I about this that I emitted a special bird-whistle that I had learned from a local Native

American tribe. The precise modulations of my whistle yielded the desired results: the condor swooped down, picked the Microphone up, and fed her to her young. Now that Microphone not only knows everything about the condors, but everything about gizzards and other such bird-digestion devices first-hand.

We watched with glee and satisfaction as the condor chicks tore at her flesh and played with her disembodied eyeballs. Her screams came in guttural waves and echoed across the canyon. She raised a bloody stump that used to be a leg, spurting velvety red ribbons of blood. The birds feasted and feasted in messy glory, waving flesh and bone around their huge nest.

We saw spine.

With Grand Canyon in our rearview mirror, the first stage of our trip was behind us. What was in front of us was 15 or so hours of the most boring stretch of I-40 imaginable, including what is, most likely, my least favorite spot on Earth; a place I dreaded passing for the first time in seven years.

I Still Think About Them

Driving through the southwest, the scenery is beautiful. It goes from the tall pines of Flagstaff to the carved rock and low scrub at the border of New Mexico. And it does this so goddamn slowly, you could swear that you're standing still. Your car crawls along the perfectly straight channel of road with only mild variations of view at smatterings of time. The only real things that break up the view into digestible chunks are the roadside attractions.

In the middle of the desert is a drive-through dinosaur park. Hurtling down the road, you might miss the rubber T-Rex watching the cars go by, warning of the exit ahead. From the looks of it, you drive down a dirt road and follow signs that point you in the direction of battling dinosaurs. So far as I can tell, none of them are animated, but are posed in postures of attack for your bloodthirsty pleasure. We took this exit happily, hoping to embrace the many roadside attractions. Alas, it was Sunday and the park was closed until much later in the day. Disappointment hung over our Honda like the full moon over the canyon.

Getting back onto the freeway, we heard the noise again. A flittery-flappity noise that seemed to come from the front of the car. But now, it was a violent flapping, like a screech owl stuck in our grill or something. Our eyes widened and we looked at each other, too frightened to give verbal acknowledgment to the problem, knowing that that would give it more life, since it clearly lived from our anxiety. Flittery-flappity-flap! It calmed down and then stopped. We didn't say a word.

There are several genuine Indian shops along that stretch of I-40. And more numerous than the shops are the road signs, every few hundred yards, promising all the moccasins, cupie dolls, pipes, petrified wood, Indian blankets, dream catchers, hot dogs, churros, sand art, and headdresses you can possibly imagine. We stopped at Geronimo's, one of the more prominently advertised of these souvenir shops. Entranced by the topaz jewelry and paintings of horses, we scarcely noticed that the two old biddies that ran the shop weren't Natives of the continent, but nearly British-looking white ladies who resented our use of their restroom without the purchase of a hunk of petrified wood. Nevertheless, we didn't purchase a thing but used the restroom in great delight. Our expressed wishes that the ladies have a good day were not returned on our way out the door.

Returning to the road, we looked at the map to see what kind of upcoming sites we could look forward to; there was Meteor City, a place that has a crater from a meteorite, but we knew we wouldn't stop, so we wasted no time debating; there was the Petrified Forest, which we had both visited independently earlier in our lives, which made the choice to pass it by at 75mph an easy one; the Painted Desert always sound like a great vision of loveliness to look forward to with gratitude, but the only thing I can really say about it is that it is less and less impressive every time you pass by; there was no way in hell that we were actually going to stand on the corner in Winslow, Arizona to watch girls—or anything else—go by. In short, our only real option was to go—as fast as we could—through the desert until lunch time. But nothing, not even sheer speed, can really save you from the kinds of lame games that you play in order to make the passing desert stomachable.

There's the alphabet game. Where you try and find words that start with each letter of the alphabet, in order of course. The pitfall of this game is that you always end up discussing exceptions that should be made for letters like Q and X. And honestly, it doesn't matter if you do make these exceptions or not, for the rest of your trip—no matter how long it is—whenever you see a word starting with one of the elusive letters, you point it out and lamely remark, "I wish we were playing that game right now" even though you really don't wish you were playing that game, not at all. There's also the…no, come to think of it, the alphabet game, as silly and poor as it is, is the only game that I think I've ever played on the road. Slug-bug doesn't count.

Coming towards New Mexico, I was forced to recount, for the millionth time, the story of the car accident to my wife. Here, the poor girl is just trying to enjoy her honeymoon, and all I want to talk about is the most horrific thing I have ever seen. It was, after all, the first time that I had driven that same road since it happened. Ever since then, for one reason or another, I had taken I-10, the southern route, to Texas.

For the sake of continuity, I will recount the story once again.

My grandfather had died, and we were headed to Waco for his funeral. My brother was already there, having scored a free ticket on a plane. We were in our old 1987 Dodge Ram van. The seats inside had been gutted and changed many times, and this, the last configuration of seats, had a bench seat in the back that was decent, a tiny bench in the middle that was falling apart and had no seat belts, and two captain's chairs for the driver and passenger.

I was driving. My mom had lost her senses with her father dying and all, and she was riding shotgun. My little sisters were in the middle seat, and Dad was stretched out across the back seat. He had been driving all night and now it was his turn to get some sleep. It was around eight in the morning or so, and we were just about three or four miles inside the New Mexico border.

We were clipping along at over 85 mph, with the speed limit at 75. We had just reached the area where the landscape changes so drastically and so quickly from low desert scrub to tall, towering rock. My eyes wandered to the surrounding hills and cliffs, but not for too long, thankfully. In front of us, there was a small red sedan, and in front of him was a semi truck. We were in the left lane, coming up to a rest stop on the right. Suddenly, the semi moved quickly into the right lane, revealing another red sedan in front of it. Only it was coming towards us.

I don't know how to explain what went through my head. First, I was just kind of sick. I didn't feel queasy, or anything, just the kind of sick that you know *something* is wrong, but you're not sure what. Then, as the two red cars smacked into each other, there was a desperate thought that occurred to me: "I've never seen this before," I thought. "This kind of thing isn't supposed to happen." The two cars were up in the air, and spinning around, smashed into each other. I looked at my speedometer, again, over 85, and decided that stopping was not an option. We were going to hit it, and we were going to hit it hard. Damn hard.

I don't know that time slows down in this type of thing. I know that it did for me; like my processor sped up and everything came to a crawl. It gave me plenty of time to think about everything I've ever wanted to think about and about every horrible thing I didn't want to think about. I was happy, had had a happy life; the steering wheel was going to feel terrible when my face hit it; at least my brother would still be alive; my sisters, sleeping, may never know this was what killed them; at least a whole bunch of questions were about to be answered; I would have liked going to college; what will happen to our dog? Oh yeah, my brother can take her.

Among the myriad horrible things that flashed quickly in my brain, there was the lesson from physics that any time two objects collide, they lose the same amount of momentum. Therefore, in a high-speed collision, it was better to be the one going faster. So I slammed on the gas, in hopes of somehow busting through.

Just as that thought was finalized, the cars bounced off of each other. The cars were at enough of an angle that as they bounced away, there was a small, yet widening, clearing between the two. Everything happened so fast that I processed the event as being one car splitting in two before my eyes. My dad yelled from the back seat, "Drive straight through it Will, drive straight through!"

In between the cars there was debris and smoke and I wasn't sure how far apart they were. I had the image of our car hitting the ends of the other cars so hard that they spun but we didn't. That was my goal. But we cleared them both, by what must have been inches. Time went back to normal very quickly. As the smoke cleared and I saw that we were all alive, my lungs filled with air and I felt like we were floating off the ground, literally. I kept my foot on the gas, triumphantly, thinking that we needed to get far away from the hell that was behind us. Then I asked my dad if we should stop, and he said yes.

Dad and I got out of the car, leaving Mom and the girls there. As we walked back to the accident, Dad asked, half sure of his question, "Were there two cars or just one?" I felt better, knowing that someone else was so confused as to think that it was one car that somehow split into two. Then he said, "You know this isn't going to be pretty, right?"

I nodded. I tried to reassure myself by thinking of movies and how much blood I had seen in them. This couldn't be that bad, I thought, not as bad as a movie.

It was much worse.

One car had an old couple in it from New York. The man had ribs sticking out of his chest. The woman, like everyone else, had blood pouring out of her nose and mouth. The other car had two younger Indians in it from New Mexico. They had been drinking. The driver was in and out of consciousness. While the passenger twitched and jerked every so often, it was plain to see he wasn't alive. The engine block had come through the car and cut him in half. His arm was out the window and his separated hand hung from his wrist.

We couldn't move anyone. We just stood with a few other people, making cars stop, wondering when the ambulance was going to get there, talking about what had happened. At one point I told the Indian driver to stay where he was; he kept trying to get out of the car. Standing and staring at the Indian's car, my dad nudged me and I saw that he was looking up. Over the car, about 10 feet or so, was a crow, just hovering. It hovered there in a wind current for a few moments, then flew off, high. Later on, my dad would say it was a hawk. I saw a crow. Neither of us will bend on the subject. We were both sure of what we saw. But we also both knew that it had something to do with the car accident. That someone had just died. We just knew.

In fact, Dad and I still disagree on which car was going the wrong way. I guess we'll never know. We'll also never know if anyone survived. We left when the ambulance got there. I couldn't drive for the rest of the day. I was haunted like I've never been haunted before. I still think of that at some level every time I get in a car. It made me very frightened of going on our honeymoon. It makes me frightened to go to work, at times. Or frightened to close my eyes.

A Quick Visit to the Rarest Animal on Earth

We passed the site of the car accident with little incident. No bizarre folding of time made me relive it, nor were there any drunks driving the wrong way with a heavy mind for irony. We were greeted to New Mexico with a new bevy of signs for tourist stops. The one that beckoned us the most was the shop shaped like a huge wigwam that had exclusive rights to the viewing of the White Cave Buffalo.

Now a white buffalo, I've heard of. They were supposed to be spiritual signs to Native Americans. They would show something of a changing spiritual atmosphere, significant world events, or the coming of a great and powerful leader. But a *cave* buffalo was another story. I'd never heard of one. And a white cave buffalo, well, that was something worth looking at!

We paid our five bucks and followed the gated walkway to the cave in the side of the rock face. There we glanced into the darkness and saw a shape emerge, quietly. Blind, white eyes looked out at us as the beast stepped out of the darkness. Huge and covered with a mix of white fur and soft, furry white scales, the miserable and lonely creature hissed an angry hiss at us, caught a huge hornet with its reptilian tongue and quickly scampered back into the safety of darkness. Charlie and I stood transfixed, silent.

Actually, we just sat in the car and drove by without stopping, but whatever.

Why our Marriage is a Sham

We stopped at an odd little hotel in Gallup for a rest stop. The El Rancho Inn brags about having the "charm of yesterday" and "the convenience of tomorrow." I suppose there is no use for today at the El Rancho. Charming, it is. It's an old cowboy hotel that used to house many Hollywood stars while they were shooting westerns in the surrounding desert. Do you realize how many shows used to be westerns? Do you realize that in the late 50s, with only 3 networks on the air, that there were over 30 westerns on TV? That's all people would want to watch, evidently. These days we hardly watch a western unless it's somehow an ironic western or a western in space or some shit. No wonder the El Rancho will take people like me these days instead of just the stars.

  The bathrooms at the El Rancho are hard to find. It's only through frequent stops that I've learned that while the women's bathroom is sitting at the top of the stairs, nestled between hotel room doors decorated with the names of various old movie stars, the men's room is on the lower floor down a winding and horrifyingly dark hallway. Honestly, I've only stayed at the El Rancho once in my life, but I've used the restrooms about a million times. I feel like I owe them some money or something for using their 'throoms and enjoying their nice and spacious lobby so often in my life. But I don't know exactly how such a charge would be classified and I'd hate to put them into some kind of trouble with the IRS by giving them a big ass check out of the blue, so I just keep the money and continue to impose upon their hospitality.

Since Gallup is the exact mid-point between Waco, where my family came from, and Fresno, where my family ended up, and since we stopped so often at the El Rancho, it has for years been part of our Plan Z if the shit goes down. Specifically, if circumstances (such as wars or natural disasters) were to force us to flee our homes in California and head east, and if we were separated, we were to meet and regroup at the El Rancho, if at all possible. And if we should stop at the El Rancho and not see anyone else from the family and if we wait around and finally have to leave, then communication should be left behind the toilet tank in the women's room. There are other places designated, should an evacuation north be necessary or should New Mexico be not far east enough, but really, what are the chances? If the world comes to an end—and no doubt it will—I can just about promise you that Gallup and especially the El Rancho Inn will be in perfect condition long after time itself has ceased. If you don't believe me, it's only because you've never been there and smelled that sense of utmost destiny in the air.

Charlie and I called our dads from our rarely used cell phone at the hotel. It was Father's Day and we figured a call from the El Rancho was surely in order. We called our folks and this is when I found out something rather dreadful. My wife and I were on our honeymoon, but she was not yet officially my wife.

"What the hell?" I asked my mom.

"You pastor didn't put down an address on the license."

"So?"

"So it was sent back to us. It's not filed. We have to track her down and get her address so that it can be official.'

But we couldn't track her down. She was out of town. Or she had turned back into her alter ego or something. Whatever the case, we wouldn't be officially married until a few days after our honeymoon was over. What garbage. What disappointment.

"And here we renewed our virginities for nothing," Charlie said.

We then wandered around the hotel gift shop, where we found topaz jewelry and paintings of horses. It's amazing the ways one is willing to spend their leisure time after a morning driving through the desert. One of the great things about looking around gift shops in the southwest is the fine line between the semi-tasteful art and the straight-up sick-funny art. In a shop like the one at the El Rancho, that line can be traced with a finger and explored from either side on many of the objects for sale. While one painting might be for sale for three hundred or so dollars and look like a perfectly capable rendering of a herd of wild horses wandering about in a snow covered forest, you will be given pause when you look at the painting's kin, right next door to it on the wall, of three or four wolves howling at a moon against the backdrop of some kind of Native American princess covering the sky. That one might also go for three hundred and is certainly painted by the same artist and now those horses don't look so serene anymore.

Getting back into the car, I decided to take a second to look at the tires. I had noticed earlier that day that there was a strange vibration happening right at 70mph. Clearly the car was capable of going that speed without flying apart, but the vibration was still very strange. It didn't seem to have anything to do with the flippity-flap noise, but it was bothersome nonetheless.

Just as I feared, the front passenger tire was looking pretty bad. There was zero tread on one part of the tire and I was afraid to look deeper into it for fear of seeing those little metal threads that really means your tire is about to fly to pieces. Every tire looked worn, but this one looked like garbage.

"What's wrong?" Charlie said, reading my facial expression.

"Nothing."

"Nothing is wrong with the tires?"

"Nope. They're fine. We'll get a few thousand more miles out of them."

"How many thousand more?"

"We'll get new ones when we get back to Fresno. We'll use the hell out of these then get new ones."

"They'll last that long."

I nodded. I knew that if I told her how bad things were, she'd stress out and then we'd have to get new tires and then we'd be out of money way before we wanted to be. So I just shut my trap and tried to not go 70. It could go 68 fine and 72 fine, so why even bother with little lame 70? Who needs that shit?[18]

---

[18] It's been pointed out to me that I had a bit of a fear of long distant trips, but no fear of this tire issue. Such is the confusion of my subconscious with which I am daily faced.

Tucumcari Tonight

Driving the length of New Mexico is a trying experience. There is a profound happiness that can be located in finally arriving in Albuquerque. A large, though strange, city full of Mexican food eating options. With a city like that, so full of the promise of authentic Mexican food (specifically New Mexican food), why would one eat anywhere else? Whatever the circumstances, my wife and I found ourselves dining on second-rate diner fare on Coors road shortly after noon. My Philly cheese steak sandwich was so bad that I just about didn't finish it.

Pressing on, one is harried by the most unpleasant suggestion on I-40 east of Albuquerque. It is the prospect constantly proposed on road signs, suggesting you just write-off the rest of your day and spend the night in Tucumcari. The signs make this rather indecent proposal through the use of the slogan, "Tucumcari Tonight!" These signs make wild boasts about the 111 rooms that can be rented for the evening throughout the dusty little town, and even wilder boasts about the quality of the dining—specifically that there is a measure of quality that can be expected or even counted upon.

While we didn't, in any broad way, ever consider a night in Tucumcari as being a possibility for our future, we did need very badly to pee and very badly to get something to drink. Now this is a slight flaw of the human body that I never could convince myself to abide by without complaint. Why in world should I be such an inefficient machine as to be at once dehydrated and overly full of wastewater? We certainly wouldn't stand for this if this sort of behavior were exhibited by a robot, for example. I dare say that the robot in question would be shit outta luck when requesting a joint bathroom and drink fetching stop of his inventor/owner. But since a person is neither perfect nor robotic, our joint trip was jointly approved by both members of our party in a unanimous landslide.

We pulled off and took the I-40 business route through Tucumcari, looking for the best spot to fill up and empty our bladders in one fell swoop. What instantly got our attention was a drive-in that boasted high quality sodas, extensive options, and awesomely small ice cubes. Drinks ordered, paid for, and straws inserted, Charlie walked around back to use the restroom. This was a very unfortunate move on her part; she should have simply gone right there in the parking lot.

First off, she had to walk through part of the kitchen to get to the bathroom. This was because they didn't actually expect guests to use their facilities, for whatever reason. You'd think that since it was only workers using the bathroom regularly, it would be pristine and might even smell good. But no. The bathroom was in disrepair. It was filthy beyond belief. There were discarded cups and wrappers strewn about the ground. Filth seemed to stick to the walls in a shallow layer, but not so shallow as to go unnoticed. A repugnant scent hung in the air that could be physically seen with very little imagination. And to top it all off, *there was no soap in the dispenser.* So the people who made our drinks hadn't washed their hands after visiting the fifth circle of Hell.

Charlotte advised that I opt for happiness and avoid the restroom, but my human imperfections drove me to the lesser of my options. I did end up regretting this choice, as I could hardly drink my chocolate cherry Dr. Pepper afterwards.

Getting back on the main drag, another unfortunate event befell us in Tucumcari. Charlie was sitting leisurely in her passenger seat, her foot and leg propped up provocatively. A small red car filled with teenage boys pulled up alongside us at a red light.

"Hey," the driver said.

"Hi," said my wife.

"Where you going?"

Instead of responding to this question, Charlie started laughing.

"Ah, come on," the driver said.

The light turned green and I sped off. And don't get me wrong, it's not that I'm such a jealous person that I can't take a little competition from a dude in a red car. It's that I was insulted—the dude apparently didn't stop to think that I might be her husband or her boyfriend or something. Or, just maybe, he even thought I was a girl. What the hell are these Tucumcari dudes thinking?

Well, just as I was thinking all of that, I hit a bird. A bird that was sitting in the road took off to fly away and do jolly bird activities, and I hit it in a splash of black feathers, leaving a smear of blood on the hood of the car. In the rearview mirror, you could see the black mess of feathers disband into several pieces.

"Oh Jesus Christ!" Charlie yelled. "Jesus! Why? Why did you *do* that?"

"I didn't do anything!"

"Will, you can't just hit birds! You can't!"

"I didn't *try* to!"

"You must have, Will! You know how many times I've *not* hit birds in front of the car? Every time!"

She was near tears. Tucumcarri can make you near tears without hardly trying. It wasn't but a few hundred feet until the freeway entrance, where we quickly joined the Interstate again, happily avoiding the prospect of Tucumcari Tonight[19], and heading out of New Mexico altogether. Flippity-flap went the noise in the car.

---

[19] Since writing this book, Charlie and I have stayed the night in Tucumcarri at least four hundred times. We found a great, cheap hotel——an amazing place for breakfast burritos—Unburritable—and we love the place fully. Can you imagine?

The Burrito

Crossing the border into Texas is an exciting thing. It's exciting for about half a minute, the time it takes the "Welcome to Texas" sign to pass from the front of your car to the rearview mirror. The scenery changes just a little, adding more vegetation and a few low Mesquite trees to your view. But once the thought of being out of New Mexico settles comfortably in your mind, like a blanket of dust on old library books, you get bored again. There are still 70 miles until Amarillo.

But once Amarillo comes upon you, you are never the same. You've spent days and days wandering through the deserts of the Southwest, with little hamlets that catch your attention and Albuquerque, which you just rush on through. Then, over the horizon, about 20 miles off, you see the lights of Amarillo lighting the sky, drawing a line that the brightest stars cannot cross. The freeway runs like a river into a vast surrounding display of what can only be called *civilization*.

Charlotte and I were hungry when we saw those lights. We were damn hungry. We had little directions printed out on a slip of computer paper to help us find our way to the Amarillo KOA, on the far east side of town. Entering from the west, as destiny had bound us, we were tormented by the vast array of restaurants in one of the best towns for eating that there is. Quickly, my nimble wife produced a small spiral-bound notebook and a fine-pointed pen. She feverishly wrote down the names and exit number of the restaurants that we might want to return to after turning back.

As we torturously watched the steakhouses, BBQ joints, and Mexican food restaurants drift by, we both knew, somewhere in the back of our minds, that there was only one real and true consideration for where to eat. We had known this since we were back in Arizona, over 500 miles away.

The Big Texan Steak Ranch.

The Big Texan bragged on billboards for hundreds of miles in every direction that it was the home of the "free" 72oz steak. Yes, it is free, so long as you eat the steak and all the fixin's in under an hour. It is dressed with a full baked potato, shrimp cocktail, a green salad, and, presumably, an entire hog. It is a feat that has been accomplished, purportedly, by people ranging from 12 to 85 and has, from time to time, been accomplished in stunningly short amounts of time. There was one dude—a professional wrestler in the 60s—who ate two of them in an hour. Take a moment out of your day to imagine the look and smell of a wood-fired steak that is four and a half pounds. Imagine sitting down next to it, taking in the bouquet, picking up the small fork and knife, and starting off on a culinary journey of epic proportions. And then imagine doing it again. What. The. Crap.

We passed the Big Texan, just one exit up from where we had to turn to get to the KOA. A massively kitschy cowboy stands out front, announcing the restaurant and bragging just a bit about his Texan heritage. And despite the fact that it was Father's Day, the place didn't look like it was bursting forth with people.

"What do you think?" I asked.

"Don't you think it's expensive?"

"Not if we're *really* hungry."

Her face adopted a stern expression. "You're not eating that. I don't want to be embarrassed."

"You'd only be embarrassed if I can't eat it. I know that I can," I reasoned.

"There's no way in hell that you're going to ruin my honeymoon by eating that much steak."

While her argument seemed—at the time—oxymoronic, I could see that by the way she invoked "ruin the honeymoon," there was no way I was going to push any further. But still.

The world of vacation campgrounds can be easily broken up into two rather large categories. The first is good campgrounds. These are places that are well wooded, private, nd exciting. You can't wait to pitch your tent, start a fire, and think about singing campfire songs. The second category is bad campgrounds. These are ones that are depressing. These are open, close together, and generally bad-feeling. You can imagine staying there as a homeless person, looking forward to the shower you might have the next day as the highlight of your week. The one we found in Amarillo fell into this second category. It would have been serviceable were we traveling by RV and just needed a place to park it for a while. But since we actually wanted a camping experience, it just wouldn't do to set up in what was mainly a parking lot with patches of unwelcoming grass.

"What else can we do?" Charlie said. "This is cheap. Do you think we can find a hotel room that's this cheap?"

"Well, no, but maybe just tonight we could stay in a hotel."

The sun was setting and we had to move. If we didn't find a decent room in a couple quick minutes, it would be too dark to fall back on the campground.

As we rushed to join I-40 once again, we saw a sign. The sign came in the form of a billboard. It was an advertisement for the Big Texan Motel. What. We had never heard of such a thing, and surely it would be too expensive and lame to really stay there. Did you get your night free if you slept in under an hour? No, actually, you don't. But the terms were reasonable. By announcing that we were on our honeymoon, she gave us a good deal on a room out by the Texas-shaped swimming pool(!).

The room was, to be honest, rather shocking. I mean, I know that the Big Texan is the ultimate in Texas kitsch, but this was bordering on the awesome. The room was, from floor to ceiling, wooden. I mean, really, really wooden. It's hard to describe the plank boards making up everything you see as anything more elaborate than wooden. The windows were covered with barn-style wooden shutters. The mirror frame was the same rough-cut wood as the walls reflected in it. It was like living in a stable for one awesome night. Or being turned into a bore beetle, tunneling through the wood inches below the bark of a mighty pine.

The only non-wooden things were the porcelain things, and the bath was a Jacuzzi bath, which made things all the better. There was a chance that a short spin in that whirlpool tub would even make a dent in the pain that both bride and groom were feeling in their feet, thanks to the long walk in new Docs. It didn't, but there was a chance, and that at least felt good.

Charlotte and I had barely a moment to discuss the intricate sensation and smellsation of the wooden hotel room before we had to bust our asses to get over to the restaurant before it closed. All the puttering about in wooden admiration had brought us dangerously close to last call at the Steak Ranch, and, by God, I needed some steak after that long day on the road and that shit lunch. In the fashion of the times, we moseyed (rather than sauntered) over to the restaurant and took a seat in a cozy booth in the corner.

The place was campy; "sick-funny," is the actual term we used for it. The walls were covered in the heads of former animals; cows, deer, elk, buffalo, and any other remotely edible large mammal had a representative specimen adorning the room. Great chandeliers hung from the ceiling, two floors up, giving the illusion that you're eating in an old Texas ballroom. The waiters paraded about in cartoon-like caricature of cowboys. The menus were printed on a slab of wood and came with a diagram of where each cut of steak comes from and how one should ask for it to be prepared.

Sauntering (rather than moseying) around the dining hall were three rather authentic looking cowboys each outfitted with an instrument; two guitars and an upright double-bass. For a small tip, they'd stop by your table and sing an old cowboy song to you and your friends. I thought it was a bright idea to invite them—for a shilling or two—to sing "Cool Water" at our tableside, one of our favorite tracks from the immortal *Gunfighter Ballads and Trail Songs* by Marty Robbins. That album, practically perfect in every way, was one of the favored CDs that we'd brought along and had gone perfectly with the western landscape of the day like some kind of wine that's supposed to go perfectly with some kind of fancy fish.

"What'd you think?" I asked my wife, watching the cowboys play a song a couple tables over.

Her face went white. "About what?"

"About..." my wife's eyes widened and any remaining color wiped cleanly away from her face. "The menu? What are you going to have?"

Charlie was ever frightened of being the center of anyone's attention. I tend to forget that when something fun like singing cowboys comes along. God help us all when we end up in the frontish rows of some fancy play and the actors come into the audience. She would really and truly shrink to nothing before the eyes of the entire audience. I had backed out of the suggestion just in time, as the cowfolk came up to our table and I gently sent them their own way before my wife had a chance to freak out.

"You make fun," my wife says, looking over the manuscript. "But it's stupid for the characters from a play to walk into the audience. Are we supposed to be excited? It's humiliating. After all, people don't do that in real life. We don't break out and go sauntering through a crowd of viewers. Imagine the reality of that."

I admired the menu a bit longer before deciding on what I already knew I would have, the ribeye. It was a forgone conclusion that a honeymoon was no place to really try and eat a gigantic steak, even though the table in the middle of the room, up on the little stage, with a digital timer next to it presented a tempting offer of free beef. Walking away as the object of every glutton-watcher's glee wasn't the right and proper way to adjourn to a wooden room with one's bride of only a few days. It was, in fact, a classless notion that just happened to be rather hard to come to grips with.

There was a time in my life when I was game for such things. One might think this time in my life shameful, but, to be honest, I'm quite open with it, you will kindly note. It was college, and while many of my compatriots happily adopted the sins of drinking, drugs, or rampant sex, I embraced overeating. I'm sure it was a coping mechanism of sorts. I went to school in San Diego, at a notorious party school, and I just couldn't manage to fit in with the crowd. None of the partying vibe interested me in the least. I enjoyed surfing—or, at least, boogie boarding—but nothing else in the lifestyle of the San Diegan College Student held the least bit of interest, for whatever reason (or, at least, if girls did interest me, I felt as if I terminally disinterested them, so kept my distance.) I didn't get terribly out of control, weightwise, but I never was in great shape. I could easily have starred in a sitcom without feeling out of place.

We had this friend. He was the roommate of a pre-existing friend and, for whatever reason, and enjoyed paying people—in the form of a bet—to entertain others with acts of public foolery. He would bet you, for example, that you couldn't eat 24 saltines without taking a drink in the middle. While this was something that you could do, you would openly hate the endeavor and make a right ass of yourself earning the twenty bucks that he bet you. One of the best parts of his bets was that they weren't bets proper; he didn't make you put up the money that he was putting up. *He wasn't interested in winning, only in the sport of it.* This made everything in good fun for everyone. He once bet me that I couldn't eat a gallon of ice cream by myself, and, when that turned out to be true, my only punishment was to put the rest of the ice cream on my head and walk to the beach across the street where I could wash off. This was agreeable terms to everyone on the beach, as well as my friend.

We had just finished working on a video project together for my brother's filmmaking class and about seven of us were celebrating at a taco shop across the street from the college. There is, by the way, nothing in this world quite so wonderful as a taco shop in San Diego. This particular taco shop had wonderful *carne asada* burritos as did they all. But this one sold a large version of the *carne asada,* called, inconspicuously, The Fat Boy.

"I'll buy it for you, if you eat it," Brian said to me.

"Nah," I said, trying to sound reasonably detached.

"I'll buy it *and* I'll pay you one hundred dollars if you can finish it in a half hour."

"Sold," I said.

The Fat Boy was a *carne asada* burrito with all of the trimmings. Besides the steak, it had *pico de gallo,* cheese, lettuce, rice, beans, and guacamole. It was made with three large tortillas, all working together to make a burrito 27 inches long. Its girth hung off on both ends of the tray on which it was served. And it smelled terrific. Besides the seven people who we knew, the five or six others in the restaurant joined in and ooed and ahhed when it was delivered to our table.

I started eating. It tasted really great. Who wouldn't want to eat so much of such a good burrito?

Twenty minutes passed and I was only six inches into the Fat Boy, and getting really full.

"Sorry man," I said. "I can pay you back for the burrito. It's not gonna happen."

"I'll give you an hour."

"No, I'm pretty full, it's not gonna happen."

"I'll give you five hundred dollars!"

Now we were talking. I knew that if I dragged it out a little, I could earn much more than a hundred for it. "Okay, I'll give it a try."

And try I did. For the first time in front of him, I ate in earnest. I knew that I had a real eating problem because I ate differently in front of people than when I was by myself. If I went with my brother and a friend or two to Jack-in-the-Box, I'd order a value meal, right? Like a burger and fries and a coke. Big deal. But when I was by myself, I'd order several items together, all from the 99 cent menu: a Jumbo Jack, a chicken sandwich, a double cheeseburger, two tacos, and onion rings with a large coke. And I would make time just about every other day to stop in at The Box before or after walking to school (it was probably the two mile walk to school that saved my ass, come to think of it.)

So I unleashed the caged beast within me and started making a fool out of the Fat Boy burrito. I got Brian to refill my Pepsi, I got my brother to run up and get a couple cups of hot sauce. I asked for a side of chips and guac. Cheers went up and the restaurant goers gathered around to see what all the hubbub was about. Those that came in late were regaled with stories about how large the burrito had started out as and how I had played my cards to bait Brian into a bigger payoff.

All the while, Brian was excited, but not worried. Fifteen minutes in, he said, "You can't do it. I'm so sure you can't do it, I'll put up a thousand bucks!"

It was just what I needed to keep going. My determination was so obvious that another crowd-rallying cheer was sent up. Bite after bite, I would make it through the last sixteen inches of it; I *had* to. I had never had anything close to a thousand dollars before.

There were fifteen minutes left, and still eight inches to go. I felt like shit. The burrito, once a wonderful masterpiece, now tasted like dirt. The chips and guac sat mostly uneaten, my showboating obvious.

"What do you need to finish this?" Brian yelled at me. "What's it gonna take, Stronghold?"

Mouth full of beans, rice, and meat, I couldn't answer.

"The Cannon XL-1!" my brother yelled out. The XL-1 was the newest mini-DV camcorder on the market at the time and cost around five grand, where you could find it. It was broadcast quality (ESPN was using the damn camera for basketball games!) and we knew that our lack of having one was the only thing stopping us from international fame and fortune. With it, we would be superstars, we just knew.

This was all explained to Brian.

"You've got it, Stronghold!" Brian yelled. "A Cannon GX-900, or whatever it is, if you can finish this thing in 10 minutes!"

The crowd cheered, once more.

To be honest, the cheer didn't help. The camera didn't help. The intensity on my brother's face didn't help. I felt like a dead seal that had washed up on Del Mar beach on a relatively hot afternoon. There was still way too much burrito sitting around on my plate.

Chomp. Gomp. Chomp. The damn thing was hardly diminishing. There was five minutes to go and still five inches of burrito, which, I might add, was now cold burrito. A good twenty people sat and stood around watching, and observing, making conjectures on my chances.

"Dude," my brother yelled. "You gotta tell us the rules. Does he have to have it down or does he have to have it in his mouth?"

Brian thought about this, but he might as well not have, since he wanted to see the same madness my brother was looking for. "He has to have it in his mouth by the time limit, but he has to eat it all for it to count."

"You hear that bro!" my brother yelled (everyone was yelling at me, as if I was deep in a gorge, climbing gear failing me, and they were motivating me to get the hell up the mountain before the molten lava took me.) "You just have to get it in your mouth! Do it, damn you, do it!"

Shove. I started to shove the last five inches of burrito into my mouth. The entire room erupted in cheer. People were jumping up and down, hitting each other on the back, asking me to sign their take-out menus. Riding the wave of the crowd as if on a boogie board during el Nino, I got the whole of the remaining burrito into my mouth and feebly started to chew.

"You did it! You did it!"

"Five thousand dollars, oh my God!"

"Holy shit! Holy shit!"

I'm telling you, there were tears.

"Get it down! Take your time but get it down!" my brother kept yelling.

I was close, folks. I was really close. I've never been closer to winning the lottery or to getting on a game show or anything else in this life that can grant such a humble man, living so poorly, such a windfall. For what it's worth, my brother and I really and truly believed that getting the XL-1 would change our lives. We really did. This was going to be the dawn of a new era for us, like having all debts paid off sounds to me now. It was going to be terrific.

But it was all just a dream. While trying to chew and swallow the mouthful of rice, beans, meat, lettuce, tomato, onion, tortilla, and God knows what else, my body took over. I had had to open up my throat to fit it all in. The plan was to somehow chew the food in the front and then switch its place with the food in the back. My body, sensing real and terrible danger, stopped me from going any further. And there, right in front of the only crowd that I've ever truly pleased with genius and unique entertainment all my own, my throat pushed the excess food out, and from there, the mouth cooperated and it all ended up on the red plastic tray, right in the middle of the climax of the crowd's adulations.

There was disbelief. There was heartache. There was cheering and moaning and a general chaos. I coughed, complained, and took a long drag of Pepsi. I couldn't look in my brother's eyes. By now, many of the cooks from the back, who had been watching, put their sunglasses back on and went back to work. People who had walked in from the streets grabbed their skateboards and headed back out the door. People who had long since finished their food gave me a pat on the back, cleared their tray, and headed back to apartments and dorm rooms to study for the next day's exams. The press was notified to get back to work on more pressing stories.

I walked outside and, in the flower bed, quietly puked. My brother was there, slapping my back as if to help it come out more cleanly.

"Dude, you tried," he said, to let me know that I hadn't let him down. "I've never seen anything like it."

"Sucks," I said.

"Don't worry about it."

It was a Sunday night now and people had to be going. The glory had died away and now everyone wondered what the big deal was, anyway. Someone had cleared my tray for me, and my brother got me a refill on my Pepsi for the ride home. Right before we headed out the door, Brian, who was in the middle of telling the story to people around him for the tenth time, came up to me.

"Dude, that's the best time I've ever had in my entire life. My *entire life*. I owe you something."

"You paid for the burrito," I said. "I don't deserve anything else."

"You were so close I nearly pissed my pants. My God I've never had so much fun. Do you want to try it again some time?"

"Never."

"What can I do?"

"Buy me a root beer next time we're at Claim Jumper's."

"I'll figure something out."

That night, I swear this to you on everything I love, I dreamed of nothing but burritos. I dreamed and dreamed and dreamed, and they were all terrible nightmares. As the rice and beans expanded in my stomach, I would wake and rush to the toilet to throw up and heave and throw up again. Around three in the morning or so, my mild-mannered roommate, who wasn't at the gathering of the century, came down stairs to see me.

"You alright?"

"I don't know man."

"I'm not complaining, but your vomiting is waking me up. Do you think you need a doctor?"

"No, man. I'm sorry. I'm dreaming about burritos."

"No doubt."

That story, every word of it, did not impress my wife. And even if it did, and though I firmly believe that the 72oz steak would not have been any more difficult than the burrito hell that I had endured, it wouldn't be becoming. No, no. The ribeye. Let it be the ribeye. Fifteen solid ounces of marbled steak, with steak fries and a small Caesar salad, that would do. I was hungry after a day's travel like I felt that I had never been before, and I thought I could have tackled the beast-steak, but I'm glad that I didn't.

The steak was fulfilling the same way a hug from God must be. Even with the pitch-black nature of the room, closed in by its barn door-shutters, our night's lovemaking wouldn't have been possible, had I gone for the gusto and had the "free" steak.

Directions

In many ways, looking back at the honeymoon as a whole, we shouldn't have stayed as long in Texas as we did. It's a great place and driving through Texas is one of the true pleasures of the driving world (for at least the first five hundred miles or so), but we ended up moving there about a month after the honeymoon and spent six years getting our absolute fill of the place. And to top it off, we spent a lot of time with relatives while there, and that, honestly, isn't the most responsible use of honeymoon time.

We headed out of Amarillo toward Ft. Worth where we were going to visit my uncle and aunt. The road from the panhandle to the DFW area, Highway 287, is a beautiful stretch of road. Prairies, rolling hills, congresses of trees, quaint small towns, and miles and miles of sky accompany you the whole way. It's always longer than you expect it to be, which is mighty long in the first place, but it's pleasant nonetheless.

I suppose it goes without saying that the folks in Texas are friendly. We stopped for a drink and 'throom break at a Dairy Queen in the little town of Childress, population 6678, and I'm telling you, the difference in friendliness level between California and Texas was instantly obvious. Everyone in the restaurant, or at least the gal taking our order, inquired about how we were that day, what we might be up to that day, and where we were coming from; all these questions and she wasn't even arresting us! This was a nice town. We talked to an old gent in the parking lot and admired his dog. "Oh yeah," he said. "I used to have a whole lot of 'em when I lived out in the country. Now that I live in the city, I only have one." And my wife and I tried our best not to laugh at the suggestion that Childress could somehow be described as a city.

Witchita Falls is the first city on the road between Amarillo and the DFW area that sports a Whataburger. It's really hard to describe just how downright decent a meal at Whataburger really is. Yes, it is fast food, but it is by no means quite so nasty as something like Burger King or McDonalds. While In-N-Out Burger in California has a great share of fan-boys, Whataburger isn't quite so hip, for whatever reason. But the food is hearty and good, and, much like In-N-Out, it is a family owned chain and not a huge corporation. If you're going to be stuffed with lard, salt, and sugar, you may as well have a family do it and not a corporation.

We stopped at the Whataburger and were once again treated with as much politeness and respect as one can reasonably handle while ordering lunch. After our order, I stood in a short line to fill our cups with the fountain drink that is as prescription in a Whataburger, Dr. Pepper, behind two rather large gentlemen. Never have I seen such massive, hulking examples of what a human can grow to become. They had smiles on their faces a mile wide (probably solely because they were in a Whataburger) and everyone kept on talking to them. It didn't take me long to catch up on my Texas trivia and remember that Witchita Falls is the location for summer training camp for the Dallas Cowboys. While I'm not one to follow football myself, I found myself slightly star struck, eating in the unofficial Whataburger of the Dallas Cowboys Summer Training Camp and all.

I found that I was outclassed in the neighborhood of orders. The Dallas Cowboys there (two of them; I suspect one was a running back and one was an offensive lineman) had triple bacon Whataburgers. In that light, my single Whataburger value meal, even with the large size upgrade, was some kind of a sick joke. I resisted further upgrading, and resisted the relation of the story about the Fat Boy burrito and settled in on enjoying my meal.

What does Whataburger do best, you may ask? The answer might surprise you. While the burgers are great and the fries are top notch, and the breakfast is easily the best among all fast food places, their greatest achievement must be their ketchup. Here in the States, we live in a world so dreadfully lost in the clutches of Heinz that you may not even notice ketchup from day to day. Bland and red, Heinz ketchup lends little in the way of flavor. Even the simple shift to Hunts may find you in a better place next time you find yourself with a plate of fries. But Whataburger ketchup, served in little sealed cups instead of lame tear-away packets, brings even men of the sternest convictions to a place where truth must be confronted and past sins lamented; the conclusion reached is this:

No. One cannot live on one brand of ketchup alone. There must be variety in all things. What does that say about our increasingly homogenized corporate culture? Why is it that you, sitting in your reading room in Florida must drink the same Pepsi, watch the same *Grey's Anatomy* episode, and go to the same lame-ass Radioshack for power adapters? Folks, this makes as much sense as having Heinz ketchup on every table. Have a large order of Whataburger fries and Whataburger ketchup, and your entire religion might just change. I promise that's all I'll say about that.

We came into Arlington in the afternoon, following little printed directions to my uncle and aunt's house. The directions led us in an unbelievable knot of freeway twists and turns. We discovered a small kink in our planning, as we had somehow, when using Google Maps, mixed things up to the point where our directions were starting at my uncle's house and ending at Amarillo. This was a conundrum. I had to twist my head a little and try and help Charlie to give me reverse directions.

"Okay, start at the end, right? But start right where we end up getting on 287, see?"

"No problem. Okay. Then we just go in reverse from there, right?"

"Yeah...no. Wait. You have to look at the direction above it and reverse the direction of the turn."

"So if it says go left, on the direction above, we go right, but from below to above? This sucks."

It was like if a map threw up on you while you were sleeping. It was severely confusing, especially since there were better ways to go than just the reverse of the reverse directions. It was like doing the mirror image of a jigsaw puzzle, except upside down, and with the image turned schizophrenic. We managed to get there and as I cheered the revelation that we could follow these directions, Charlie just sat there and nodded her head in approval like Admiral Ackbar when the Super Star Destroyer *Hammer* is destroyed in *Return of the Jedi*.

Visiting family in Texas is fun. It's fun because—among other reasons—you get to eat good things. Charlotte and I took one day to ourselves and went to the Stockyards in Ft. Worth. The Stockyards is a decidedly touristy place, full of shops and restaurants and a rodeo place. It used to be the heart of the cattle trade in Ft. Worth and its roots as a cattle yard are evident, if, at times, contrived. We shopped around looking at boots and hats and other native garb and ultimately picked a place to eat. Can you say "unlimited beef ribs"? I can, and did, to our waitress. It's sort of amazing how different the result is from saying that phrase to your waitress from just saying it to yourself while reading a book. One of the above methods stops you from being hungry.

While it's not the time or place to complain about unlimited ribs, and Risky's BBQ isn't something I'd complain about, I would recommend a different place to eat, should you ever be anywhere near Ft. Worth. The reason—and only reason—that I hesitate to recommend

Joe T. Garcia's Mexican Food to you is because there's an off chance that I'll be there someday on a trip and that you'll be there because you read this book and then you'll get in line ahead of me and I'll have one more group to wait for before sitting down to eat myself. And that really, really sucks. Probably you'd be talking to your posse and I would overhear you saying, "I read about this place in this totally decent travel novel thing that I picked up at my local bookstore on a whim. No, I don't know if the whole book was really that good or not, me being some kind of prick who didn't read the whole book, but I totally flipped to the page that dealt with the DFW area to see what restaurant was recommended before coming on this trip. Actually, I just did a word search because I bought it on my Kindle (see, here's my Kindle, awesome, isn't it? I totally have one and I read books while riding on my Segway from my Kindle and it's boss, man, boss. I love having a million dollars) and I searched for 'Ft. Worth' and struggled through the chapter and read about this place. Man, why am I having déjà vu?"

Trust me, when that happens, I'll totally regret it, because Joe T's is no secret and the wait can get rather long. When my aunt and uncle took us there, the wait wasn't too bad. We sat out by the pool (there is an extensive variety of seating options available) and it was damn hot. The shade was just right and my folks ordered a pitcher of margaritas on the rocks that helped to cut the heat a little as well. The food there is beyond reproach. If you were to try the fajitas and later learn that they are, in fact, poisonous and would kill you if you ever had more than four orders in your life, you'd happily have three orders in as many days and split a fourth with a friend, then probably have another half order on your deathbed however many years later. The tortillas are really good, too.

We Hang out with the Aged

Driving around Texas, visiting and eating, we decided to apply for a few jobs. Previously, you will recall, to go to grad school at Baylor, seeking a PhD in Literature. That didn't work out, so one of our mandates for the trip was to find some other sort of plan in life. In a few short weeks, I would have my MFA degree and fully capable of teaching English at a college. I didn't have my sights set on Baylor—they had turned me down to even attend classes there—but that left two other options in town.

I trucked my little resume out and went over to the other two colleges in town; McLennan Community College and Texas State Technical College. I didn't get a real good vibe from either one, but especially not from TSTC. I walked into the Human Resources department to apply for a part-time job teaching English 101 and you would have thought that the lady wanted to get rid of me like a bad Charlie horse.

"You don't have enough experience for us," she said, shooing me away.

"How so, ma'am?"

"This is a transferable course. You need to have at least three years of teaching experience to teach a transferable course. It transfers to universities, so you need to be able to do that."

"Ma'am, for a year I did teach this very course at a university. So I taught not only the transferable course but the course at the college where a student may very well transfer."

"Sorry, come back in two years."

It was a fine compromise, her not wanting me to work there and me not working there, but I couldn't help but to feel insulted. I mean, here I had already told CSUMB that I wouldn't be back in the fall, and now I was adrift on the highways of the country hoping to find a place to live and there was this old lady telling me that I couldn't work at their technical college teaching welders and computer technicians how to write an essay. What in the world did this say about my chances at the other schools where I wanted to drop off a resume? Was Ithaca College going to laugh in my face? Was Portland State going to trip me on my way out the door? This was grim. Grim.

My grandma took us to the Dr. Pepper museum. This was the original Dr. Pepper bottling plant in downtown Waco, where Dr. Pepper was created, or, discovered is really a better word. In the lobby of the museum, an animatronic pharmacist tells you about how and why he made Dr. Pepper in 1885. Apparently he wanted to make a drink that—get this—tasted like a pharmacy smells. Um, yuck. The robot waves around his robot hand, clutching a robot cigar, but never smoking it. It makes one wonder about the self control a robot must have. Does the restraint fade away with the crowds? Or does the programming allow for addiction without satisfaction? Where do robot tears come from?

The museum is really quite a chronicling of the history of soda. They have old machines from every decade and bottles of rare and obscure sodas from around the world, as well as a history of Dr. Pepper advertising campaigns. The most amazing way that one has ever tried to sell Dr. Pepper is there, trapped as if in amber, the written and illustrated suggestion that one should "Serve Dr. Pepper Hot." There, in the picture, they showed a teacup of Dr. Pepper steaming hot with a slice of lemon floating in it. OMG, folks, OMG. The amazing thing, at least to me, is that I still haven't tried this. I mean, I don't have to like it and if I don't like it, I don't have to finish it, but I do enjoy me a good Dr. Pepper and I do enjoy hot beverages and, though it seems revolting, it appears to at least be possible to try Dr. Pepper hot. Maybe I should go try it right now and then write about the experience…no, no I won't.

One floor of the museum was dedicated to the anniversary of the Waco Tornado. During a period of a few days in May, several tornados touched down in the Waco area. Of them, the most devastating, the Waco Tornado, and F5, is tied as the most deadly tornado in Texas history, killing 114 people. It apparently damaged the Dr. Pepper bottling plant, along with much else in downtown Waco, leaving piles of brick everywhere and taking days to dig all the bodies out. The museum showed huge pictures of the destruction and some old codger standing near us started talking about how "That car right there was my daddy's" and reminiscing about the tornado.

My mom had a Waco Tornado story that I heard all time while growing up, and naturally enough for my mom, it was totally TMI. The story was that my grandpa, working downtown at the time, decided to come home early to plant flowers in the flowerbed, for whatever reason. Had he not come home early that day, he would very likely have been a victim of the tornado. And—here's where the TMI comes into play—that night my mom was conceived. Yuck, right. Totally yuck. I deserve a settlement check.

The bottom floor of the museum is mostly made up of gift shop. It was here that my wife and I bought tons of Dr. Pepper post cards and a T-shirt or two. It's just really hard not to. There's also an old time soda fountain on the bottom floor, and each paid admission to the museum gets a free Dr. Pepper made the old fashion way with the syrup and soda water added separately. Man, it was about the best Dr. Pepper one could possibly hope for.

Our last night in Waco we spent playing cards with my grandma. Triple solitaire. It's a rather intense game, once you get going, and everyone is trying to pile their six of clubs on top of the only five of clubs on the table and you have to wait for the hands to be pulled away to see who's card is really the bottom most. Charlotte won, which is quite a feat, since my grandma is an awful cheater.

If she had the same determination for painting that she has for cheating, her paintings would hang in all the great art museums in the world. She cheats cleanly and effectively, like a smart bomb going through the window of a ruthless dictator; cheating you can believe in. The only defense you have against her talent is to watch her like a hawk and then what you do is spend all your time watching her and none of your time playing your own cards. Before you know it, the scrap of table in front of her is picked clean and yours is still covered with cards. Perhaps it was my stubborn policing of my grandmother that aided my wife to her victory. Gloating is a matter of ritual at my grandmother's card table, and Charlie took to it with flying colors, sternly and unforgivingly rubbing our faces in her astounding victory, winning the best of 20 hands. Her bragging took her well into the morning and still, once in a while, her victory is mentioned when we, say, see a pack of cards for sale at Target.

On our way down to Austin, Charlie and I stopped at Salado for lunch. The little town about halfway between the cities is picturesque in a sort of western version of a Currier and Ives print. The main street is lined with old buildings, shaded by massive oaks, selling arts and crafts to day-tripping Texans, smattered by a few old hotels and restaurants. There's a small creek that runs through town that, every time you pass it, you or whoever is in your car says, "Oh look, pretty," as the water slips down a small series of waterfalls and goes under the bridge you're driving on.

The place where we ate (yes, yes, we ate again, goddamn it) is a restaurant attached to a hotel, The Stagecoach Inn, where my grandparents used to eat when they were our age. It's been around forever and boasts that it was a stopping place for Jesse James and his gang, as well as a place where Sam Houston gave some rather large speech about why Texas shouldn't leave the Union with the rest of the south. Dude probably just wanted the state to branch off into its own country so he could be a sovereign president again.

As usual, the restaurant was filled with old people. Just chock full of them. We sat at a nice table and listened to the menu—that's right, listened—to our three or four choices for the afternoon. We were in Texas, so we had chicken fried steak and iced tea along with several other courses served homestyle. Charlie and I sat and talked about plans for the rest of our honeymoon and a little about what we had been through before. The window next to us looked out at an oak tree hundreds of years old and the dining room was quiet with the tinkling of ice against glass and the occasional knife against plate. It was a peaceful lull in our travels, a calm in the middle of so much moving about. It felt like we stopped for a breath and took the time to reflect on what it was we were doing.

At the table next to us, an older couple stood up and started putting on their jackets. Central Texas is the only place in the world that I know of where old folks still put on jackets for lunch even though it's a hundred degrees outside. The man came over to our table and I was afraid, for whatever reason, that we had said something to offend him. He leaned over our table and spoke rather quietly.

"You two just got married?" he asked. We verified his accusation. "We're here celebrating our fiftieth anniversary. Just looking at the two of you, I can tell you will be as happy as we've been." His blushing bride smiled over his shoulder at us, her heart, no doubt, as warmed as his.

I'm somewhat of a bastard, I've come to find out over the years. I know that for sure because, in the moments after that couple left, all I could do was come up with comebacks for that sweet little message that they left us with. To be fair, Charlie joined in.

"I hope we're a hell of a lot happier than that!"

"What? You spent the last 49 years overseas?"

"You must have misheard us, we didn't marry *each other*."

And so on. I hope you don't think ill of us now, having totally tossed your sympathies aside by being so crude to the old couple. One or more of them is most likely dead at the time of this reading.

We Consider Splitting Up Again

Driving into Austin, we nearly got divorced. We had printed directions to get to the main offices of Austin Community College, where I was going to drop off some application materials. The directions were faulty to the point of foolery. The damn sheet of paper kept having us take an exit and go for miles in the wrong direction. It was obviously the wrong direction and yet, printed there in black and white, it was easy to trust; its sincerity was written all over the page and it refused to be silenced. We followed, realized we were too far away from town, and came back. We did it again. We did it a third time. We yelled.

Charlotte was always talking about this time at the circus when she really, really had to pee. I don't remember when in our relationship it was brought up, but once it was, it kept rearing its head. The story was that when she was 10 or so, her family went to the circus. At the circus, she had too much punch or something and really, really had to pee. But the thing was, the circus was far too entertaining. One supposes that there were clowns and acrobats, savage lions and unforgetful elephants. Perhaps a man had trained dogs to stand in a reverse pyramid atop a rolling barrel in plain sight of a plate of sausages that the dogs were refusing to attack, all out of pure discipline. Clearly, all these sights to behold, one after the other, were far more interesting than a five minute trip to a scummy old port-a-potty outside the big top, so poor little Charlie simply crossed her legs and smiled, as if nothing were wrong.

This little war story of hers would always pop up when she had to pee. "Oh my god, I have to go to the bathroom! Where the hell is the next gas station? It's not as bad as the time at the circus, though." And so on. In our years of knowing each other well enough to discuss going to the bathroom, she had never, not even once, had to go to the bathroom as badly as at that circus, where she held it in for the sake of pure entertainment.

And now, as we drove around and around Texas' state capitol, she had to pee terribly.

"Like circus bad?" I asked.

"No, damn it, not that bad."

"So do I need to stop?"

"Yes you need to stop!"

"But you held it in during the circus and you don't have to go as bad at that. And the HR department is going to close soon."

"Stop! Stop right here!"

She was terribly angry and just couldn't let it go until I stopped. I was perturbed myself. While I knew that it wasn't her fault that she had to go so bad or her fault that it was 4:30 and we were no closer to finding the place than we were at 3:30, but I still registered on the irritated spectrum. We ended up stopping at ITT Technical institute and moments after she relieved herself, Charlie asked about the presence of their rival college. She came bounding out of the building with a smile on her face, no doubt because she was feeling three or four pounds lighter in the bladder.

"Across the highway," she said. "Five minutes away."

And sure enough, we weren't far from ACC after all. And while I wasn't laughed at or made to feel like a solemn and inconsequential part of the world, I wasn't much assured that they were going to hire me to teach English or Creative Writing, both of which I put in applications for.

"Call tomorrow," the lady on the 8th floor said. "Maybe someone will be here who can help." I did and they didn't, just so you know.

Bats Waste our Film

Austin is one of the best cities in the world. It still retains the quaint feeling of a small town while holding a large enough metropolis together to have some of the finest music, food, and culture you can find anywhere. The capital building in the heart of the city is a sight to behold—and behold it you will several times an hour while you're in Austin. The city is surrounded by greenbelt and borders hill country, making an afternoon escape into nature not only possible but desirable on all but the hottest days of the year. You can spend your day and night in Austin without much of a game plan and still stumble into several live music venues to catch one of the reportedly hundred live events that takes place every night in the city.

It was during our honeymoon that Charlotte and I discovered the greatest church of all churches, BookPeople. An independent bookstore in downtown Austin, BookPeople has an awesome variety of titles and attracts the best authors from all over the world for appearances and signings. I can easily spend an entire day in the store without the want of outside air or outside distraction, perusing through categories of books that are just plain hard to find at the retail chains. It's also a great place to buy souvenirs for those people you left behind to get to Texas who may or may not have funded your honeymoon.

Across the street from BookPeople is the perfect way to spend the rest of your money at Waterloo Records. The extensive selection of new and used CDs is very impressive, but even more so is the extensive collection of new and used vinyl records. The store has anything that a music lover could want and much for someone who just enjoys music in passing but has no real emotion for it.

Not knowing the great many places to eat in Austin, we stopped in at a Joe's Crab Shack. It was situated right across the lake from downtown and had a great view of the city. We sat on a wooden table outside and looked at the view. The edge of the lake, just yards away from us, had several turtles of various sizes sitting around, swimming around, and poking around.

"Turtles!" Charlie said. "Did you guys put them there?" she asked the waitress. This question confused the waitress a great deal. It revealed that Charlotte was a true central Californian. Being born and raised in a desert that has the sprinklers on, one never really sees a lot of wildlife, and something like a wild turtle becomes downright magical. There was a note of innocence in her question that, I think, made the waitress feel for her. From that moment on, she acted as though she were our personal waitress and personal host to the world of Austin. She seemed to be there before you'd call her, refilling your Dr. Pepper or giving you advice on where to catch a show that night.

It was unlike Charlotte to go to a seafood restaurant, even one that had a bunch of campy crap nailed to the walls where the waiters would get together and dance to the occasional disco song. She wasn't a daring eater and I know that she never had eaten crab before. And yet, before my eyes, she ordered none other than a big ass plate of crab. It far outclassed my shrimp order. When the crab came, intimidating and spider-like, she had no freaking idea what to do with it.

Enter our best friend.

The waitress, still adoring my cute little wife for thinking the turtles were somehow a tourist attraction, sat down next to her, produced a metal shell cracking device, and started opening Charlie's crab for her. She manhandled a couple of legs before handing the wheel over to my lobster-bibbed wife.

"Here, you try a couple."

Once she was certain that Charlie was ready to trade in her learner's permit for a license, our waitress left us to our meal in peace. It was not without some effort that I crushed the notion that the girl had a crush on my girl and should be invited to an evening of deviance. But, I'm sure, it was worth the effort.

Sunset found my wife and me joining every other tourist in Austin under the Congress Street Bridge. We sat on a grassy hill with at least 200 other people, all looking up at the bridge and waiting for the sun to go down. Sometime, just before sunset, we knew that we'd have a chance to see a bunch of bats. What could be more exciting?

We brought a little video camera with us. We had taken some footage at Grand Canyon and were interrupted by a microphone explaining the nature of the California Condor. We hadn't used it since then, except to document the woodenness of the hotel room in Amarillo. So far, the honeymoon video we'd bore our friends with had a know-it-all and a wooden room. Real exciting. I just knew that these bats would liven things up a little, move the audience to their feet at the sight of bats.

We got to our grass patch a little too early, it turns out. We waited and waited, watching more and more people arrive to their grass patches a little early. A grass patch just a few patches over, it turned out, housed another microphone. Apparently, this dude knew everything there was to know about bats and he would gladly entertain the masses by talking way too loud.

"Now, these are Mexican free-tailed bats. They're small, but live in a large colony. Every single night they eat between 10 and 20 thousand pounds of bugs." And on and on. The crowd around him didn't give him any encouragement, but luckily he didn't need any. All I could think about was that the dude had either visited a website or had our same waitress at the Crab Shack and now he was just regurgitating everything that he had memorized to try and impress everyone.

A brief fantasy played in my mind where the microphone became covered in mosquito and started sounding off everything he ever knew about mosquito and just in time for the bats to come out. The bats came out, started eating the hundreds of bugs all over this dude, but their proboscises were dug too deeply into his epidermis and the helpful bats carried him off to the cheer of the crowd. At least in my mind, justice was served.

After about 45 minutes, a few bats started coming out from under the bridge. They'd fly out of a crevasse in the cement work only to fly into another, making tiny noises all the way. Flashlights started shining small spots of light into the tunnels where the bats flew within and without[20]. I started filming.

Turned out, it was the wrong time to film. This strange bat warm-up ritual just kept going on and on and on for another solid 45 minutes. I kept starting and stopping the video camera, intermittently deciding that the shit was about to go down and that things were stalling out. To be fair, it's hard to know that it's not impressive to see a few hundred bats fly around. I mean, every time three or four hundred bats would come out, we'd think it was the beginning of a deluge. And they'd just go back in and tell their friends that it wasn't dark enough yet, or something.

Once the bridge was painted in burning red light by the setting sun, they started coming out in earnest. And once the light on the bridge turned to purple, the bats poured out like a tidal wave. One and a half million bats filled the sky. I filmed away, but it was too late, anyone watching the honeymoon video was just too

---

[20] It's hard to imagine how much spirits soar when the bat flight looks near. Watching a presidential candidate, say, or an ex-Beatle take the stage has nothing on it

bored already to care that there were so many bats at last. I had done a terrible job and ruined every chance of impressing family and friends with bats when we got home.

We walked up around to the top of the bridge and got a different point of view of the bats. From above them, you were looking down at a solid river of bat. It seemed like you could jump off and ride the bats into the sunset. I briefly considered putting the microphone down below into an arm lock and rushing him to the top of the bridge to toss him off so that we could see the bats carry him away after all. But I couldn't spot who he was from my vantage point so I decided to be the bigger man and just give up on it.

Interviewing Waco

We brought a cell phone along for emergency purposes. We didn't like the idea of being bugged by friends and family while on our trip, but we figured it would come in handy if we had a blowout or if, say the flittering flapping noise that our car made became some sort of disastrous problem that we needed to call the police about or something. For the most part, we told our folks not to call. Just don't call, okay? What's wrong with that? We'd call and check in and all, but we didn't want to feel owned by the cell phone.

Man, those were the days, when it was socially acceptable to tell people not to call your cell phone. You could even make the excuse that you don't have enough minutes or that it's too expensive because you're out of state. And now that the cheapest possible phone plan includes all these damn minutes and includes free long distance and roaming and whatever, people just call and call and you can't stop them. Anywhere you are in the world, people can call and bother you and act like it's their right. Hate.

So we were really surprised when our cell phone rang as we were getting dressed in our hotel room. We were even more surprised to see that it was a Texas number. I answered and discovered that MCC, the community college in Waco, wanted to interview me before I left the state. We set up an appointment for the next day. No problem, we'll just leave Austin a little early, drive to a Target or Penny's[21] and buy a nice shirt, and I'll do an interview. Stress-free honeymoon, right?

So I was all stressed out for the rest of the time in Austin. I didn't have any teaching materials and I didn't have any lesson plans and I didn't have a tie. I tried to keep my mouth shut and not stress Charlotte out with it all, but it bled in, little by little. When we went and bought a shirt, I felt a little better.

Back in Waco, we stayed with my other grandmother. She was an English professor at Baylor. She gave me some copies of writing assignments that she used to do so that I could fake like they were mine and I was all prepared for the interview. She also gave us a fat check, as she wanted to help fund our trip. With that money, we put the car in the shop to try and figure out what the flippity-flap sound was. I decided that even though it was clearly going to be an expensive problem, it would be a better way to spend the money than on the tires. The tires would last. They had to last.

I took my grandma's Mercedes to the job interview after Charlie and I dropped the Honda off with Manny, Moe, and Jack. I half hoped that the gentleman interviewing me would be out near the parking lot and see me pulling up in the Benz and be all, "Oh shit, a Benz! We totally need this professor here." But he wasn't, so he didn't and I had to rely on my interviewing skills.

---

[21] Really, this is just an expression; I would never buy anything at a real department store on purpose. Hell, it might not even be an expression; it could just be a typo that I'm too lazy to fix.

It turned out to be a fine interview. Mostly we just talked about both my grandmothers, as he had known them as writing instructors, then we talked about Iraq, since his son was shipping out there, then San Diego, since that's where his son was leaving from, then the giant burrito, since that was in San Diego and on and on without too much talk about writing or teaching or jobs or anything. He made it clear that they only had part-time positions available and I made it clear that that was fine, that's all we were looking for; part time work in a place that was cheaper to live than Monterey and we would get other jobs to support ourselves.

I got back to my grandma's house, where Charlie was waiting, and we got our second phone call on our little cell phone. Moe had apparently found and solved our flippity-flappity problem. I gritted my teeth when he said, "It'll cost you" imagining it would be the rest of our honeymoon fund and we would just drive home, heads hung in shame, and sneak around our parents' attics for a few weeks so no one would know we had to come home. We would live like feral raccoons.

But instead, it was just fifty bucks.

"What?" I asked.

"Yeah, there was a paper towel stuck in the intake on the passenger side. If you had just ducked down there, you could have seen it."

Relief made a brief stop in my heart before it was drown out with disappointment. "And that costs fifty bucks?"

"That's our diagnostic fee. I didn't charge you for labor," he laughed, knowing he could have speared me for another fifty, had he wanted. "You know," he continued, "you might want someone to look at these tires…"

"That's fine, thanks, we'll come down and get it, thanks." This dude didn't realize that even though I was proven a fool for ignoring the flippity-flappity issue, I would do nothing like pay any attention to the tires. If I were to properly ignore these tires, I had to deceive myself into believe that there wasn't a problem. This dude just couldn't—or wouldn't—let me live a happy little life without tire trouble. I wasn't about to waste four hundred bucks this early on the honeymoon. What an ass[22].

---

[22] Which of us is the ass? Read on! Read on!

Joe King

We had one more uncle of mine to visit in the DFW area to make sure that no one was overlooked or left out. Charlotte was a bit fed up with the hanging out with family thing, as was I, but it did cut down on our costs a little, despite the lack of privacy on our honeymoon.

This other uncle of mine made a mean smoothie. That's what I remember most about our stopping there. The dude had perfected smoothie manufacturing the way some people perfect an old family chili recipe or alchemy. While his kitchen looked nothing like a Jamba Juice or Smoothie King, if you sat in the living room and just listened to the tinkering and clacking, followed by the violent blending, you'd think there was an army of teenagers with stylish hair pouring liquidated fruit into a Styrofoam cup just for you. The smoothies easily tasted that good and cleanup was so quick that you'd hardly know the guy was put out at all.

My aunt was out of town, working for an airline as a stewardess, I mean, airline hostess…no, wait…flight attendant. One shouldn't insult her or the industry by using any other such terms. The 60s, apparently, in a mad rush to fill seats with business men ruined the name "stewardess" before they had the chance to resemble something classy like, say, a waitress or a coroner. Knowing that businesses had the cash to send a guy from coast to coast for a meeting, they started marketing the appeal and availability of their air crew as lures for the men who would have to spend time away from their families. Some airlines ran ads that said, "Shortest skirts in the air" and showed pictures of ladies lounging about in the laps of business travelers, taking orders for, presumably, scotch on the rocks. Northwest Airlines, I believe it was, ran ads where the individual ladies would introduce themselves to the happy magazine reader with the text, "I'm Susan, Fly Me!" Their eyes looked longingly into yours in a way that let you know—not think or suspect—but know that clothes were coming off. It's silly and entertaining to us now, sure, but don't call a flight attendant a stewardess; it's practically a form of sexual innuendo.

In an effort to show us a good time, my uncle, forever mystified at my dislike, or at least avoidance, of wine, took us to a tapas bar. Tapas were the new thing for the upper-middle in the Dallas area that summer— some kind of Spanish appetizer, round and bite-sized to be served with distilled grape beverages of various breed. To be honest, I didn't see what all the hubbub of the tapa was, but the bar was a pleasant and soft place walled in cubbies for wine bottles.

After tapas, we went to Finn Fest. Some fresh-mex restaurant (you know the kind of place, fish tacos, cilantro, lime and all that) was having a small music festival with the headlining act of Joe "King" Curasco. The self-proclaimed King of Tex-Mex Rock-n-Roll played a rollicking set, some kind of mix of calypso, Tejano, and zydeco. While it wasn't my favorite music or my favorite venue for a concert—the parking lot of a strip mall—the dude had a spirit about him and an enthusiasm that made it easy to watch. The burger I had was pretty damn decent, too.

Banjo Buddies

We got up early to leave for Memphis. We had a good time in Texas, loved Austin and the food and all, but we just had to get the hell out of there already. We spent nearly a week of our honeymoon surrounded by people who came to the wedding. We yearned to be on our own again, so leaving before the sun came up was a damn good idea. We had one last smoothie of my uncle's design—this time a little tart—and hit the road.

I had only been through Arkansas once in my semi-adult life and was excited to see it again. Growing up in California, it's easy to discount what is widely seen as the "lesser states," thinking California to be the most beautiful of places. Trust me, California does have its moments; the central coast, the northern forest, the majestic Sierras, all places that can't be missed for one who loves natural beauty. But driving through Arkansas, a Californian is blown away by just how freaking green the world can look. Arkansas has an overgrown look to it, full of rivers, trees, vines and snakes that just beg to be looked at. We wouldn't be staying there long—just passing through on our way to Tennessee, but it was a wonderful site nonetheless.

There was a bit of a conundrum going through a state where we weren't staying the night. We had seen this problem earlier in our trip in New Mexico, and we were encountering it again. What problem, you ask? Okay, fine, fuck it, I'll tell you.

We had this hare-brained idea before we left on our trip that, since it was our honeymoon and we were going to be going through so many new places, that we should have sex in each and every state that we came to. This became seemingly impossible just a few days in since we left Grand Canyon in the morning and knew without a doubt that we would not be spending the night in Tucumcari but going on to Amarillo. I had this bright idea though, since we both smelled like campfire and s'mores and didn't have enough coin for the showers at the campsite, that we should stop for a shower at one of the large truck stops. It dawned on me that it was a brilliant idea because we could easily share a shower and have it be—you guessed it—a sexy shower! The very thing I had been pushing for since well before our honeymoon was looking like a reality.

Look, the place was clean, okay? We were newly married, madly in love, and I wasn't writing a book about it all at the time, so it didn't seem at all sleazy. For real, it really didn't seem sleazy at all, but adventurous and exciting. The people had no problem with us sharing a common shower room, which was also easy on the pocketbook.

Even with the cleanliness of the place, and the fact that the door shut and locked and the whole room was well-lit and pleasant, as far as public bathrooms go, things just didn't, you know, work out. There was nervousness and pressure and we were standing up and all and the energy, ultimately, just wasn't there. I spent a good deal of the afternoon feeling bad about it, dealing with those common feelings of worthlessness and suicidal fantasies and all of the terrible things that comes with not being able to please your girl in a truck stop shower in the middle of the desert.

And now we were going to embark on that journey again. We were fueled by the freedom of knowing that we were out of the clutches of relatives and the energy that comes with having a totally decent smoothie at the break of dawn. We spotted a nicer looking truck stop and pulled of the highway. Shower bucket in hand, we walked inside and ordered a shower as politely and unnaughtily as we could. And you know, it should have been a sexy little endeavor, right? Walking off to go and screw under their noses. But instead, there was that same nervous feeling.

And let's face it; Charlie wasn't that in to it. Shower time was cleaning time. She may have seen a great deal of the world as a backdrop for sexual exploits, but showers were never it; I knew this and understood it. There didn't seem to be a lot of other options for us at the time. Our car was too filled with gear and luggage to consider parking somewhere in the dark of night, plus, we were only driving through in the daytime. The shower thing was our way of taking a risk without it really being risky.

Once more, it didn't pay off.

Cleaned up and dressed, we left the truck stop. Charlotte was more than a little perturbed, and I was more than a little humiliated. On the way out the door, I picked up some drinks and snacks for the car, while she went to put the shower bucket away. Then, right there at the register, I saw something that was going to make it all better.

A "newspaper" headline boasted indisputable evidence that Saddam Hussein and Osama bin Laden were lovers. Excited by this information, I shelled out the $5.99 and took it to the car with me.

The article, complete with pictures, showed proof and fulfilled its promise to break the little bit of tension between Your Humble Narrator and his bride. One shot showed Saddam leaning back, holding a rose, in the comforting arms of his terrorist lover. Another showed them riding a shared horse on a beach. A third—and perhaps most amazing shot—had them dressed in tuxedos playing banjos, the caption reading "Banjo Buddies!" I wasn't aware that playing banjo (one of only two American instruments) was a common activity for Muslim hard-line homosexual terrorists, but there it was in black and white.

There really isn't much like watching my wife laugh. She really lets go and bellows, teeth open to the air, when she finds something funny. And this article and the accompanying pictures were absolutely priceless. At least, they were worth much more than the six bucks at this time in my life. The silliness of our sexual romp dissipated into the wind, and we never did try the truck stop quickie again. I can't say I'm sorry for it.

A Novel in Braille

Trying to plan ahead, I had called from my grandmother's house to make reservations at a KOA in Memphis. The lady on the other end of the phone told me that all the cabins were taken. I told her not to worry, because unlike the schmoes in the cabins, my wife and I were hard-core and wanted a tent site. We didn't mind that we hadn't seen the place, we just wanted to save a little cash.

"Trust me, you do not want a tent site," the lady said.

"Why not?" after all, ten bucks seemed like a steal.

"The mosquitos are *unreal* around here right now."

That was enough to discourage me from thinking we should camp along the banks of the Mississippi. The biting bug problem in Texas had been one of unreasonable proportions. While they never did develop a taste for my blood, they hounded my wife like she was some kind of rock star in a cloud of teenage groupies. I have little doubt in my mind that her blood is sweeter and tastier than mine, her being all cute and me being all dude, but I didn't realize that such slight blights on society had discerning pallets. I was bite-free while Charlie's legs felt like a novel written in Braille.

No worries, though! We didn't need a cabin and we wouldn't mess with bugs: we had the internet. I simply got on to a discount hotel site, made a silly offer on a hotel in Memphis and waited for it to be taken. Taken it was, and the Lucky Strike Inn had sold a room. We printed directions and were happily sated.

We crossed the grand Mississippi into our sixth state of the trip so far.   Crossing the Mississippi, I couldn't help but to have a long feeling of nostalgia for a place that I had never been. I have always been a fan of Mark Twain and admired the life that he breathed into the Mississippi for me. Naturally I had read *Tom Sawyer* and *Huck Finn*, but I had also read his mostly non-fiction book *Life on the Mississippi* and stood in amazement of it. I had never seen a place come off the page like the Mississippi did for me while reading that book. He took something so meaningful to him and made it absolutely tangible for me. I remember reading it one day while sitting in a hot tub in San Diego and thinking, "I've got to go there, I've got to ride that river." Besides crossing it a few times, I never have interacted with it much.

This wasn't true for my grandfather, I have come to find out. My grandpa piloted a B-25 bomber in North Africa during the war. He was a hot-shot hero-type, the kind of larger than life person you hear about but rarely meet. When he and his buddies returned from the war, they wanted something exciting to do, so they planned a trip down the Mississippi on a boat of their own making.

They made a boat out of old telephone poles and outfitted it with a tent for a cabin and outboard motors for steering. They started somewhere north of Memphis and had a mind to make it down to New Orleans. Reading about war heroes sold papers back then and the news caught up with them whenever they made port in a new town down the river. My grandpa, being the captain of the ship, was quoted in several articles down the Mississippi valley, some of which are still in my family's possession. At the termination of their trip, in the Big Easy, they put on tuxes that they brought along and went and had a night on the town. The town had been expecting them and gave them a warm welcome. When he was asked, in New Orleans, just why they did the trip, my grandpa said, "Durn'd if I know."

Some macho thing for a bunch of veterans to do, now that the war was over. And what an awesome experience. For years many of us in my family wanted to repeat the trip, along rather more civilized lines, and we never got around to it. I guess we just didn't feel like it enough.

Darth Monkey

Memphis was an exciting looking city. Driving over the bridge, you see a huge glass pyramid sitting on the banks of the river against the backdrop of downtown. As hungry as we were and as much as we wanted to see the city right away, we really wanted to check into our hotel first to clean up and change clothes. As usual, getting to the hotel turned out to be a bit more complicated than we had planned. By the time we found the Lucky Strike—much farther from downtown than our online booking site suggested, Charlie had to pee terribly. Again there were images of circus clowns dancing in her head.

Some kind of transformation comes over that girl when she has to pee. It's hard for me to imagine that she worked so hard to hold it in while watching the circus that once because her mood must have slid down the desperate pit of despair where happiness goes to drown and positivity is a strange nostalgic feeling somewhere in the dark. She gets snappy, irritable, and just plain downtrodden. Before we checked in, she was pretty sure she didn't want to see Memphis anymore, she wanted to go to sleep and be done with it.

"Oh, come on. How often are we here?"

"I'm just too tired. We shouldn't have gotten up so early," she moaned.

"You just need to pee. I can tell. Just relax and have faith."

Unfortunately, nothing was that simple with the hotel. This Lucky Strike Inn that had looked so promising online was rather trashy in personal experience. Even though our discount booking site promised that all rooms booked were non-smoking, ours smelled like a burning tobacco field. It was serviceable enough to help Charlie empty her bladder and her mood improved just a little. I called the front desk and insisted on a different room. We switched, only to find the new non-smoking room to be rather less smoky, but still very clearly smoked in. The Lucky Strike was true to its name, and Charlotte crashed out on the bed.

"What pillow is that?" I said.

"I brought it from the car."

"That's *my* pillow again! I brought that for me!"

"But it's the perfect pillow. Just let me take a nap with it and then we can go. Take a shower or something."

Shower. Fuck. That's what it was that was making her so sour, I figured. Her mood, damaged by her need to go to the bathroom, clearly brought back the negative feelings from the failed sexual escapade. The feelings were drowned away by the Weekly World News only temporarily. They'd surfaced again now, and what we needed was a prescription from Dr. Love. Medication administered, moods healed, we got dressed again and left for a night on the town.

Needless to say, we headed straight for Beale St. My dad had recommended a restaurant that he claimed had the best BBQ pork ribs in the world. It was strange being in Tennessee for the first time and taking the trip down the road of pork barbeque. Texas, clearly a cattle state, found ways to use parts of the cow that were originally too tough to eat, thus the invention of slow smoking the brisket and turning it from a tough, fatty knot into God's gift to man. We were now in the land of pulled pork and baby back ribs. I had to open my mind a little and let go of the old ego to try and experience the food of the locals without a bent judgment of superiority.

The Blues City Café was a hell of a place. It was clear from the get- go that this wasn't some kind of fancy place, but a legit dive that had made a name for itself. Walking into it was more or less like walking into an old diner that you can find in just about any old Main Street in the states. The place was packed, though, and full of life. I really like a loud, noisy restaurant. Many times in my life I have just walked away from a place that looked like it featured plenty of good food because it was either empty or too quiet. I love going out to eat (in case you haven't noticed) and I love it much more when there's action around, people to watch, excitement to be had.

We sat down right in the middle of the action at a table crammed next to several others. We both ordered a rack of ribs (we could smell them, for God's sake, and man, were we hungry) with fries and a Dr. Pepper. The Dr. Pepper was a good one—I've become quite a connoisseur—and it was served in a huge plastic cup, making excessive drinking not only a pleasure, but much more easily accessible.

And when the ribs came? Oh my. These ribs were just about out of their minds with flavor. They were clearly out of their heads in the tenderness department (beef ribs, for all their savory goodness, can never be considered tender). The meat fell off and left clean little white bones that you could use to make little log cabins on your plate to house your French fries. We didn't do this, but we probably should have.

We filled ourselves to the point of popping and then wandered out into the nightlife.

The first and most remarkable thing that caught our eyes was the monkey. A gentleman had a monkey right outside the door of Blues City and was charging people to have their picture taken with it. I don't know what kind of monkey it was, but we can describe it accurately through what it wasn't. It wasn't a gorilla, an orangutan, a chimp, a howler monkey, a gibbon, one of those ones with the big noses, a baboon, a spider monkey (though we're getting closer here), or any kind of lemur. It was one of those monkeys that's mostly black but with a white circle around its face. You know, a hoppy little monkey with a long tail that was on that lame movie *Outbreak* and a couple episodes of *Friends*. I should have just checked Wikipedia or something.

At any rate, Charlotte had always had an irrational fear of monkeys. I'm not sure if she thought they'd bite her or carry her off like Dorothy, but she generally shies away from the very thought of them and covers her eyes at the unsightliness of their primate presence. Now, however, she was not running for the river, but rather looking at the simian with her eyes wide open and her breathing slowed.

"I think," she said quietly, almost to herself, "I think I have to."

"Have to what?"

"I have to do this."

Watching Charlie approach the organ grinder was like watching Luke Skywalker rush to confront Vader. I mean, here was Luke, brave and all, but he still had to face his *own father*. I mean, he had grown up hearing stories of his dad's heroism and even thought that Vader *killed* his dad, then he finds out that his dad is the supreme asshole of the whole galaxy, right? And he has to face him or else he has to forfeit the freedom of everyone in the galaxy. It's not like he wants to kill the guy, and he knows his dad can totally kick ass, and he knows that the shit is going to go down. His own sister tells him to get the fuck away, to hide and he's like, no, no I won't; I have to face him. I mean really, the guy didn't want to but knew that he had to and it was like beyond bravery for him to do it. My God, I'm tearing up.

So Charlie was the same way. She knew that, for whatever reason, she had to face her own Vader, this little monkey. Stoically, she approaches the organ grinder and asks if she has to pay to have the monkey on her. He says no, just for the picture, if she wants one. The monkey gets on her and her face is beyond disbelief.

Her eyes widen and her jaw lowers. The monkey starts playing with her hair. It was really an amazing sight to see.

Then, of course, she yelled. Not a huge, guttural yell, but a high one. Not like she was dropping from the side of the Grand Canyon, but more like a foul ball was headed her way and she was ill prepared to catch it. And, what was this? The yell turned into a laugh. A *good natured* laugh. She took a coin out of her pocket and handed it to the little simian. He put it in his tiny monkey apron and kissed her hand. Proud? You bet I was.

We left the scene of the monkey-madness, and took a stroll down Beale. The street is, at least on the weekend nights, shut off to car traffic. It was filled with people out enjoying their night surrounded by bars, clubs, gift shops, and street performers. We stood for a while watching a few guys impress the crowd with a bevy of running flips and somersaults. I don't know if these were the same dudes, or same troupe or whatever, that was on the Tom Cruise movie "The Firm" or not, but they were good. I thought about pulling out the video camera and filming, but I knew in my heart of hearts that I wouldn't know when to start filming and they'd end up taking a break for a long time while I turned on the camera to catch them stretching or something.

We had consulted our guidebook before getting to Memphis to see fun things to do on Beale. B.B. King's night club was going off, but we didn't really want to deal with a place quite that crowded or expensive to get into. The other thing listed in the book was the Police Museum. It was supposedly filled with artifacts and exhibits that we wouldn't want to miss. Plus, it was totally free! How could such a thing be offered?

Since our guidebook was about the entirety of the United States, and since the USA is a big and generally interesting place, we figured that even though each section was going to be relatively small and devoid of detail, that it would surely include only the most interesting and exciting things. So this Police Museum, being only one of two things listed on Beale St., had to be great.

It didn't take long to find the museum, and it took even shorter for us to decide that we had been ripped off. That's right. Even though it was free and we spent five minutes finding the place and three walking through, we wanted our money back. We wanted more than our money back, as a matter of fact. We wanted like fifty-thousand dollars back. That only seemed fair, considering the trouble we had gone through, going all that way, from California to Tennessee, just to be met by this museum. I mean, at this moment in time, our entire existence had led to this place. It was the culmination of our beings. I had traveled miles and over years and years to get there. I had been born in Texas, traveled to New York, Chicago, lived in California, went to school, had dozens of field trips, gone to college, met people, rented apartments, worked jobs, fell in love, got married, and finally driven to this, the very finality of all my experiences up to that point, this museum. It was beyond worthless. It's exactly like if I were some sort of super Christian who had worked and devoted his whole life to get to Heaven, only to find out that heaven was ten feet squared and filled with bric-a-brac and being looked over by a guy in a fake uniform watching Maury Povitch on a snowy television screen. Where is my fifty grand?

We left the museum, anxious to get back to the hotel, where, in bed, I whispered my memories of the ribs from Blues City, trying to find their place in the pantheon of best foods I've ever eaten. Charlie was asleep before I had finished detailing their texture.

Waffles in the Rough

Elvis. Freaking Elvis. We wanted to go a pretty long way that day, but Elvis was standing in the way. Clearly, he wasn't literally, but, you get it. Our original vision of the trip was stopping at all the little touristy areas. We had missed Carhenge, by mere miles and not gone there. That seemed some sort of a travesty at the time. And even though we wanted to get to Virginia by that night, it just didn't feel right to ditch out on Graceland. I mean, we did do the goddamn Police Museum, and it was too lousy to even be kitschy.

In the months leading up to the wedding and honeymoon, we spent hour upon hour in the Borders[23] bookstore in Sand City, California. It was a pretty good bookstore, as far as those chains go, and we'd check in every weekend and pull out some travel books, state by state, and see what there was to see. We'd bring along our atlas because we weren't even sure on a route, just a few places that we wanted to hit for certain. One book that we kept coming back to was something like *Weird Travels* or *Roadside America* or something. Or maybe there were two of them. We were always on the lookout for Mystery Spots or ridiculous statues.

---

[23] Borders keeps popping up in this book. Poor giant corporate bookstore! May you rest in peace! How I loved your layout and your café! Your chai latte, vastly superior to the Starbucks variety, lives on only on the tongue of my memories!

Why, you may ask, were we in a Borders instead of a library? I honestly can't answer that question very well. It seems like the big chain bookstores have almost transformed their private stores into public places on purpose. I am of the generation that would gladly sit and study in a Barnes and Noble because of the pleasant lighting and expensive coffee, taking notes from books that won't be bought, while a library down the street sits empty. Older, wiser, and poorer (or at least with a better understanding of money), we spend our time much more in libraries these days. But I'm telling you, I know people younger than me who think that there's little difference. With an iPod on and your blue tooth and cell phone handy, every public place is transformed into a private space, and vice versa.

A night at the Smoking Inn came with a breakfast in the morning. This was a handy moneysaving device that just about compensated for not staying in a tent the night before. Well, almost. And the breakfast was much better than the buttered toast in Kingman. Her head still resting on my perfect, perfect pillow, Charlie opened her eyes and looked at me. "I'm exhausted," she said. "We were out too late last night."

"Gotta get to Virginia," I said, cheerily. "And there's breakfast!"

"Why don't you go ahead," she said. "Bring me something small back. I could use the rest."

I grabbed my book—essential gear for eating alone—and headed down to the lobby, a corner of which served as a service area for food. There was the usual array of prepackaged muffins and Danishes, but there was also—what's this?—a waffle iron. Ahh yes, a waffle iron. If God didn't invent iron for the reason of making waffles, he is indeed a silly God. Nothing in this world makes a free breakfast a legitimate meal like fresh, hot Belgian waffles.

The only thing better than a real and true free meal? A real and true meal and a show.

A young black lady, about 16 or so, was the hostess of the breakfast area, walking around the five or six tables with a wet rag and making sure that the little cups of waffle batter remained filled. While going about her duties, the girl was humming. But not content to keep so silent, her humming, slowly and gently, turned into full-force singing. Once she would burst out with song loud enough to drown out the little TV playing CNN in the corner, the manager at the front counter would yell out, "Shut up, Markeshia! No one wants to hear your singing." The girl would stop singing, return to quiet humming without looking up or acknowledging that she had been disciplined. I started to think that she was the daughter of the manager.

This cycled through several times while I sat there. I stayed there for a spell because I was reading a really good book, Tom Robbins' *Fierce Invalids Home from Hot Climates* and enjoying the hell out of my third or fourth waffle. I was also—really and honestly—enjoying Markeshia's singing. She had a voice, that girl did. A hell of a voice. It was full-bodied and powerful. While I was eating my last waffle, she burst into song (something from *Annie* I want to say, but I can't remember) and the manager shut her up again. This time, being the only one in the room, I spoke up.

"She has a great voice," then, to the girl. "Your voice is great. Please, keep singing."

"You hear that?" the girl called. "Someone appreciates me."

"He's not a record executive, is he?"

"You a record exec or somethin'?"

"No," I conceded. "But please, go on."

The rest of the time that I sat there, reading my book, I listened to her sing. I took my time making a waffle or two for Charlotte and finished a chapter in my book. I felt good about myself, and then realized that it was possible that feeling good was the motivation behind my giving this girl a little boost this morning and that was selfish. So perhaps I wasn't such a great guy after all. Here I was, benevolent little me, playing with the emotions of a 16 year old singer just so I could feel good about myself.

It was lose/lose, I tell you, because I would have felt awful if I hadn't spoken up and, no doubt, I'd be writing something snide about her right now. Instead, I took her habit and her talent and turned it into a reason to like myself a little more. Where has sincerity gone?

The King of my Sympathies

I have some advice if you're planning on visiting Graceland. My advice does not vary, no matter the reason behind your visit. Some people go there because they love Elvis and want to see his home. Some people go there because they love Rock-n-Roll and want to see a piece of it. Some go there because they love tourist attractions and kitsch. I can say that I went there for a slight combination of those reasons, though I never was a devoted Elvis fan or anything. It's not that I don't have respect for the guy; it's that I like The Beatles way too damn much more and there didn't end up being that much room for Elvis in my growing up because of it. If I was the worse for that, I am sorry to myself; I doubt Elvis gave a crap.

My advice for your visit: don't go there.

It's a sad bit of advice to have to give, but I have good reason for it. Graceland is, quite honestly, the most depressing tourist attraction I have ever been to[24]. It is a testament to the folly of fame and the misguided nature of the untamed human heart. Elvis built his own prison there, not unlike Charles Foster Kane, and now it is on display for everyone to see. One can't help but wonder what staggering loneliness crushed down on Elvis every single day. He filled the void with tasteless opulence

---

[24] I haven't been to a mass grave or to a concentration camp, but I have been to Alcatraz.

and abundant pleasures. All of this on top of a pretty hefty price tag.

From the visitor's center, where one pays something in the neighborhood of twenty dollars a ticket (for the regular tour, not the one of his jets and his cars and the like), a tram takes you across the street to Graceland proper. This is probably the most exciting moment of the trip, when the gates swing open and let you in. From there, you disembark in the hot, humid morning sun, and go into the house with thirty or so other vacationers.

If you go to Hearst Castle in California or Neuschwanstein in Germany, you are constantly hounded by the daydream of living in such luxurious surroundings. You look around yourself in those places and you understand how someone with vision and money can make an art museum out of their homes. That just isn't the case with Graceland.

Maybe it was the times in which he lived (or, more likely, died.) Maybe it was the unlimited wealth. Maybe it was his taste. But I did not want to live in Graceland. In the basement, or the Jungle Room, as he called it, Elvis had a waterfall installed and several TVs and, finally, a recording studio. There was just something about being in this little basement room with a waterfall and a bunch of old TVs that let you picture the man, lounging about, watching three channels of television just because he was the only one in the world who could, waiting for his cook to bring him a fried peanut butter and banana sandwich. Shag carpet. It was just downright lonely.

The rest of the house wasn't much better. The only thing I can really liken it to is walking through the home of a grandma who has too much time to go to little craft stores and shop around, times a billion. Eventually you walk through museum rooms, featuring instruments, records, and—for God's sake—jumpsuits.

Once you're really and truly ready to go home, and you find yourself inordinately glad that the tour is almost over, you're led out into the garden. It is there, in the garden, where people start crying. For real, crying.

Sitting in the middle of the garden are the graves of Elvis' parents, a memorial to his stillborn twin brother[25], and, at last, a huge stone covering the King himself. People from all over bring trinkets and flowers making even the man's final resting place a gaudy sight. The poor, poor man.

I have since seen pictures of Mike Tyson's abandoned mansion. If some visionary man would only buy that place and sell tickets, it would easily out gaud Graceland. Filled with room after room of white tiger carpet, gold fixtures, an indoor pool the size of Lake Tahoe, and a huge ice cream sundae bar, the place must be the tackiest example of wealth gone awry. I can find little more depressing than the rise and fall of Iron Mike. Think of how many people have become millionaires from that guy's career and no one would sit down and

---

[25] A memorial to his goddamn stillborn twin brother. Did you read that? Are you depressed yet?

say, "Mike, bro, you need to make some wise investments. You need to put some money away. Stop buying cars and houses for people. White tiger carpet is just plain trash. Cut that crap out!" But no one would.

Hell, the same goes for Elvis. On the way back to our car, sweating in the swampy air, we caught site of a couple of Elvis's jets. On the tail fin of one was a lightning bolt with the initials "TCB" written above it. We had learned that this little ill-designed logo ended up being a motto of his. It stood for "Taking Care of Business," which, to us, sounded like a covert way of saying, well, referring to what one does by themselves in the, you know, shower or something. You know, you take care of business, TCB, right? Maybe our minds are just in the gutter, but it made perfect sense and the term has really stuck over the years. Poor Elvis.

Pigs Fly

Nashville. Charlotte I had never been to Tennessee, though it was a place that I had plenty of associations with, thanks to the magic of TNN, The Nashville Network on cable. Of course, TNN had long since turned into SPIKE TV and dressed up their image to have very little to do with country music and rodeo, but it was no matter. The damage was done. On Sunday mornings my parents would sleep in and there was nothing on any channel except TNN. My brother and I would sit and wait impatiently for our parents to wake up. My dad always made a big breakfast on Sunday and insisted that we eat nothing else until then. It was maddening. But TNN had a lineup of shows that would keep us entertained until the eggs and biscuits were cooking. They would play drag races and follow it up with Mesquite Championship Rodeo. Yes, it was broadcast from Mesquite, Texas, but because it was on the Nashville Network, we thought it must be a huge part of Nashville culture.

Of course what Nashville is really about is country music. It was a genre that I had never listened to until I met Charlie. I enjoyed the occasional old Country and Western song; Patsy Cline was a favorite of mine. But I couldn't figure out for whom all these damn country stations were for.

One day I met Charlie at a bar after she got off of work. It was a day or two before we started dating. I had walked to the bar to kill time, but now that we were leaving, Charlie was going to give me a ride back to my place. As we walked toward her Saturn, she turned to me and said, rather self-consciously, "I listen to Country, is that okay?"

I actually laughed in response to this, assuming that she had made a joke. Then, when we got into the car, a Toby Keith song was on. Ha, I thought, she thought of this joke earlier, knowing she was going to give me a ride home. I started getting really excited about the facts that a) she was so clever and b) she was planning on taking me home. Then, she changed channels and I saw that she had a Country station programmed in as a preset. Wow, elaborate. Two and three more stations ended up being preset to Country stations.

This was no joke. Holy shit. I liked a girl who listened to music I was entirely unaware of. Not even to mention that she listened to the *radio*. I hadn't listened to the radio in years, except when catching the occasional NPR show[26]. To be honest I was, and am still, somewhat of a music snob. I majored in Music in college and really enjoy listening to it. I don't like to have music simply as something that goes on behind my life, like some kind of soundtrack, I like to actually sit down and listen to it. When I go to a concert, be it orchestral or pop, I enjoy

---

[26] Charlie snickers at this. "You're such a pretentious bore," she says. "What's the word for someone who is a douchebag but in a pretentious professor way? That's you. Dr. Douche."

the act of listening and get annoyed by those who are there to meet and be met, to be seen, or any other motives besides the ritual listening. And beyond anything, I cannot stand the annoying deadening of the art through radio play, commercials, and all that crap.

Yet there was something endearing about watching Charlie croon along with Blake Shelton as he sang the parts of an answering machine message. Charlie explained the little story playing out, how the woman had moved away and here he was, years later, still leaving outgoing messages on his machine telling her he still loves her. It was corny, to be sure, because all I could do was imagine the dude's friends calling to invite Blake out for a beer and going, "You really got to let go, bro. I have this girl, a friend of my cousin's, who you should really meet. She doesn't run off to Austin without telling you and otherwise treat you like crap. Get your head out of your ass." But whatever the reality of this little country novella, it was the narrative structure of the story that kept Charlie interested. And that interested me.

Since then I have been exposed to much of the Top-40 country music scene. I can say that there are some artists out there who have real and rare talent, putting out songs of artistic worth. And then there is the other 99%, which is total and absolute garbage, put out by heartless record execs to sell albums to 11-16 year olds who are too young to think for themselves and must rely on others to know what speaks to them.

Shortly before we got married, The Dixie Chicks came out with what is no doubt their greatest musical achievement, a bluegrass album called *Home*. The album was totally acoustic, featured many traditional bluegrass instruments, and had some really great song writing from the likes of Bruce Robison and Patti Griffin. During their opening track, a shout-out of sorts to the world of the old country greats like Williams, Cash, and Haggard, they mention playing for tips on Broadway. I thought it was really strange in this sincere country song on a sincere country album to mention the likes of the theater capitol of New York City. But as we drove into Nashville with no particular destination in mind, I saw that an upcoming exit was for Broadway. I started to make the connection in my mind an audible one, but stopped myself short as this was no doubt a conclusion that Charlotte had known all along.

"What?" she asked when I shut up.

"Nothing. You want to get off there, on Broadway?"

"Sounds perfect." Here she strategically injected silence so as to eye me suspiciously. "You thought they were talking about New York, didn't you?"

"No."

"Yeah, you did. That's kind of sad."

There was a comfortable quality in Nashville that really spoke to me, not unlike the atmosphere in Austin; a big city with a small town vibe. We drove around a bit, looking for something to do or somewhere to start. After just a few minutes there, we started to regret that we didn't plan on spending more than an afternoon. The streets were filled with attractive restaurants and bars, many of which had live music even at this afternoonish time of day.

But what we needed at the moment was a Kinkos. After the interview with the gentleman at MCC, I wanted very compulsively to check my email for any word. We had scoped out a few colleges on the internet in Tennessee but concluded that their starting pay was a little too low in their many college systems to warrant a move from California. Kinko's located, very adjacent to the action on Broadway, we parked and started walking. My email box was empty, as were our stomachs.

Being in tune with the idiomatic pork style barbeque, our taste buds were instantly enticed by the sight of the neon pigs sprouting angel wings on the sign of Jack's BBQ. The very mockery of the pigs that gave their lives to the heavenly aroma we were smelling left us with confused, entertained emotions. The place was a perfect example of why hickory smoking pork is as legitimate of an art as mesquite smoking beef. We took our pulled pork sandwiches and fantastic potato salad to the second floor of the establishment where we could look out on the city below.

For probably the millionth time on our honeymoon, we referenced the fact that we shouldn't be indulging quite like we were. In the month leading up to the wedding we, like many other couples out there, went on a diet. Charlie wanted to trim up and tone her shoulders for her wedding dress, and I wanted to complete my life's dream of being in reasonable shape. We joined a popular meeting-based eating program and never skipped a meeting or a weigh-in. The process was much more rewarding than I had hoped, and in the four months before our nuptials, I lost a staggering fifty pounds. Just because we were getting hitched and were tramping about the nation was no reason to damage that kind of good and valuable accomplishment. Nevertheless, here we were eating like crap for the millionth day in a row.

    And really, how could we argue with it? With the sight of Nashville below us, the sandwich was a perfect compliment. Nothing communicates a sense of place better than that place's native cooking—at least if it's in the south. We didn't travel two thousand miles to have a McDonald's salad or a can of Slimfast from the local Piggly Wiggly. There were other factors besides money and weight to consider here. There was the concern of truly visiting a place, for one. And, for two, there was the concern of feeling like a king with all the great food that was to be had across the country. We progressed with our meal, absolved of guilt, but even now I can't understand why I didn't run a mile every morning or something. Stupid fifty extra pounds.

Jackson's Triumph, Hanover's Suicide

We were only a few miles outside of Nashville when I saw a sign for The Hermitage, Andrew Jackson's former home (at least I hope former). I really, really wanted to see The Hermitage, as I was a great fan of Andrew Jackson. As it turned out, it was closed and there wasn't much to see in the dark. Disappointment overwhelmed me. It was like reaching for a huge-ass milkshake and finding it full of bugs and bug shit, or something. But on the road to find it, we started seeing the glows of lightning bugs under the trees.

Little clusters of lights danced underneath the trees on either side of the road. It was something like looking at stars up close, but they would blink in and out, like a fast-motion view of the galaxy. It reminded me of being a kid in Texas, chasing the little lights with a jar and always coming up empty handed. Charlie's eyes lit up; she had never seen them before. I beheld in her all the awe and wonder of a child seeing Santa Claus. It divided her life, she now says; there was her life before seeing those fireflies and there was her life after. "I've never seen anything so magical," she exclaimed. Indeed it was magical. She was grateful that we had taken the detour to try and see Jackson's home, even though she didn't care much for the president. It was up to me, of course, to try and correct that.

I never was such a fan of Andy Jackson until I had a teacher that greatly changed my mind on the subject. I took a summer school class in between my final two years of college in an effort to speed things along. American History was the last of the general Ed requirements that I had left lingering so I could do a double-major. I expected my prospects of getting a decent history teacher at a community college were rather light, until I met Dr. Hannover.

Dr. Hannover was an exciting man. He took care and pride in his work and loved History intensely. I had always been a fan of studying things that actually happened, so I found myself excited every morning at 7:30 when I walked into the class. It was held in a huge lecture hall with seventy or so other students. I found the various attitudes of these other students painful to be around. They all felt more or less forced to be there and saw Dr. Hannover's love of the subject he taught as some sort of evidence that the man was lame and unworthy of their attention. It's always the case that most students will find themselves too cool to let their guards down, even when the subject and delivery of the course is impeccable. Regardless, Hannover showed up every single day and made history a living subject for me.

The best story that he told was about Andrew Jackson. He talked about Jackson's military career, how he marched to New Orleans to stop the British in 1815. During that time, a pirate, Jean Lafitte, was terrorizing the waters around the Louisiana territory. It was such that the governor of the territory would put a price on Lafitte's head, and Lafitte, in an act of defiance, would place twice the price on the governor's. Jackson, arriving a few days before the British would get there (even though he was slowed by killing off countless "troublesome" Indian tribes along the way) stopped in at the governor's mansion for a polite dinner. During the course of this dinner, Lafitte showed up at the door. Oh my god, folks, the pirate knocked on the door and asked to speak to the general.

Lafitte said that he would pledge his pirates in the war against the British in return for a pardon for his crimes. Once pardoned, he promised to give up piracy. These terms angered the governor, who clearly had cause for complaint. But Jackson, being a practical and sporting fellow, insisted that they be carried out. Hardcore.

I sat in my seat, amazed that all these years the guy on the twenty dollar bill had been so awesome and I didn't know. Then Hannover blew my mind again, relating the story of Jackson's wife and how she died. One morning Jackson's wife picked up a newspaper and saw that a writer had called her a whore. Heartbroken and shocked, her heart broke, and she dropped over dead. It just so turns out that she had always been sensitive about the issue of being called a whore and it had everything to do with her relationship with Andy.

Jackson was boarding in a house in Tennessee. The lady of the house was constantly beaten by her husband, who was many years her senior. One day, it seems,

Jackson had had quite enough of this wife-beating nonsense and he took the old cuss out of the house and beat him in the street. He beat the living hell out of the guy and left him for dead. Good man, no? He ran off with the lady and married her, not bothering with divorce proceedings, since they assumed the husband was dead.

It later came to light that the man was still alive. In an effort to thwart Jackson's political career, people would often bring this up, though the annulment was taken care of once the former husband was discovered living. Whenever his wife's chastity would come into question, Jackson would stand up for her and challenge the slanderer to a duel. And the dude would always win.

It just so happened that one day a political rival hired a professional gunman to call Jackson's wife a whore. He did so, publically, and Jackson was tricked into challenging the killer to a duel. When the duel came, the pro fired first and hit Jackson square in the chest. Right there in front of the crowd, Jackson took the shot and held his ground. He didn't budge. The bullet lodged in Jackson's well-developed pectoral muscles and he stood there, his boot filling with blood. The gunman, in disbelief, started to walk away.

"Stand and receive fire," Jackson yelled. Or something thereabout.

Jackson took careful aim, fired, and hit the man in the throat, killing him. No one ever called Jackson's wife a whore again, until in that newspaper article that day, and it proved fatal to the woman.

Again, I sat in awe of this man, Jackson. And I further sat in awe of this professor, who related the story so well, like a medicine man sitting next to the fire, speaking calmly and matter-of-factly until the sun starts to peak up over between the trees and the fire burns its embers in the dirt. I looked around me, expecting everyone to stand and cheer, to celebrate Jackson and Hannover in amazed enthusiasm. But most people were just texting or napping.

Things didn't turn out too well for Hannover, alas. It is the case with many geniuses—and I do not hesitate to call Hannover a genius—that they may be wonderful at their talent, but poor at living within the realms of society. I've seen this to be the case with the best of my professors the same way it was with the best of artists throughout history.

One day Hannover showed up in the costume of George Washington. He would come to class in uniform often enough, at least once a week, so this wasn't strange. Actually, the dude had fired a musket in class once, too. It was impressively loud. He gave his lecture—about what, I can't remember any more—and about thirty minutes before class was to come to an end, he abruptly stopped talking.

Hannover's eyes wandered the classroom and his gaze fixed on some distant point, invisible to the rest of us, as if he were looking past his surroundings and seeing into his own thoughts. "I haven't eaten," he started, "or slept in many days." He paused. Looking at him, I thought that he was going to transition into a monologue about Valley Forge. But even though he was wearing the Washington getup, we were way past that in the semester and getting very close to Lincoln, as a matter of fact. Nevertheless, we all figured that it was Washington talking, not Hannover.

"There's a girl who I'm in love with," he continued. "An old student of mine." Nope. This wasn't Washington. "We've been seeing each other, going out for coffee, dinner, listening to music. But-" and again he stopped, his eyes not moving from that distant point within himself. "But she wants to be friends."

The classroom was quiet. Deadly quiet. His genuine and confused emotion was able to do something that the high drama storytelling about Andrew Jackson couldn't, capture the class's attention.

"I don't know what to do. She's all I have and I'm madly in love with her. And now, you are all that I have. Teaching this class is the only reason I get up in the morning. After this class, I go home and get in bed. I sit there, not sleeping, waiting for the sun to go down and then go back up so I can come and teach again. And the weekend is coming and I don't know what I'm going to do."

By now, half the girls in class were crying. There was a hypnotic quality in his voice, so full of sadness and loss. He wasn't fucking around and we could all tell.

"I think I might kill myself. I *know* I would if I didn't have this class." Suddenly, his trance was broken. He shook his head free from his thoughts. "Or I might check myself into the hospital. Have a good weekend, class. I'll either see you on Monday, or I won't." We left, silently, unable to speak to each other.

On the following Monday, I came to class early, hoping to talk to him. I had always made a habit of getting to know my professors through office hours and talks before or after class. I never had to have the best grade in the class, but I always wanted to be a favorite student of those teachers whom I respected. When I got there, though, there was an ambulance in the parking lot. I walked to class and saw two police officers taking Hannover away.

"Will," he said, cuffed and pushed, "Tell the class I won't be there today. Tell them I'll be in jail."

"I don't think you're going to jail, Dr. Hannover. There's an ambulance out there and I guess that's where they're taking you," I said.

"Whatever. Tell them I'm sorry."

I told the class what I had seen and not many of them seemed to care. It was the last time I saw Dr. Hannover, though I heard that after a semester of sabbatical, he was teaching again. What a miracle academic tenure is.

The Pamphlet

When you drive in California, big rig trucks are little more than an annoyance. Local laws—I assume—and custom has these trucks beaten into submission as they crawl along at a lower speed limit in the far right lane of the highways. But in Tennessee, trucks are like demigods, racing down the asphalt with blood on their minds. Leaving a slight burning smell behind them, one never sees the brake lights because they are usually disconnected, the truckers using the wire for more productive things since the brakes are never depressed.

I never thought of myself as the granny type, but I was ready to hand out five dollar bills to any kid that sent me a Christmas card, I was so beaten down by the driving. I'd stay in the right lane as much as possible, only getting over to pass the slowest of the slow. Just as my front left tire crept into the lane next to me, some trucker several hundred miles back would get the memo, speed up, honk their horn, and nearly run me off the road. Dust and laughter would swirl around in front of me while I held the wheel tightly, hoping not to swerve.

As the sun went down, the really wild truckers hit the roads. The tyranny of the beasts was total. They did not take kindly to me or my California plates. I had some limitations as far as speeds I could attain, the front right tire still making terrible vibrations between 68-72.

There wasn't anyone friendly around, not a single, living thing that would take pity on me and just let me drive my little wife to the next state. On at least two occasions, the trucks actually managed to hit my car up into the air for brief periods. The feeling of helplessness when all four of your tires leave the Earth is disheartening and mournful. I tried my best to ignore it, but at one point two of the trucks were ping-ponging me back and forth over the lanes, our tires bouncing in the center lane, hitting a truck on the right, bouncing left through the middle lane again, then hitting a truck on the left. We briefly considered trying to sleep through this, since the steering wheel did nothing for us anyway, but finally decided it was too frightening and annoying to ignore any longer. We pulled off the road to a gas station just to get away for a while.

In addition to buying up newspapers with silly headlines about US enemies dating each other, Charlie and I liked to pick up selections of pamphlets for local tourist traps in the entry ways of gas stations. As of late we had found ourselves, through necessity and habit, in a bit of a rush and didn't have time to stop in at every tourist trap. It was too freaking bad, too, since there were so many terrible looking places that one could stop to waste time and money—my two favorite things to do, when it all comes down to it.

But on this stop we found a pamphlet that was just too rich to pass up. The pitch was so goddamn passionate that we were persuaded to stop everything—

the driving, the honeymoon, the marriage—*everything* to stop and stay a while.

Let's pretend that you are in the Smokies. Where would you go? I know, Pigeon Forge, Tennessee.

Okay, so you're in Pigeon Forge, Tennessee, cool. What are you going to do there? Attend a show, right? Right.

Now, you're planning on seeing a show in the Smokies, right? I mean you're there and you're in Pigeon Forge, so go for it. What show are you going to go to? The most attended show in the Smokies?

No, actually, you won't. For whatever reason, that sounds unappealing to you right now. Who wants to be a follower? Not you. Not today.

So what show *are* you going to go to? The most attended *non-dinner* show?

Yes, that sounds about right. Who wants to eat while watching a show? Not you. You're not that hungry. You've had a long day of eating and one more meal—a dinner, for example—would make you throw up for sure.

Your itinerary is set now. The evening is perfect. The stars are peeking through gaps in the clouds. The warm summer breeze is igniting the passion you have for your loved one. You're wearing your favorite casual suit or your best, most comfortable cotton dress. Well fed, rested, maybe you've had a couple of drinks but, no officer, thank you, I'm fine to drive, after all I have an elaborate evening planned with my loved one and those drinks were pretty weak, to tell you the truth, and if we are too late, they'll sell our seats and we'll never catch the show and won't you feel like a dickhead?

And this is where you end up: The Louise Mandrell Theater.

Glowing, glowing remarks written by not some copy writer, no, but surely an adoring critic shined at you from the glossy pamphlet you picked up at the Conocco. This show was the show to end all shows.

Singing, dancing, costume changes, set designs that rival any set on all of Broadway, this is what was awaiting you.

And through it all, the polished, shining, crystal-perfect voice of Louise Mandrell; younger sister of Barbara and older sister of Irlene Mandrell. You've seen her on *Hee-Haw*, you've seen her on that Mandrell Sisters Christmas Thingy in the 80s, and she is in no way kin to Bobby Mandrell, so far as I know. It's Louise, in all of her glory, Louise in all of her majesty, Louise setting you aflame from the stage with her multi-million dollar production.

And when, at the very end of the show, balloons fall down from the ceiling from unknown pockets to cover the audience, the only word you can think of is "This." *This* was the reason that you drove all this way, braved all these dangers, made love so many times. *This* was the reason you worked so hard in school all those years with the promise of job and money and possibility of travel. *This* was the anchor you needed in the endless sea of human suffering.

A perfect moment. A perfect evening. A perfect performance.

Perfect like delicate expressions carved by Michelangelo.

Perfect like the smile of your daughter the very first time you held her.

Perfect like God's forgiving light shining down upon you, lifting your heart, lifting your spirit, ascending to Heaven with Death defeated at last!

Life has meaning in the Smokies. You can find it there. You can feel the blood within you take on a greater purpose. You can evolve to a perfect expression of kindness and love in the Smokies. All of this promised in the pamphlet for the Louise Mandrell Theater. Take a quiet moment and consider all of this. A pause, perhaps, in your reading.

Breathe.

Blink.

And yet, we didn't go there. Even with the whole world promised us, we didn't slow our pace for fear that we would never again find meaning in any other thing. I was afraid that the gentle embrace of my new bride as the sun rise poured light through the draperies would be a dead moment to me if I attended a show half as good as the one promised to me in the pamphlet for the Louise Mandrell Theater. I knew that someday I would be watching the sunrise over the Alps, the light painting shadows and highlights on deep crevasses, and though I'd be with those whom I loved, without cares or problems, and though there would be only beauty and majesty to behold as far as the heart can wander, and though time could stand still for that moment and a perfect little diorama of life could be observed bringing a tear to even the most alien of hearts, I would turn away in disgust for the lack of balloons falling over the audience.

I may be a fool, but I am not *that* foolish. We pressed on, out of Tennessee.

Carnal Conference

We pulled into Bristol, Virginia just after two in the morning. It had been against our philosophy early in the game to make such late stops. We had wanted to take it easy, camp as much as possible, not make such a big rush out of things. But I have always has instilled in me this unhelpful need to make good time. It didn't matter that we were mildly ahead of schedule and had nowhere to be for at least a week or more, I just couldn't see only traveling across one dinky little state in one day. I pushed and pushed, especially while Charlie was sleeping.

It had also been against our philosophy to call our folks while on our honeymoon, except for the occasional "we're alive" call. But I was so tired heading into Virginia that I couldn't see wandering around and looking for a hotel that had vacancy and was cheap enough. It was my bad fortune to call my mom on this particular night going into this particular town.

"Oh, I know Bristol!" she exclaimed. And that started her off again about her summer camp in the mountains of Virginia. In all my life, only two things have truly haunted me in the sense that something happened long ago and I would never, ever get away from it. The first was my mom's geology field trip. We would be doing something, anything, while I was growing up and my mom could produce a parallel story from her geology field trip. It was, evidently, some trip she made in college with a geology class that was, again, evidently, the most exciting, real, and enlightening experience that anyone has ever had. I mean, for all I know, they made a stop at the Louise Mandrell Theater.

The second was my mom's summer camp in Virginia. While the geology field trip served the purpose of negating any excitement that we ever had and put it in perspective of the penultimate human experience, the summer camp in Virginia was reserved for lesson teaching. We didn't want to go inside during a rain storm? Well her friend from Summer-Camp-in-Virginia was struck by lightning in her backyard and died! We didn't want to brush our teeth? Well she knew a girl from Summer-Camp-in-Virginia who had dentures in the sixth grade! We wanted to be famous? Well Sara's Dad at Summer-Camp-in-Virginia was a Rolling Stone and being famous was miserable! Anything and everything that could be learned about life was taught to us through the lens of that damn summer camp. And now I was, I guess, close to it and she acted like I had never heard those stories before. And once my mom starts talking, she's not likely to stop until some cosmic force acts on her.

"Mom," I had to yell, "We need a room, I'm tired, I know all about that damn summer camp, I feel like I lived there all my life!"

"Well, okay," she said, pitifully. I went too far, I guess, and hurt her feelings.

"I'm sorry, mom; it's just that it's so late and we've been driving and the trucks are on some combination of speed and acid."

"It's fine, let me see if I can find a hotel."

All this fuss woke Charlie up and she lifted her head off of my pillow to see what all the commotion was about.

"Oh my god, look how late it is. I thought you were going to stop two hours ago."

"I got another wind."

"Wind of what?" my mom asked on the phone.

"Nothing mom, I was talking to Charlotte."

"Is she having fun?"

"You called your mom? It'll take her forever to get us a room. We may as well build a hotel."

"My dad wasn't there," I tried to say quietly.

"So-rry if he's better on the internet than I am. Let me look at Priceline."

"Mom, not Priceline."

And on and on. Honestly, it's not worth even writing.

We did find a hotel, eventually, and it happened to be the only room in town, so we were told. "But," my mom warned, "it sounds strange."

"What kind of strange? We can't stay in a smoking room."

"It's non-smoking. It sounded like he said it was near the conference room, or adjoining the conference room or something like that."

What did I care if the room was near or adjoining to a conference room? I didn't care, not even if a rather large conference was in session. No amount of noise or conferring was going to keep me awake once I was basking in hotel sheets.

When we got to the hotel, things were a bit stranger than all of that. The gentleman who checked us in was dressed in the nicest suit that I've seen at a La Quinta at 2am *anywhere*. The guy gave me a little smile when I walked in. "Smith, right?"

"Excuse me?" I said.

"Sol Smith, right? That's your name?" the little deskman said.

"No," I replied. And yet, the name...hearing that name was like dust being blown off of my brain. I was superiorly confused while also enlightened. I was keenly aware of myself, and I heard the clicking of computer keys, like my own life was an imagined composition of the self. The hotel room briefly faded, and I saw a glimpse of a living room, packed with kids watching a television while I typed on my computer in a corner. It was miraculous and frightening, all at the same time.

"Oh, no, sorry," the deskman interrupted. "Here you are. William Stronghold."

I nodded.

"I've been talking to your mom. Seems she went to camp around here."

"God."

"So you don't mind staying in the conference room?"

199

A pause followed. I was sleepy, but I was pretty sure my hearing was accurate. "No," I finally said. He led me down the hall to a room labeled "Conference Room 1."

"There is no Conference Room 2, but they thought there might be some day," the suit told me. We walked through the door and sure enough we were standing in a conference room. A modest one, about three times the size of a hotel room with a big table surrounded by chairs all facing a whiteboard, easel, and a teleconferencing TV thing.

"Don't worry," he said, seeing the shock on my face. "Bathroom right there, complete with shower. This sofa turns into a bed and that closet hides a Murphy bed. Breakfast is at 7." With that, he walked out. I went to the car to park it and take Charlie in. I didn't explain anything but just let her walk in and see for herself. After much laughing, we decided the Murphy bed was more comfortable. We flirted with the idea of having sex on the conference table (Virginia was for lovers, and all that), but figured it would be unnecessarily uncomfortable and, besides, it was 2am.

Our hunt for pillows proved fruitless. "Oh," said the suit guy, "We must have forgotten. I'm afraid all the pillows are in use. You can use cushions from the couch, if you'd like. And the big conference, by the way, starts at two, so I'm afraid we can't let you stay an extra night."

This was heartbreaking, in the most sarcastic sense.

The suit left the room and the scramble for bed began. Indeed, I did use a cushion from the couch. Charlie, however, used my perfect pillow that I brought along. I stayed awake for a half hour or so, unable to fall asleep, looking at the vision of comfort that was my wife. I briefly considered folding her up in the Murphy bed out of misplaced disappointment.

"This is fine," says Charlie, tossed the manuscript down on the table, "but it's not right."

"How so?"

"We stayed in the conference room in North Carolina two years later."

"What?"

"You had a job interview, remember? In Virginia? And *that's* when we stayed in that conference room. We stayed in a Super 8 motel in Virginia on our honeymoon."

"I'm not sure that you're right," I say.

"And, we did do it on the table."

"Are you sure?"

"Yes. We did it on the table and laughed about how lame business men were and it was two years later."

"Should I change this?"

"No point. It's funny."

Arriving East

We knew that breakfast would be good before we even left our room. We knew because the paper-thin fold-away wall that separated the conference room from the breakfast room let happy gasps of breakfasting delight bleed right through so that the earliest ones to break their fast at seven had the honor of waking us. We pajamaed out to the breakfast room, smothering the urge to just unlock and fold away the wall to take breakfast from the surprise side of the table.

After a hot waffle (again! What luck! Two days in a row) we got dressed for real and hit the road. Shortly into the day, we came down the hills and onto the floor of Virginia proper. It was strange because for the first time in my life, I had driven all the way to the wrong coast. Now I could tell—like really tell in my blood—that the ocean was to the east of me. This was really something that only happened to me a couple of times before, and those times I had flown which instantly stops all bets on oceanic orientation.

I don't know how exactly I could tell the ocean was out there, it just seemed to be the case. The light was different, the feeling was different, the pull was coming from a different direction. I always have felt that the ocean pulls you toward it with a mix of seductive and predatory intentions. It is undeniably majestic and beautiful, but at the same time it has always seemed so full of dread and deceit, hiding all those horrid animals and water zombies and everything.

Whatever the reason for the feeling—whether it was just placebo or the actual will of the ocean trying to catch me in its web—we had reached a huge milestone on the trip. We had driven from a Pacific Coast state to an Atlantic Coast state (don't tell me, by the way, that Texas is an Atlantic Coast state; technicalities won't work here.) It felt good to have come so far together.

After gassing up, Charlotte took the keys and the wheel. Here, on the other side of the Blue Ridge, the girl who had sworn she was going to drive "at least half the time" took over for the first time since we were in eye shot of the Sierras. I wasn't one to argue with her. I was one to argue about what route to take. We would be spending the night in a cabin at a KOA campground near Fredericksburg, but we wanted to spend the day at Williamsburg. We were a ways away and there was no clear best path to take. This was long before we ever owned a GPS system for our car, long before those would be affordable. These days we'd clock it in and if we weren't happy with the "fastest route," we'd try the "shortest route." But in this case there was one interstate route that went way to the north and one highway route that, while it looked a little more direct, looked like it could be pretty slow going.

We added up the mileage and were unimpressed with our options. We just couldn't decide which of the two to take. So instead of just making a decision, we did the worst possible thing we could.

Charlie drove north taking the interstate route. She learned very quickly that the trucks in Virginia were every bit as ruthless and terrifying as the trucks in Tennessee. These Virginia trucks didn't mind that it was daylight outside either, like a mobster who shoots you in the head while you're eating spaghetti in a crowded restaurant, never worrying because the other patrons will be so frightened that they'll politely look the other way. That happened once, I heard.

"What the fuck are these trucks thinking?" Charlie yelled as four or five of them ran us off the road. After about 30 miles of it, Charlie got to thinking. "You know," she said without a hint of terror in her voice. "I think that we should take the more direct route."

"You're kidding."

"No, for real. This is silly. The highways will be more direct and won't have all that city traffic." She had a point, and a reasonable one, though we had already traveled for 30 minutes and would waste 30 more before getting to the more southerly route. "Let's pull off here and turn around."

I suppose it had nothing to do with all those trucks bearing down so frighteningly that Charlie took back the passenger seat when we pulled off to change direction. I suppose it was simply time for a switch.

As I got out of the passenger side to resume my piloting, I took a quick glance at the passenger side tire. It was getting bad. Who the hell knew there was that much steel under the rubber on the tires?

Longings for Independence

We were nearing Williamsburg. It was later than we had hoped to get there. As we pulled off the main freeway to get to the Colonial attraction, we saw a Walmart. "Hey," Charlie said. "I think we need to stop there." Two problems had been bothering Charlotte that day that she felt could be solved by stopping in at the Wal. The first was something that had bothered us both since Grand Canyon. Her feet were eaten up. Breaking in those Doc Martins by walking the rim of the Canyon was as terrible an idea as has yet been had by man or beast. Charlie was lamenting the condition of her feet, especially since they had been locked into the same Docs ever since. She figured that stopping to get even flip-flops would be an improvement on her day.

The second issue she wanted to throw money at was a new one to me. "I think I left my pillow in that damn conference room," she said. "I need to have a pillow to be comfy in the car."

Yes, folks, this was my pillow she was talking about. My very own, most perfect pillow. It was, as we spoke, being used by some conference-goer as a butt rest, so far as we knew. Poor, dearly departed comfort maker was now a prop for CEOs meeting in Bristol. It wasn't anger that I felt, but lament. Sadness overwhelmed me.

Charlie apologized for the loss of my pillow, but was sure to point out that it wasn't like *I* had used it this whole trip. Besides, I was free to buy a new pillow now, too.

I didn't end up buying a pillow, for whatever reason, but Charlie was lucky enough to find the perfect pillowcase for herself; a Care Bear pillowcase. On it, three or four Care Bears lounged about on clouds, showing off the lovely little pictures on their stomachs. It was either identical or exceedingly reminiscent of the pillowcase that Charlie used to have when she was a kid. The light in that girl's eyes with her new pillow and flip-flops was enough to erase any negative feelings I might have been harboring.

We got to Williamsburg a little late. Things were wrapping up in the visitor's center and the little chart of events for the day showed none remaining. Once again, it appeared like we were rushing things. I had always heard how cool Colonial Williamsburg was and I'm a real sucker for theme parks, but now I was going to half-experience it.

The walk from the visitor's center to the actual little town was surprisingly long. We had to use a footbridge that crossed over the street and wind up a little pathway before the colonial period houses started appearing through the trees. Colonial Williamsburg is a very well done recreation of a Colonial capital city. There's a mix of actual old buildings and reconstructions that are done so well that you never are sure which you're looking at. People walk around in period clothing and are easily distinguishable from people in tourist garb. There are myriad shops, restaurants, and museums, all done up in the period fashion, except for their futuristic cash registers. I was relieved, actually, that they had cash registers that took credit cards, as we had next to nothing for bartering.

Walking down the main street, we caught the tail end of a redcoat procession, complete with fife and drum. It was interesting to see, though the sight of the troops surrounded by people in t-shirts eating ice cream did detract from the urge to fight the *lobster backs* Indian style. I guess there was a part of me that was a bit bothered by the sight of the redcoats and another part of me that was grateful to see no dirty Hessians about. The whole idea of these guys quartering in my house really served to affirm my support for the Third Amendment.

Actually, I've been a longtime supporter of the Third Amendment. When my brother joined the naval reserves, I threw his duffle bag full of clothes out of our apartment because I felt the government was quartering him with me illegally. I turned out to be wrong and my apologies to my brother and President Clinton were quickly procured.

We walked up and down the street, watching the little stores close. Many of the restaurants were still open and it was about damn time that we had something to eat. We found a little place at the end of the lane that had nice seating out under the shade of trees on a back patio. Our server, dressed like a colonial servant, spoke with an affected accent that I found a bit boring and a bit embarrassing at the same time. I thought it strange that she would adopt a pseudo English accent for her part. While, I get it, the people were technically British, it still didn't add up. I have always heard and read that our accents as modern Americans are much closer to how the English spoke back then. Please forgive me if I'm misinformed, but I've always heard that that simple fact makes it easier for Americans to play Shakespearian roles, though you often see them done with English accents as well. Our hygiene is more evolved, our accents are less.

We ordered iced tea (should have checked for unfair taxes,) which ended up being pretty weak, but very refreshing in the hot afternoon. Birds surrounded us waiting for handouts. I felt bad for them because they were sure to get none; I was too damn hungry to support the lazy lifestyle of the avian community that day.

The menu was on the expensive side of the spectrum. And on the British. We were worried about spending all of our money on dinner when what we really wanted to do was have some kind of desert later anyway. We decided to totally half-ass things by just ordering appetizers. What a fool thing to do, really. Why spend 2/3 of the money for half the amount of food? It doesn't make sense, but that's what we did.

And what did we order? Only the worst.

We both ordered a combination of some kind of little British toast and some kind of British spread to go on it. Charlie had little round toasts with some kind of thick, horrid cheese spread. Honestly, Cheez Whiz would have been better. Or moldy milk. But, in the end, her choice, lame though it was, was the better of the two made that late afternoon. I had little round toasts with some kind of salmon paste. It wasn't just a little inedible, it was totally unreasonable. I finally came to the conclusion that it probably had gone bad, and for good reason. I figured that people ate it so seldomly that the restaurant itself had no need to keep the salmon in-date. They figured that one bite wouldn't kill you and that no one would eat more than one bite. They were right, I'm certain, but I do feel for those birds who ended up being the recipients of plenty of out-of-date salmon paste that day.

  We walked slowly back to the parking area, stopping in a few buildings to film inane footage, trying to resurrect some kind of a honeymoon video. Watching a dude in pantaloons play the fiddle in an authentic looking pub just doesn't make for exciting watching, it turns out. Not much was open and even with the new footwear, our feet ached still from our canyon excursion. We walked out of the park, promising that we'd visit another time for a more detailed trip. We briefly considered coming back the next day, but we knew that we wouldn't; there was just too much else to see.

The Circus, Dethroned

On the way up to Fredericksburg, there was much talk about what we were going to do the next day. We were staying in a cabin for two nights at the Fredericksburg KOA. We had originally planned to spend the next day at Williamsburg, but we sped things up to give ourselves an extra day. Even though we were on the ultimate vacation, we kept harboring the feeling that we were rushing along so much and that everything we were seeing and doing was so damn *important*. We decided that the next day we would spend frivolously, just the two of us, wasting time and money and doing nothing of any importance whatsoever.

There were a couple options on the table, thanks to brochures we procured from a local truck stop. The front-runner was a visit to Busch Gardens. We knew it was a little far away, but probably worth the drive. We were addicted to Disneyland in our former Californian lives and we had always heard that Busch Gardens was a top notch park as well. The second option was King's Dominion. It was a Paramount park, no doubt thick with rollercoaster. It looked fine, somewhat like Great America that we used to go to as kids in northern California. The attractive thing about Busch was that the park looked more heavily themed, being some kind of Bavarian village.

In the middle of talking, with the sun setting overhead, we saw that there was some kind of problem up ahead of us. I had to slam on the brakes to avoid a pile up, and the car behind me skidded to a stop. All the cars on the freeway were stopped cold. Somewhere, way up ahead, we saw blinking orange lights signifying a sign that would tell us the score. Accident? Construction? Presidential funeral? It would have to wait a few hundred yards.

There was one problem. "Will," my wife said. "I have to go to the bathroom. Take the next exit, okay? Even if it doesn't look promising."

"We're just a few miles from our exit."

"It doesn't matter," Charlie said, "I need to go."

We waited. And waited. Little did we know that we were on the cusp of something big. We were about to see two records destroyed right before our eyes.

I was used to sitting in traffic. I was totally Zen about it, to tell the truth. When I lived in San Diego and my folks lived in Fresno, I spent lots of weekends driving up to visit, do laundry, whatever. This meant that I had to drive right through LA. LA is notoriously bad for traffic. It really didn't matter what time of day I left, I'd hit traffic. I'd get stuck something terrible.

I remember the worst traffic I had ever been in. I wasn't far in LA, still down near Anaheim, and that made it much worse, mentally. I was at a standstill, only inching forward every few minutes. On top of the normal rush-hour traffic, a truck had turned over. The cargo of the truck had spilled out and was being blown all over I-5. And what was the truck carrying? Black thong panties.

The bounty was such that one could reach out their door and scoop up as many pair of pristine thong panties as one was inclined to carry. I wasn't inclined, at the time, so I left them alone except to gaze at them when stopped. I mean, let's face it, they weren't doing that much for me, but they were more pleasant to look at than the concrete and smog. And while one could reasonably hope for a truck to turn over and spill out money, and it would be great to pocket a few Ben Franklins while stuck in traffic, this was still pretty high on the scale of what you'd want to be blowing all over the street. It's not like it was whale oil or, god help us, chlorine, these were genuine, actual panties; a near perfect distraction to the long, labored wait in traffic.

But this traffic was much worse. The highway was filled with Virginia trucks, bearing their brights on the pathetic underlings stuck along with them. And it just wouldn't move. Not at all. We saw an exit sign telling us about the bathrooms that were just a mile away, but it took us a solid four hours to make it that mile. That's right, we traveled at a quarter mile an hour for four hours. I can run faster than that—literally.

And it was this delay to the bathroom that broke another record of ours. Not only were we in worse traffic than I had ever experienced, but Charlie broke her long standing record. She actually had to pee worse than she ever had before.

It started like this, "I can't believe this. I really need to pee."

It progressed to cussing: "Holy shit, what the fuck is going on."

There was bargaining: "I would do *anything* for this shit to clear the fuck up right now."

Then it moved to the exploration of options: "What do we have that I can pee in? Can I pee on the side of the road?"

And finally: "Oh my god, Will, oh my god! This is worse than the circus! I never thought it could be but this is twice as bad as the circus! What the hell are we going to do?" I was blown away at this. All the time I had known her, the circus was the gold standard for urinary urges. I couldn't even fathom something being superior to it in any fictional way, much less an actual way.

"Are you totally serious?"

"Christ, motherfuck, yes! Holy fuck-fuck! It's worse than the circus!"

With this kind of super-cussing, I knew things were bad. I mentally prepared myself for her pissing herself right there in our new car. I accepted that it wouldn't be so bad, that we'd clean it up easily enough, and that I would never, ever make fun of her for it. Worse than the goddamn circus! My lord. I finally suggested, rather firmly, that she just grab her Care Bear pillow and go to sleep. I insisted that she escape the situation with a nap. She has always been really amazing at slipping off into sleep when things get rough. It's some kind of internal shut-off mechanism that has never, ever worked for me. I can't even stay asleep when I need to pee, much less actually go to sleep. But she shut her eyes and escaped her body. I was still ready for the accident and willing to comfort her through it, if need be, but she wasn't there anymore. The shell of a human stayed behind and I sat with it while the traffic issue dragged on.

In the end, road construction was to blame. We finally got up to the problem and saw that this was some kind of planned closing of the highway down to one lane. Somewhere in the middle of things, evidently, a car broke down in the middle of the single lane and confusion ensued until a tow truck was able to break through the dam of stuck cars to free up the logjam.

When our wheel started spinning at over 20mph for the first time in hours, Charlie woke up. "You'd better be heading for a gas station!" she said. I was. Amazingly, even with the circus dethroned, she didn't lose her water all over the seat. I had prepared for the eventuality for nothing. When we pulled up to the station, she did the tiny-quick-step-super-march into the gas station and wasn't seen or heard of for a good many minutes. When she got back to the car, it was like riding with a new person. Happy and spry, she bounced back from the whole ordeal. She even joked about it a little, which was really above and beyond what I hoped for her that night.

Wa-wa-wa

We woke up in the cabin and took a look around the campground for the first time in the light. It was and still is the best KOA I have ever stayed in. I should mention that I'm not always a great fan of the KOA when it comes down to it. But they have something to offer campers that no one else does: organization. You can pick up a little map and know exactly where to find a campground that will have a reasonably clean shower anywhere across the 48. This truly is tremendous. While we really prefer to stay in National and State Parks, they can sometimes come with hefty entry fees for the park and can lack a shower, leaving you either dirty or trying to do it in a truck stop. The cabins are seldom much cheaper than a hotel room and the bathrooms are a far walk from your bed, which sucks. But the advantage of them is the clean, outdoor air. And if you find a good KOA, you're still surrounded by nature and trees and birdsong.

The Fredericksburg KOA was a great one. The best ones are far from the freeway, we have found. It took us forever to find the place in the dark, even with very explicit directions from the owner. But once we found it, we knew we were in luck. The grounds were surrounded by forest and you couldn't even hear a car engine all night long.

In the wee hours of the morning, we had decided to go to King's Dominion instead of Busch Gardens purely for the reason that we'd have to go down that same wretched stretch of interstate to get to Busch. We didn't want to chance road construction for another night; we didn't have diaper money in the budget.

The brochure for Kings Dominion signed some pretty hefty checks, I don't mind telling you. While the copy was sparse on details about the park, the pictures showed people who were clearly the most excited people on Earth. They may as well have been watching Louise Mandrell during her Christmas Special, their eyes were so wide. Not only that, but the brochure also pictured people of every age, race, sexual orientation, political affiliation, and car stereo demographic. This let us know that we were totally welcome there and that their King was a good King, indeed.

We had breakfast at the Waffle House on the way there. I have to say that with a name like Waffle House, I really expected a better breakfast. My waffle was fine, but my eggs were uninspired and my bacon was downright thin. I didn't see any cost-effective way to order both waffles and biscuits and gravy, so I had to swallow my desires in lieu of the gravy. This was all firmly disappointing. The only place where the Waffle House really came through was in the jukebox department.

The jukebox—one of my favorite inventions, by the way—had a nice selection of oldies on it. But where it really ran away with the cake was in the category of songs about the Waffle House. There must have been 10 or more songs that directly dealt with the Waffle House, and I must have dropped five bucks to hear them all. I can still hear one of them ringing in my head and it just wasn't any good at all. I think it went something along the lines of "Wa-wa-wa/ Wa-wa-wa/Wa-wa-Waffle House" or some such nonsense. I have since been in many more Waffle Houses and been sometimes been disappointed by my breakfast, but I have never put another dollar down to hear a song about the place where I was eating while eating there. I am the worse for it.

We were stoked when we got to King's Dominion. We sat on a bench under the shade of trees and looked at a map of the park. It was a freaking hot day. Some kind of heat wave had been following us since Texas and conditions in Virginia were hot and muggy, not unlike hanging out in someone's mouth. The park had just opened and we knew that later on, lines would be long. We wanted to hit the best looking one first: The Volcano.

The Volcano was a hell of a coaster. It's one of those suspended coasters that have your feet dangling under you. And instead of doing the traditional slow climb up a long, high hill, you do some kind of silly blast acceleration that ends up shooting you right out of the crater of a volcano in an inverted loop. It felt almost chaotic and out of control, like really flying out of a volcano, but without the being on fire. It was indeed thrilling, and the thrill was added to the fact that the

Volcano looked like it could use a little cosmetic maintenance. There were these huge chunks taken out of the rock face, exposing the Styrofoam. Kind of lame. We learned that the Volcano itself was used for years for a number of different rides before the coaster came along.

The next ride we hit was called the Avalanche. This ride was a totally non-traditional rollercoaster. Instead of being on tracks, it was some kind of rolling bobsled that would go down a tube-like path, twisting and turning. It was supposed to be a snowy thing or something, though it was hot as hell.

I really, really hated this ride. It made me sick in the head. It was like the rolling made my stomach roll and the heat drained me of all hope of not throwing up. For the next couple hours, I felt heat exhausted and hellish. I sat down drinking water while Charlie rode rides. I insisted that she keep riding, especially the freefall ride and other such things that I'm not really that keen on in the first place. The Drop Tower has the largest drop in North America. Well, the largest one that you can survive, I assume. I can't vouch personally for the extremeness of it, but Charlotte seemed to enjoy the hell out of herself.

After drinking a gallon of water and having a subpar lunch, I felt much better. We hit more rides and had fun. They have a great collection of wooden rollercoasters, which are my favorite. The Rebel Yell is really hard to beat. But the most amazing of these rides was one called the Hypersonic XLC. I say it is the most amazing, which is very true, but it was by no means the best ride, just the most amazing. While waiting in line, things got stuck for a little while. The locking system malfunctioned and left a guy sitting in the rollercoaster, all by himself. He sat there, grumpy, with a worker holding an umbrella over his head. In the line, we were standing under shade, but the discomfort this guy was feeling was plainly visible. His shirt soaked with sweat as he sat there. Another worker came and gave him a frozen lemonade. The delay lasted something like half an hour, and many people in line left, complaining that the ride always got stuck. We stayed there, uninterested in leaving the shade. When, at last, the maintenance crew freed him from the ride, he stood up and left, without saying thank you or anything. Grumpy, grumpy.

Finally, it was our turn.

The Hypersonic XLC went from 0-80 in a second and a half. Then it went up a ridiculous hill, straight up in the air for 165 feet, and then down an insane 87-degree drop. It loops back to the start, the whole ride lasting under 30 seconds. I really don't think that dying would be any more horrible than that ride. When I was at the top of the drop, a full two seconds into the ride, I thought to myself, "Oh my god, this is actually going to be over soon, praise the Lord!" When it was over, I was relieved and satisfied with my position among the living.

The XLC is no more, alas. It had so many problems breaking down that they put it up for sale. No other park was interested and it is currently sitting, dismantled, in the lot next to the park. It is now for sale as scrap. I find it liberating that I have outlived the beast that made me feel dead by at least these last few years, though I can't help but feel sorry for it, too, and all of those who have never come so close to the abyss without falling in.

The Fair Sex

Later that night, we decided to go out on the town. Fredericksburg is a hopping place and it seemed like we had endless choices for where we would go and what we would do. In the end, the infinity of probability waves were collapsed down to this: We had dinner at Hooters and then went to see *Alex and Emma*. I guess the universe wasn't nearly as exciting a place as it could have been that night.

It was Charlotte's first time setting foot in a Hooters. I had been to one several times in college and always found it a satisfying experience. Look, the place has really amazing chicken, so just drop it, okay? We both had the strip-cheese sandwich which, so far as I can tell, has gone the way of the XLC and is no longer on the menu. The restaurant is worse for their loss, I can tell you.

Our waitress was a perky redhead. Hooters is a strange place; when recounting a meal, the looks of the waitress is almost always involved. The place bills itself that way, you know, delightfully tacky, or whatever, but that's still really strange. Charlie learned something at Hooters that I had always known about the place: it's not really about the boobs. While the name seems to suggest cleavage, and you may well find it there, the waitress outfits are really about the ass. Little orange shorts that show off the bottom of their bottoms. Ass,

ass, ass, that's what our waitress was showing off. She had an amazing butt and Charlie and I had many delightfully tacky conversations about it.

The movie that we watched was not as good as the strip-cheese sandwich. The movie that we watched was not nearly as good as our waitress's ass. The movie that we watched was just plain garbage. I'm sure you haven't seen *Alex and Emma* and if you have, I'm sure you didn't do much in the way of enjoying it.

I don't need to tell you much about the movie. But I have some universal questions that the film brings up. Why is it, why, why, why, that in movies, a man is always looking for a girl that represents his psyche? Why is it that the man is uptight, troubled, conflicted, whatever, and this girl comes along who's all mysterious and freaky and free in every way that the man is not and she saves the man from a life of repression? Is this what men are looking for in their women, another aspect of themselves? Men are wandering around the world as we speak being total assholes, thanks to society, and they're looking for women that represent their inner hopes, dreams, and behaviors. That's what I learned from this movie. And I think that it's six or seven kinds of bullshit. I think that it's white cave buffalo shit.

Yes, partners should complement each other, I don't doubt that. But I can't imagine why movies always depict this compliment through turning women into nothing but Freudian shadows of the men. There's a real imbalance, still, in how women are shown on TV and movies. And it's a damn shame that they can never be as fully human as men.

It's the Smurfette thing all over again. The Smurfs are full of 100 different dudes who show different aspects of humanity, from clever, to wise, to brave, to lazy, to smart-ass. But then there's a girl. A girl is another example of how one can be. A girl is one way, and then there's a hundred different other ways someone can be. Lame, lame, lame. I have four daughters now (spoiler alert!) and I'm raising them in a society that depicts women as complimentary accoutrements of men and little else. Thanks, *Alex and Emma*, for reminding me why I got married: I found my own inner impulses in a body I could have sex with. Not true.

In short, it was a night of veiled sexism, followed by a night of cabin sex. I prefer one to the other; you may not, I don't know.

Misinformed

I couldn't freaking wait to get to Washington D.C. I went there on a field trip in the 8th grade and just couldn't wait to get back. I found the whole thing so damn interesting back then, I knew it would be more so when I was older. We had planned to spend a lot of the day at the Smithsonian, before a leisurely walk down the mall all the way to the Lincoln memorial with a quick stop by the White House for lunch with the first family in between. If there was time, we'd drop by the Library of Congress to check out some microfiche that struck our fancy. The country was our oyster.

KOA bathrooms are really nothing special. This particular one was enjoyably clean and the showers had reasonable water pressure; those two things together solved six or seven problems by themselves. But something else this KOA bathroom had was the first automatic motion sensing paper towel dispenser I had ever seen. I waved my hand next to where the picture of the hand waving was, and then a robot issued me a small square of paper towel. I eyed the machine skeptically, wondering if it could see fit to give me a surface more sufficient for my hand drying needs. Another wave was in order, then another. It was clear to me that this little robo-towel dispenser could benefit from a mind-control function. There wasn't time for me to make any such modifications, so I left the bathroom.

I heard a throng of giggles issuing from the women's room. Now, we men know and understand that a women's room is full of jolly merrymaking a good deal of the time, what with their furniture and couches and table lamps all around, they're always either relaxing, gossiping, or having a bit of fun comparing breasts in there. I know this and I'm used to it, but a bevy of giggles is hardly customary; they're usually much more careful to keep their secret clubhouse antics secretive, so the male population doesn't catch on.

Charlotte came out, laughing a little to herself.

"What's the deal?"

"There're a bunch of little girls in there playing with the automatic paper towel thing. They're totally tickled by it."

"Whatever," I said. "It's not like there haven't been robot butlers in women's rooms for years."

"What?"

"Nothing."

Leaving Fredericksburg, we had to find a Kinko's. We stopped at a bagel store, had breakfast, and asked for a Kinko's or any other place where one could find online connection.

"I'd tell you to go to the library," the bagel-slinger said. "but it's closed on Sundays."

"Sunday?" I asked. "It's Saturday."

"Oh no, it's Sunday. I'm sure. I don't work on Saturdays."

Charlie and I looked at each other and started counting on our fingers. "Okay, we were in Memphis four days ago? Wait, we got there the day we left Dallas. Oh crap. We lost a day in there somewhere." It hardly seemed possible, but we were a day off.

"Well," Charlie said. "I guess we have time to stay in the night in D.C. after all."

"But where?"

"Let's find the Kinko's, I'll check that while you check your email."

The bagelman remembered where a Kinko's was—about a hundred yards across the parking lot—and he sent us on our merry way. The rest of that day, the bagelman did what he could to help a city full of people purchase and eat bagels. He buttered and/or creamed cheese their bagels, toasted things, and brewed certain brands of top quality coffee, all for a public that desperately needed his services. At one point during his shift, a certain girl came in, ordering her regular order—probably an everything bagel with a savory roasted tomato cream cheese and a diet coke—and he made her order with all the love in his heart, for he had loved her for these past three years and though she was engaged, he trusted that someday she would see just how bad Greg Penner was for her and she would come running to the bagel store and ask Jeremy Bagelman for his hand in marriage. But that would be for another day. Today, his boss would arrive toward the end of his shift and say, "What the fuck are you doing here, Bagelman? You don't work on Saturdays!"

But the bagelman was the lucky one. We wouldn't know that it was Saturday and he was wrong for several more days. Damn bagelman.

The Nation's History Condensed to Five Hours

Washington was hopping. I mean, terribly hopping. We knew this was the case before we got there because there were so few hotels with rooms available on the internet. Those hotels that did have space were of the extremely expensive variety. We considered, for a scant few seconds, the idea of pulling out our sleeping bags and sleeping under the domed roof of the Jefferson Memorial, basking in the great man's statuey shadow the night long, dreaming of independence. This proposal was quietly and forever shut down by a roll of Charlie's eyes. Instead we opted to adhere to our original plan, to pass on through D.C. on our way to Philadelphia.

Parking was rough. The streets were crowded with cars and pedestrians, all in a fervor. You'd think the president was in town, or something. As it turned out, there was some kind of street fair, or craft fair, or international fair or some such thing covering the entirety of the mall. Suck. I spent a good twenty minutes pouting about it, since Charlie had never seen the capital before and would forever be stuck supposing it always to be such a literal circus, and not at all the comfy and beautiful space I remembered. Or, we wouldn't be able to go there at all, since it appeared that every single parking spot in our fair nation's capital had been taken.

At last, deep underground, somewhere near the secret tunnels that Kennedy had made for illicit affairs with busty blonds, we found a parking garage that didn't have a "full" sign hanging out front. Its lack of a full sign was remarkably deceptive, as it turns out. Instead of admitting that they had no free spots, this lack of a sign was a signifier that the parking attendants were willing to pack car after car into the garage, moving the clusterfuck of parked autos out of the way for people coming to fetch theirs out. The attendant told me, in his broken Pakistani, to just park the car next to the dam of other cars gumming up the garage. He motioned for me just to leave it there and leave him with a key. I kindly declined. As we were leaving the garage for less frightening circumstances, a small BMW gently pulled out of its space right near the entrance, far from the clustered collection in the deep underground catacombs of Car Hell. I managed to park our car in the small place by using a quiver of backing up and driving forward moves. I paid the parking attendant and happily kept my keys to myself.

There is just so damned much to do and see in Washington. Where does one start? The museums, the monuments, and the actual chance to watch the government in action all present temptations, making sure that if you don't have an infinite amount of time, you walk away from the city wondering if you could have seen things more compelling, or regretting all the important things that you didn't stop by to see. And yet, my suspicion is, that if you were to stay there too long, you'd get bored at all the majesty and sick of all the walking through hall after hall of exhibits.

We were parked near the Capital. We decided to check out a few museums and meander all the way down the mall to the Lincoln Memorial, catching every monument we could along the way. The first stop was my favorite museum when I had visited in the 8th grade, the Air and Space Museum. Now that I was older, I wasn't quite as enthralled as I had hoped I would be. You walk among myriad planes, jets, rockets, and landing modules until you're totally desensitized to everything. You stand there looking at an actual lunar lander, and you just keep telling yourself over and over and over, "This thing has been on the moon. The motherfucking moon, up in the sky!" If you pause before every single exhibit, you can manage to totally trip yourself out. Otherwise, it's just a bunch of clutter. "Oh, The Spirit of St. Louis. Oh, the X-1. Check it, some space ship."

While I could manage to spend the needed amount of time tripping myself out on each thing in the Air and Space Museum, Charlie was pretty uninterested. My guess is that she never saw *The Right Stuff* or something. We moved on to the National Gallery.

I really do love me some walking around an art museum. Even though you're generally looking at similar objects—paintings—there is just so much variety in an art museum. You never know who the next painter will be, what the next subject will be, the period, the medium; it's like taking in a thousand stories with one little stroll. Think of how long it would be to read so many novels or listen to so many symphonies, and with the paintings you can decide how long to spend with each one, passing ones that don't speak to you and pausing for as long as you like for paintings that transcend you. The National Gallery is full of goddamn fantastic paintings.

The National Gallery is the only place in the United States that has a da Vinci painting. Standing and looking at his *Ginevra de' Benci*, we were captivated by his eye for detail and control of color. The woman in the painting stands in the foreground in front of a landscape, much like his more famous painting, but this woman wears a distinctly stern look on her face, eyeing you without joy or sympathy, her face circled by small ringlets of hair. Her skin tone, while fashionable pale, was so richly textured that you think you would know what it felt like if you brushed the back of your hand against her cheek. You don't do this, of course, because you don't have to be told not to touch the Leonardo da Vinci painting, because you're not some kind of an idiot. And if you had kids, they'd know not to as well, if not from the reverent atmosphere of the onlookers, surely by a simple "don't touch anything" before entering into the gallery, right?

Well, this one kid lacked the ability to respect reverence and the ability to follow the orders that his parents must have given him. Right there, in front of us and in front of a dozen other art fans, this 7 or 8 year old kid marched up to the small painting, cocked his hand back over his head, and slapped his palm right onto the face of poor Ginerva. Everyone in the room inhaled at the same time and put a hand over their mouths.

"What?" the boy yelled back at us all. "It's just glass."

It just so happens that this particular painting is the only one in the whole gallery that is covered with glass. What great planning. My guess is that Ben Franklin saw this boy coming two hundred years ago.

Shock was overcome quickly and the boy was seized by his parents and a security guard at the same time. He was marched out of the room and is now, so I've been told, serving out a sentence in Gitmo.

We spent the rest of the afternoon going through a few other museums, the Natural History Museum and the American History Museum, especially. Remembering back on these museums, it all becomes a wash of images and objects, difficult to distinguish and categorize in the memory banks. I know, for example, that the fossils of the giant ground sloths(!) and the Hope Diamond were in the Natural History Museum. But where the hell were those mummified oxen? Or the Barbie dressed as the virgin Mary? And where can I get a virgin Mary Barbie to display for reasons of cultural irony? I feel like, in many ways, rushing through so many museums at once left me with more mysteries than answers.

We had lunch in a cafeteria in the basement of one of the museums and then watched a 3-D Imax in one of them. The movie, I believe, was about bugs. And unless those bugs were dressed in powdered wigs, reenacting the meeting of the first Continental Congress, the movie must have been in the Natural History Museum. Just imagine, the praying mantis as Washington, some kind of wise, redheaded cricket as Jefferson, a stag beetle as Franklin, a silly-looking grub as Adams, and who wouldn't cast a cicada as Patrick Henry, squawking away about liberty in his trademark manner? But, as hard as I try to remember, I cannot accurately remember the movie in that fashion, no matter what. The fact of the matter is, it was about bugs, actual ones at that, who founded nothing but their own offspring in eggy rampages of natural order. Yes, this movie must have also been an article of the Natural History Museum.

We progressed down the mall, passing the Washington monument and respecting the length of the line as unwaitable. When I was in the 8th grade, I took the elevator up to the top of the 555 foot obelisk. From there, I took a picture out each of the four views, capturing a postcard like shot of the Capital, the White House, the Lincoln Memorial, and the Jefferson Memorial. I was as proud as could be when I picked up these pictures from the drug store and rushed to show my classmates. I saw that each of us had spent four frames of film on identical shots and then reasoned that the damn thing was placed right in the middle with the utmost of intention and that it wasn't my keen photographer's eye that caught the views and made perfect frames.

Do you remember picking up pictures at the drug store? Even on our honeymoon, in 2003, we had a film camera along. This is rather amazing to me. I had a digital camera at the time that I got for my job at a weekly newspaper. I paid $400 for it and it was just over one megapixel. We decided to take along Charlie's Cannon Elph instead, because my digital camera didn't blow up pictures quite right. The Elph was a great camera, too, using that long-dead APX photo system, so you could frame your pictures in different ways, from a regular rectangle to the panorama. I mean, you couldn't photoshop them, after all, unless you had a mega scanner handy.

Back then, you'd take your pictures and then wait weeks before you actually got the film in to the drug store. I never paid for one-hour processing because it was so damn expensive and because it often turned out wrong in my very limited experience. So they would mail the film off to their processor, and it would come back to you two weeks later. So by the time you saw pictures of your trip, it was a month or more after your trip was over. You would sit with your family or friends and get to truly reminisce about the time that you had and evaluate which pictures came out as you had hoped, which ones failed outright, and which ones were surprise treasures.

Last Christmas, as I write this, we went to Disneyland with my little sisters for a day. We were riding in "It's a Small World" and my middle daughter (who was the youngest, at the time) was enamored with the little animatronics waving and singing. My sister snapped a picture of her, eyes wide, mouth agape, and showed me the picture on the back of her camera. It was a cute shot, to be sure. But when I looked over the camera, I could see that my daughter was still in identical pose and attitude. So there we were, my sister and I, reminiscing about something that was *still happening*. Man, this world has sure gone crazy.

These days, we hardly ever get pictures made. We have a printer that does a fine job of it, but, to be honest, printed pictures seem somewhat irrelevant. It's nice to have a portrait or two of the family hanging up, but for the most part, we don't bother. What we do now is publish pictures to Flikr or Instagram. That seems to be as official as pictures get to us. People all over the world can ooo and aahh at our kids and we save a mountain of ink. It's really, really weird when you realize that you live in the future.

Because of time constraints, we had to skip out on our Presidential dinner. We walked by the White House, shielding our faces from view, lest we be recognized. We pressed ahead to see the Vietnam Wall, the Korean War Memorial, and the Lincoln Memorial.

The two war memorials are full of emotion. There's something so dark and deep about that volume of names written in the stone at the Vietnam wall. And always, whenever you visit, there is someone who knows a name on the wall, who stands there looking at his or her own reflection against the name of a lost friend, and you just can't stand to look at them or connect with them because it's too heartbreaking.

The Korean War Memorial, just across the way, was new to the city since I had been there. The statues of soldiers trudging through the wilderness of a distant country are as emotionally evocative as any sculpture I have seen. You can walk between them and look at them in the face, as if wandering through a captured moment in the lives of these men. They are each larger than an actual person, dwarfing you with not only the gaze on their face. The 19 statues represent a squad on patrol and are a mix of the four branches of the armed forces. Near the statues are the statistics of those who died, were wounded, and went missing. Standing and looking at these numbers, you are forced to see each one as a collection of individuals instead of just statistics. You've just looked into the faces of the individuals and you can no longer separate yourself from them. It truly is a painful experience. I think there is much to dislike about war and about governments in general, but that a government has the vision to give a project like this over to true artists is somehow comforting. Or it's a good way to stay in power. I'm not sure.

The Lincoln Memorial is endlessly interesting. You can't stand there in the presence of the man himself and not feel small. This is partially because of his enormous size, of course, and partially because even if you accomplish your greatest goals in life and do it with as much humility and grace as imaginable, you will never have a culture build such a monument to you. I can only hope that no matter what else happens to our people and our species, that the Lincoln Memorial is left as intact as possible so that some future society can discover it and imagine what in the world kind of man deserved such a godlike stature among his own people. Oh, how much fun is that to think about! I smell a speculative fiction novel coming on.

We paid as many respects as we could to Lincoln before deciding that it was time to head to our car. We were behind schedule, as the bagleman had so kindly pointed out, and we needed to get all the way to Philadelphia to spend the night with a friend of mine. Our feet hurt like hell, our long walking that day tearing out whatever flesh had grown over our wounds since the canyon and Williamsburg. With no cash in our pockets, we flagged down a taxi.

The taxi smelled like some kind of curried and buttered falafel but with a breathy quality that helped it to really grab a hold of the fabric in your clothes and dig in. For about five or six years to come, a breath taken anywhere near the shirt I was wearing would smell like a diner from half way across the globe. The weird thing was, the dude was as much a white American as I am, just, evidently, a more convincing chef. We talked him into taking us to the parking garage with a short stop at an ATM machine to get payment for the guy. On the way there, we passed quite near the FDR memorial, another new addition to the city since I had been there last. We didn't feel that we had time to pay homage to the architect of the New Deal, but pressed on .

The mall was empty now, the hustle and bustle from the day's celebration—or whatever it was—having died down. Vendors—or whatever they were—took down their tents and packed their stuff into nearby cars and trucks. The streets were full of people leaving, by foot and by car, and the sun was low, painting the sky. Our parking garage, once the gravitational center of the automobile universe, was now almost completely empty and navigating out of it was a breeze. We passed by a few more sites on our way out of town, the Jefferson Memorial and Robert E. Lee's former home, reminding us that there was so much more to see. If only it weren't goddamn Sunday.

What we didn't know was just how long it would take us to get out of town. Even on a Sunday, evidently, there was way too much traffic to be believed. And no turned over trucks with panties, either.

Half-Service

We burned through something like 19 states that night. Well, nowhere near that many, but still far too many to be believed. There seems to be a rule back east, that no state should have anything resembling size. If I remember from American History class, England sent a group of governors over to the land to be colonized and had them all stand together. They each got as much land as they could throw a baseball across. Of course, back then, instead of a baseball, they would have used a mutton ball, which is the product of a castrated ram, and instead of throwing it for distance, they would have bought it or, that is to say, bought the favor of the king through acts, deeds, and monies or some such ways, and instead of states, they were colonies and the colonies were full of Indians and one of them was Squanto. Something like that. The point is, those states are really small and we drove through a lot of them. Stop quizzing me.

We stopped in one state, Delaware, I believe, or perhaps Maryland, or something, to have dinner. We ate in a Ruby Tuesday in a mall. I was heartbroken to learn, upon entry to the restaurant, that it was not, as I had expected, a Rolling Stones themed restaurant. I imaged such items as the Jagger Burger, the Charlie Watts ham sandwich, and the Keith Richards scrambled fucking mess. Instead, it was just called that with no real reason.

Anyone who has eaten in a Ruby Tuesday already knows this.

Our waitress left a lot to be desired, specifically in the health department. She was coughing up a lung, pale white, and had huge bags around her eyes. When our waitress talked, she sounded like she was perpetually about to sneeze. We ordered anyway and specified that we preferred our food SARS-free (this was the year of SARS, btw, and it was always faintly in the back of our minds that we were sure to get the mysterious disease somewhere along our journey.) What was most troubling of all was that we were seated in the waitress break area and were forced to hear her talking from the booth behind us in repose, complaining to her friends about how awful she felt. "I think my heart stopped this afternoon," she said at one point.

You know what, I hate sitting in the waitress break area. Anyone who has kids knows what it's like to go to a reasonably nice place for dinner and watch the hostesses scramble to find some out of the way place to seat you. You're led through a labyrinth of tables and rooms before parting some heavy curtains and entering a room full of other families full of kids. The kids in this room are perpetually yelling because the people in charge have already expressed their expectations for the behavior of the kids and kids tend to float at about the level where you set the water. You take your seat and you get knowing glances from the other parents. And then the kids menu is way too expensive, anyway.

But even before having kids this seemed to happen to Charlie and me. I don't know why, exactly. Maybe they can tell that I consider myself more child than adult. Or maybe we're terribly unappealing to have around in general. But we would often be seated away from the excitement and noise of the busy dining room and instead be in the back next to hosts and hostesses wrapping silverware in napkins at the next table. Don't get me started on answering questions over the phone from banks or phone companies. Somewhere in the mix of things, we became an afterthought of the service world, filed away for later attention.

This may well be the plight of every individual, I suppose, in a world that is bent on mass service. Every time you get on the phone with a computer or are put on hold, the masses are being served, but you, the individual, are not. An image comes to mind, that of army ants building a bivouac to ford a rushing stream. We, as people, have linked arms and legs to make a structure of ourselves so that the species can survive. We sink ourselves in debt, making sure our kids will have food on their plate and a roof over their heads but will never go to college, so that the kids of bankers can go to college.

The good news, I suppose, is that our dinner was fine and that we didn't get sick. Strange that I either remember or have convinced myself that the waitress sneezed in my root beer and took it back, supplying me with a fresh one. As much as I can see and remember this image very well, I logically know that this just couldn't have happened; I never, ever would have had a drop to drink from that second root beer, my thirst gone, if not quenched. I leave it to you, gentle reader, to separate the fact from the fiction in my own mind.

Two Birthplaces, One City

We pulled in late to our friend's house in a suburb of Philadelphia. Roger had been like an uncle to me growing up, my dad's best friend since they were playing cowboys and Indians in Waco. Now he was a stay at home dad and a hell of a musician. Since it was summer, he didn't mind that we came in the middle of the night. As a matter of fact, he and his oldest son, who was about 12, were having a contest to see who could stay up later. This contest, evidently, goes on night after night in their house during the summer. Oh, to be a stay at home dad!

But what was this? It was 2am and his wife was awake?

"Wow, good to see you, Jane. Don't you have work tomorrow?"

"Tomorrow? No. Not till Monday."

"I hate to tell you this, Jane, but it's Sunday tonight," I said, not totally vacant of smuggery.

"No, it's Saturday. We're surprised you guys got here a day before you had planned."

Well, that was the last straw. It didn't matter how good my bagel was that morning, I would never forgive the bagelman. How dare he, the little ass-badger, play God in such a treacherous fashion? The very fabric of time was dealt a cruel insult that day. Our calendars, every one of them, were made a fool of by that little guy schmearing bagels from sun up to sundown. Sunday. Sunday indeed! Not only did we end up showing up at our friends' house early, but we missed out on so much D.C. action. I felt a total fool.

We stayed at Roger and Jane's house for more time than we had planned. His two sons were lots of fun to play with, especially in the Nintendo room. The basement of their house they had converted into a grade-A rumpus room. Fully finished, carpeted, a fully equipped entertainment center, and a well-appointed bar. The basement was, essentially, used as a Nintendo room.

My wife and I kind of rocked at Mario Kart. Okay, not kind of, but really, really kicked ass. The Mario Kart of the day was the Gamecube's Double Dash. It was a quick and hectic take on the Mario Kart game, where each player picks two characters to work as a team, each one wielding a weapon. Man, when four people get going on this game, it turns into a battle royal with so many cartoon voices yelling at once that it's hard to discern exactly who is doing what.

It was really great to find competitors worthy of our time. Ever since the game had come out, Charlie and I had wasted at least an hour a day playing it. We worked hard to unlock a mode where you play through every single race of every single circuit—16 courses—all in one sitting. It took 45 minutes to go through and we'd often go play two or more rounds of it well past our bedtime. We were polished and we were awesome. We tried not to team up on them; as Charlie really is no team player at all, it was easy. But, at the end of the day, we had our way with them. We turtle-shelled them off the roads, lightening bolted them into ditches, and even hit them with a few bananas thrown in front of us—the homerun of Mario Kart.

In between our Mario Kart games (my family always called the act of playing Mario Kart against one another "busting." It is a right proper term that you may use now with your friends with all of my blessings) we had to eat. And ever since I had eaten the limp, tasteless mess of a cheese steak sandwich in New Mexico, I had wanted to try a real one in Philly. Roger told us that there were two places, right down the street from each other, competing for the title of the originator of the Philly Cheese Steak. He was going to take us to Pat's King of Steaks, the one that is held in highest regard by a slightly larger number of people.

Look, I love me a Philly Cheese Steak. Really, I do. When I was in college, my brother and I shared an apartment and our phone number was one number off of the number for Balboa Cheese Steaks. It was a little sandwich joint about a block or two away from us that served some very reasonable sandwiches for when one wasn't in the mood for Mexican food. They had this low-budget commercial for the place that showed the workers making the cheese steaks and in the background the only noise was a group of men all chanting "Cheese steak! Cheese steak! Cheese steak!" over and over again. The phone number would flash on the screen, ending with a 1054 where ours ended with a

1055. For a last, crowning moment in the ad, the number would change to the message "We deliver!" The best part was that whenever this ad would come on, usually in the afternoon during Jerry Springer, our phone would start ringing. It would always be a different person asking about the cheese steaks and/or wanting to have some delivered. It was annoying at first, but the irritation gave way to fun when we started just taking their orders and promising that their sandwiches would be there in fifteen minutes or less. We never did figure out the Holy Grail, how to get someone to buy us cheese steaks through a phone scam, but we had fun nonetheless.

Now, earlier I had said that the place in San Diego, Balboa Cheese Steaks, made a pretty good sandwich. But in light of how damn good Pat's was, I must rescind that earlier statement. Pat's King of Steaks made what I can simply say is my favorite non-barbeque sandwich I've ever had in my whole life. It tasted so good that I really and truly did go up and buy a second one to split with Roger. I only split it because it made me feel less like a heathen.

You walk up to this little outdoor place, much like an old burger stand or something. They have this sassy little menu telling you exactly how to order, saying first what kind of sandwich you want, then specifying if you want it with cheese whiz or a provolone or neither, then stating your onion preference, "wit" or "witout." I ordered my cheese steak wit whiz and wit onion. And my God, what a sandwich. It's a messy little sucker and not terribly pleasing to look at, and for nearly nine bucks, you could almost buy an actual steak. But I've never had anything like it. In fact, I'm not entirely sure I've ever ordered a cheese steak again or if I ever will unless I'm standing there on that corner.

On another outing, we went to see the Liberty Bell. The bank my parents used when I was little had a replica of the Liberty Bell in it, and it being a familiar symbol, I assumed it was the actual one. For whatever reason, my parents tended to spend a lot of time standing in line to talk to people at that damn bank. I would sit my little three-year-old self down near the bell and look at it. I'd get bored a minute or two into it and start looking for someone to give me a sucker or something.

I hate to say it, but seeing the actual Liberty Bell wasn't much more interesting than seeing the one in that bank so many years ago. We stood in a rather long line and entered the futuristic looking building where the bell is housed with a rather large group of people. The park ranger introduced us to the Bell and acted like we were privileged to receive an audience with it. I half expected the bell to start pontificating about the sanctity of liberty right then and there, but it just sat, dormant and cracked, for far too long while we watched and watched.

The ranger went on and on. He told us every tall tale associated with the bell and now I no longer remember when it actually cracked. Was it at the same time as the first shot of the Revolution? Or was it when

Thomas Jefferson finished signing the Declaration? Or perhaps it was when Washington turned down the army's suggestion that he be king. I know, in my mind, that it was none of those times. What I can't figure out is why the hell the ranger mentioned all those times and so many more over and over and over again. Struggle as I might, I do not recall a single fact about the Liberty Bell that I would be comfortable relating to you, as the facts are so gleefully mingling with the fictions.

Right outside the building where the bell is housed is Independence Hall, a far more interesting place, no doubt replete with objects of never ending interest and satisfaction to look upon and hear about. I don't doubt that a walk through Independence Hall would be enlightening and entertaining and that the whole of our American heritage would be made relatable and digestible just standing within its walls. Even though I don't doubt these things, I cannot know them for sure, as the Hall was closed to visitors by the time the Ranger was finished yammering on and on about the statelihood of that pompous bell.

What Roger and Jane's family gave us was a wonderful gift on our trip. It was a moment to feel like we were at home in the middle of it all. It was a moment to rest and regenerate. Also, Roger has one hell of a music collection and he was happy to let us burn all the discs we wanted from his library. We were supplied with new music for the road, which was certainly a valuable acquisition. When we left there, early Tuesday morning, we were ready for New York.

Full Service

Getting gas in New Jersey is a silly thing. First of all, you have no clue, driving along the turnpike, where the hell a gas station is going to be. The only things visible from the freeway in New Jersey are trees. Trees, trees, trees, as far as you can see. You have to actually exit to find a place to eat or pee or get gas, so it's a total shot in the dark.

We had been going along all morning without a break and needed to fill up. Not only that, Charlie had to pee so bad that images of clown cars were swimming in her head. We took an exit, at random, and found a small gas station. It was by no means a perfect place to stop, as the bathrooms were on the outside of the building, which always means that they're going to be dirty and smelly. Why is it so much easier to keep a clean restroom when it's inside?

Even worse, they didn't have pay-at-the-pump. Not only *that*, but the whole place was full-serve! Full serve! It was the only time in my life that I've ever had someone pump my gas for me. I hopped out of the car, like a normal human, and reached for the pump. My hand was shooed away by the hand of a slight little guy wearing a sweatshirt. It was almost July and he was totally wearing the hell out of a sweatshirt. I didn't get it. He gave me a smile, to disarm my alarm, and pointed me towards the restrooms. I walked into the building slowly and backwards, to make sure he wasn't up to any funny business. What the hell was going on? Was he going to hotwire the car, steal my bride, my identity, my *soul*?

Charlie relieved herself of discomfort and reported the restroom to be clean enough that she didn't have to hover. Girls, honestly. She was astounded to see that a man was pumping gas for us and we both kept our distance until it was done. What the hell was going on? Was there going to be a rumble? If he was jacking me, why didn't he at least let me pump my own gas like a man before he stripped me of my one and only vehicle? It made no sense and the hairs on the back of my neck knew it.

But the guy seemed nice. At least not overly aggressive, save his aggression in pumping my gas. He seemed almost docile, except for that strange habit of his. He had this clumsy smile on his face, as if he was happy to pump my gas for me. Maybe, I allowed myself to think, he was a bit of a simpleton, New Jersey's own Baby Huey.

For years, when I was younger, my family was familiar with this strange character in Fresno who we lovingly named Baby Huey, thanks to his uncanny resemblance to a little known cartoon character from the '50s (google it.) He was an unfortunate soul who lived in a little house behind the 7-11 on Blackstone, the town's main drag. Every day, without fail, Baby Huey would don a three-piece suit and walk out to the intersection next to the convenience store. There, he would spend the day waving at the passing cars with a huge smile on his face. He'd stand on one corner for a few hours, then walk across the street (obeying all traffic laws, like a good boy) and wave from the next corner. Baby Huey's face would shine and glow as he waved, and the bald spot on his head would create a glare visible from space.

One of my earliest encounters with social injustice occurred when Baby Huey's house was moved. No, he wasn't evicted from his home, but his entire house was picked up by a machine, put on a trailer, and taken away. Evidently the land was rezoned or something and it was removed to make way for a much needed used car lot. This effectively ended the reign of Baby Huey over his corner of Paradise; he was never seen or heard of again. And yet, his smile lived on in the face of this guy in New Jersey, who pumped gas without being asked. Could it be?

It wasn't. No, the mystery of Baby Huey stayed put, as this guy was much too young and functional to be him, regardless of his earnest and simple smile. We were shocked to see another car pull up and another attendant rushed over to begin gas-pumping operations. The driver of this car just stayed-put, sitting in his car waiting for his tank to fill, like a man being waited upon by a robot butler.

Not only wasn't this Baby Huey, this wasn't even a guy with any particular issues, so far as we could tell. In fact, it turned out, there was nothing wrong with this guy whatsoever. He was just doing his job, and his job, we learned, was a result of the very law of New Jersey.

We later learned that it was a mandate of the state to let no citizen pump their own gas. That's right, by law, every gas station in the little place they call a state is by law decreed to supply each citizen with a robotic gas-pumper in the form of an actual employed human being. This gas-pumper was further programmed to take your credit card, walk inside with it attached to a clipboard, and run it through one of those credit-card-impression-making-slide-thingies. You then have to sign the slip of yellow paper that holds your credit card's numbers in relief and the pumper guy sends you on your way.

This was one of those truly cavernous moments in my life when I felt so far from home, stuck in an alien land with nothing familiar around me so far as the eye could see. We may as well have been driving on the other side of the road. We may as well have been served Bovril on toast. We may as well have been asked to give a solemn word of prayer for the Queen before proceeding with our day. It was all that alien to me.

"What the hell are we doing here?" I said to Charlie.

"I don't know, but that was some weird shit."

We drove on with the radio off, contemplating what it meant to be a free people in a union of states that could each furnish its own laws. These laws, in this instance, created a state personality of sorts, allowing — or forcing — all citizens to participate in a ritual of leisure while another class of citizen participated in servitude.

Was there not a war somewhere in this? Was payment enough to keep this servant-human living in an arrested past, acting the part of a slice of Americana in any sort of consensual way? Were the people of the New Jersey maliciously voting to extend such unadulterated mistreatment to create a quaint-feeling nature that passers-by can relax in—an ancient familiarity bringing to the mind speeches of Ward Cleaver and to the lips the taste of chocolate Cokes fresh from a malt shop?

Put simply, it was all too much. Somewhere over the horizon, the scent of the alien Atlantic wafted to the turnpike, peppering my wife and me with nostalgia for the grand Pacific with its familiar tides, comfortable grey whales, and shores lined with self-service stations.

Look, Don't Touch

We saw New York. And I mean saw. It loomed on the horizon and decorated our trafficked surroundings with cosmopolitan abundance. I called my brother on our seldom-used cell phone to mention that we were looking at New York City. We weren't planning on seeing the city at that time, but figured that we would in the next few days. Our next stop was going to be with more relatives, taking care of a few hundred dollars' worth of room and board. This time it was Charlie's aunt and her boyfriend or husband or something. They lived in Connecticut and we figured it would be easy enough to hop on one of those underground train things that they're always riding back east and see the capital of the industrialized world.

Just to cut the suspense, we never did bother to see the city. We'd both been there before, though that's little excuse. Much of our anticipation about our trip revolved around seeing the Big Apple as independent and consenting adults. We thrilled at the notion of seeing a Broadway show, of going to the New York Public Library, of strolling around Central Park in a handsome cab, ordering lunch from the Soup Nazi, trading complaints with Woody Allen, and everything else that all New Yorkers do each and every week. But, as one thing led to another, human relationship trumped human experience—or so I tell myself. It's altogether likely that we actually got lazy or didn't want to spend money or were tired of just experiencing new thing after new thing, as alien as that concept may seem to me now.

We got to Charlie's Aunt Heather and her Maybe-Uncle Chuck's house in Groton, CT. in the late afternoon after a long day of driving. They were perfectly hospitable hosts, providing us with a bedroom should we wish to take a rest after our long day of driving. Take the room, we did. Rest, we didn't.

After not resting, it was time for dinner. We could tell because we were hungry. Aunt Heather and Maybe-Uncle Chuck (we never did find out if they were married or not. It seemed to be veiled in secrecy) took us out to a small shack on the shore surrounded by picnic tables. It was here that they ordered for each of us a lobster. An entire, scorpion-like creature for each of us to enjoy. If you've not had a lobster, you might be surprised just how enjoyable such a creature can be. Especially with butter.

Charlie experienced another lesson in culinary ritual. Just like in Austin with the crab, there was a learning curve with this beastie. Maybe-Uncle Chuck was patient with his student, explaining the intricacies of lobster ingestion, explaining in detail what parts are edible, which parts are not, and which parts are debatable depending on your courage. If you've ever seen anyone practicing a Zen art, you are familiar with the peace and gentle concentration that their face adopts while practicing. This is how my wife looked while disassembling her lobster, dipping it, and finally devouring it.

In addition to lobster, Maybe-Uncle ordered fried clams. Now, I am not exactly friendly with clams as I really have no idea exactly what the hell they are, and I suspect they don't either. I think each and every clam spends its days and nights folded into its shell deep in the ocean or under sand, wondering what the fuck it got itself into. Occasionally eating—Christ knows how—and occasionally spitting and always fashioning useless pearls, they while away their days in stern self-damnation. Why are they here? Why don't they have a proper form? What does this shell protect them from if every creature on God's Earth is constantly prying them open and eating the wholly edible creature? What is this talk about a foot? No, clams are not a favored creature of the earth, and if that distinction says anything about texture and flavor, I'll have nothing to do with them. I didn't try the clams, filling myself instead with the noble and level-headed lobster.

On the way back to the house, we were given a tour of the area. It seems that the major employers of the Groton realm are Pfizer, the evil drug company, and the extraordinary bevy of submarines housed in the harbor. While I found the brief excursion to the submarine base area rather interesting, I didn't care to see the large factories sullying the surrounding woods filled with people making money by ripping off all of our grandmas with inflated drug prices.

Our last stop on the way home was the most tedious of all. They took us by the Mohegan Sun—what they claimed was the largest casino in the world. It very well may be the largest in the world. But regardless of stature, I didn't care to be given a tour of its size alone, which is just what they did. They drove us around the casino and through the parking garage to impress us with the footprint of the building, explaining to us at each and every turn that this was, "All casino. All gambling."

This, as I said was tedious. But also, it was torturous. Tedious because I expected that by "seeing the biggest casino in the world" there was the suggestion that we might go in and have a look around. Torturous because I really, really had to use the restroom. And not in the easy way, either. When I realized that we weren't going in, I made up my mind to stay the course and wait for the return home for a more private experience. Besides, any request to stop at a gas station and my resulting use of time would result in the shared knowledge about the generalities of my experience. I found that notion disgusting with people I had pretty much just met, so I toughed it out.

In toughing it out and making it back to Aunt Heather's house, I discovered something about her. One thing was that she keeps an ashtray in the bathroom, which I found disquieting. But another fact that dawned on me in the bathroom was that Aunt Heather had a fascination with Betty Boop. There were Betty Boops everywhere I looked. The toilet seat was a padded Betty

Boop one. Now, I hate padded seats in the first place, adding Betty Boop doesn't make it any better[27].

There was much still to discover about Charlie's family, it seemed.

Aunt Heather represented a branch of Charlie's family that was expatriated from California and took up camp on the opposite coast under somewhat mysterious circumstances. Heather had had a husband who fathered a pair of kids with her years ago in the comfortable lap of Fresno. But the husband turned abusive and she fled with her kids to Florida for a while, expecting to find a substitute for the state where she grew up. Landing in Bumpkintown, Florida, however, was a total disaster for the family and nothing like California. Where the gentle dryness of California had embraced her family and her dreams, the sticky weather and bastard culture of Florida left her feeling sick to her stomach. New places were sought. The Carolinas sounded kind of like California, but they were strange and alien, too. At last, Connecticut was tried out, and while it was nothing like California, it offered culture and excitement and by now California was a distant and forgotten dream—a place that had been and was no longer for her and her children. As far as I know, I'm making most of this up. At least three-quarters of it.

For whatever reason that this branch of Charlie's family found themselves in Connecticut, they came together in a huge bunch to greet us. She had one

---

[27] It doesn't make it terribly worse, either. Since it has zero effect on functionality, it really doesn't matter how the thing looks at all.

cousin, Johnny, who showed up with his wife and three-year-old daughter. I don't know exactly how to put this gently, but Johnny is not the flagship of the family. He fought in the Gulf War (the more popular one) and came back home to find himself unable to hold down a job. A dozen or so ailments sort of worked in unison to hobble him—physically and emotionally. He was wrapped up in a lawsuit against the government involving Gulf War Syndrome. He talked about it a lot and elicited a good deal of sympathy before he talked about it too much. While the class-action case was still in litigation, he self-medicated with tobacco and alcohol, the only medication that seemed to ease him. His daughter—a cheerful delight—was the only non-smoker in her household. But in all honesty, she may as well have smoked, for a cloud of black tobacco smoke followed her like a halo for a good four or five minutes after the poor thing came out of the car.

Then there was Charlie's other cousin. She didn't make it out to the wedding, so this was the first time I had met her, though I had long heard stories of her. While everything I had heard led me to believe that she was a charming and sophisticated girl, nothing had prepared me for what she looked like.

Maggie was a few years older than Charlie. She had started a family and had two very funny little girls in tow. Her husband was of the tall-nerdy type—easy to get along with and not at all threatening. But Maggie, while not bearing a *Patty Duke Show* sized resemblance, did look an awful lot like Charlie. It was like a longer-haired, slightly more mature version of my own wife was standing there and talking to me as if it were perfectly normal that she existed.

Fetching, is the word that I finally settled on to describe her. She was a fetching lass. That tame way of describing her shielded my true feelings from myself. She was hot. Dead hot (in case that means anything). I had been with Charlie for about two years at this point and hadn't thought much about the existence of other girls. While I worked with them and interacted with them, I found myself in the unique position for the first time in my life of being able to act as if they were totally normal people, fellow inhabitance of this world and not at all distracting. Helpful, in fact, and friendly in many cases. Often they were even terrible or reprehensible. They were individuals, actually, just like we regular people have always been. An immense discovery.

But seeing Charlie's cousin, I was reminded that there was a time in my life when I saw the population of females in the world as nothing but a troublesome, beguiling, and magical breed of superhuman sexuality. Being with Charlie, I realized at that moment, had been a liberating experience for me. I was free of the cage of attraction that I had previously been captured. I remember, when I was a teenager, hearing people talk about men and women relations, wondering if they could ever truly be friends. I remember thinking that it was a silly notion; men and women, it seemed to me, would always be the deadliest of enemies. The world opened up for me when Charlie and I got together. The population of reasonable beings who I could spend time with without fear of danger more than doubled. In fact, I discovered that I found women to be quite congenial company, not at all irrational or over emotional, like everyone says they are. (Do you realize that "hysterical" means acting like a woman? Did you know that "lunatic" was a word to describe a woman who was experiencing PMS, being driven mad by the moon?) The world is full of men like me who are so vastly intimidated by women and our own attraction that we heap upon the whole of our own irrationality and emotions and feel like it's coming from them.

    I'm taking a rather long time to say this, but Maggie was the first girl who I had seen in two years that I was attracted to. Now, I wasn't out of control or a jerk or an asshole, like many times I had previously found myself attracted to a girl, but I did note the attraction. I came clean about it with Charlie and she thought it was funny. I hope that she found it comforting that the only girl who was able to break through my wall of female blindness was someone who looked like a long-haired more mature version of herself. If she didn't find that reassuring, at least I did.

Pick and Choose

We hit it off with Maggie and Karl. Charlie and Maggie hadn't talked for years, but fell into comfortable company without missing a beat. Karl and I talked about *The Legend of Zelda*, something that I could talk forever about. They were more our age demographic than Heather and Chuck and understood, without doubt, that a trip to the Mohegan Sun was not complete without actually entering the building.

On our second night in the strange little state, Maggie and Karl took us out to dinner. While it was our wedding gift, they chose the place. The buffet at the Mohegan was talked about in great detail all over town in the form of bus signs and radio ads. And for once, advertising didn't disappoint me. The buffet was excellent, having such items as lobster tails and prime rib. It was priced to match the quality, leaving our hosts with a hefty bill. Not only would they not hear anything about us paying, but they gave us another wedding gift, a hundred solid dollars.

Now, this was a valuable acquisition. We'd been wandering for a while now, and it was getting expensive. But it is always a tricky proposition, being handed a hundred dollars in the dead center of a million-some acres of casino. Especially since Charlotte is genetically predisposed to gamble.

Charlie's whole family has a gambling problem. Both her father's and mother's sides. Her dad has told me stories of losing sports bet after sports bet over a single weekend, losing thousands. When she was little, Charlie's mom and step-dad used to take them on family trips to Las Vegas, handing the five kids—all under 13— money for the day and telling them to be back by bedtime, even though they wouldn't come back all night. Then, on the way back from Vegas, they'd stop at the Nevada border at the last casino for another couple hours of gambling while the kids waited in the casino breezeway.

Charlie's grandma was always taking trips up to the Indian casinos in the mountains above Fresno. She once told me that she lost six thousand dollars the night before up there. I found it surprising because I had no idea that she had anywhere close to six thousand dollars. I asked for further clarification and learned that she actually *won* about a hundred dollars, but since she was betting only one quarter in a five-quarter machine, she could have won six thousand dollars if she had placed the maximum bet. But in her twisted gambler mind, she didn't see this as walking away with an extra Franklin, she saw this as actually losing six grand that more or less belonged to her.

Charlie's brother had his own issues. For weeks in a row, he would lose his entire paycheck up at the Indian casinos. He would occasionally win—once he won ten thousand dollars—but then he'd lose that money within the next few nights playing poker. His gambling problems finally got so bad that he up and joined the military one day. I'm not sure what he expected the correlation to be, but so far as I know, the army hasn't cured him of gambling.

Now, I'm not slamming her family here. They have a gambling problem for one really good reason, so far as I can tell: they win right off the bat. When I step up to a machine in a casino, I can put in $20 and dispose of it in less than five minutes. I lick my wounds and start looking around for something else to do. Charlie, however, finds a quarter on the ground, pops it into a slot machine for the hell of it, and comes away with 20 twenty or 40 forty bucks. Now, she has a level head about these things, but I tend to get carried away. I start thinking that if she just won that much money from one quarter, why, look at how many quarters she has *now*. I mean, it's all free money, right? I start looking at those progressive jackpots and imagining what it would be like if she scored us enough money to buy a house. Suddenly, that 20 or 40 bucks doesn't seem like so much; I know she could do much better.

Luckily, through a smattering of maturity and wisdom, Charlie understands that this winning is a mere illusion. She knows that her family's condition is the genetic equivalent of a Three-Card-Monty. She is not taken in, and she walks away.

Ah, three-card-Monty. I've got a story about that.

There was this friend of ours growing up, Balto. Now, I have got to have about 600 million stories about Balto from over the years. He was, and no doubt is, an extraordinary person who seemed to get into different situations without even trying. But I respect the fact that the art of the Balto Story, as they are known in our part of town, is not mastered by me. My brother is the true master of the Balto Story and I really must abdicate to him, should he ever decide that he's going to write a book of Balto Stories to be handed down like the fables and just-so stories of the ancients. But this Balto Story is as much mine as anyone's and I'll lay it down here.

During high school, living in Fresno, there wasn't much to do on a weekend night. This led to the inevitable acts of petty violence and vandalism that we all engaged in. And this led to the youth being blamed for a lot of the town's problems. Which led to a curfew. But that's not what I wanted to talk about.

One of the ways we occupied our nights was good ol' fashion cruising. We'd cruise the drag, Blackstone, up and down looking for girls. What we'd do if we found them was a bit of a mystery, but in the many years of cruising, so far as I know, no man has ever found a girl and done anything about it. So there was little pressure, but we were still able to feel as if we were doing something. I suppose that cruising is to sleeping with a girl what praying is to dying in a plane crash.

Eventually, cruising was outlawed. There was a huge fine and cops all over Blackstone watching for cruising suspects. It was enough to deter us that if we were under 18 and out without an adult after 8pm we'd be arrested for the night. We didn't risk cruising once it was outlawed, balancing in our minds the risk of arrest vs. the likelihood of sleeping with a gaggle of girls. We had to find a place to hang out.

There were two places to hang out for us at that time. One was the McDonalds on Herndon and Marks, and the other was the Taco Bell on West. This may sound lame, and that's because it was. We'd all gather — about every single person from our high school — at the McDonalds. Some would order food, while most would just hang around in the parking lot, flirting and talking. Eventually, this led to a fight. The fight was the main event of the evening, really, and it was always exciting when one would break-out. But once it did break-out, you had to start getting closer to your car because you knew that at any minute a cop would show up and it was time to split.

Once the fight was nearing a conclusion, you wasted no time. You sprang into your car like those people in the movie theater who can't stand seeing credits. The cars would split up, going every direction, only to come back together two miles away at the Taco Bell. There, the whole process would start over. You'd hope that the next fight would be spaced out long enough that McDonalds would be clear to go back to, otherwise you had to waste an hour or so driving by some girl's house in case she was having a pajama party on the lawn or something.

The Taco Bell parking lot was the real place to be. It was the cooler of the two destinations because it was very, very dark. This darkness made one braver and made things sketchier. To this day, the Taco Bell parking lot is the only place that I've been threatened with a gun, though the threat predictably went nowhere. The parking lot was so dark and troublesome, as a matter of fact, that before I graduated from high school, the Taco Bell moved across the street to a more well-lit place and the whole party died there.

So. Balto.

One night we were at the Taco Bell parking lot and happened to have a few dollars on hand. This Taco Bell was the only one I knew of that had a walk-up window for ordering so that no teenagers needed to be confined within the actual store. Every few nights, a 30 year-old black guy with sunglasses would show up and set up shop on someone's hood. He'd pull out three cards, each with a big fold in the middle, making them easy to pick up while lying face-down. The cards were a Queen of Hearts, a King of Clubs, and a Jack of Spades. Every time he pulled out these cards, he would say, as poetic as Wordsworth himself:

> *Red you win,*
> *Black you lose.*
> *The name of the game*
> *Is Pick and Choose.*
> *Red will set you ahead,*
> *Black will set you back.*

All the while, he'd be shuffling the cards around, making them jump and hop over each other on the hood of the car, his siren song bringing kids out of the shadows, snuffing out joints to see what the big deal was.

I never once played this game with him. I was what I thought of as a wise kid. I had listened to stories that my dad told and really listened. I knew that this was an old game and that this guy was much better with cards than you are. I knew that when you tried to pick the Queen, there probably wasn't a Queen anywhere on the table. But he made it look so damned easy.

Like I said, we had money and we were going to have some burritos. We walked quickly by the card dealer and he grabbed Balto's shoulder. "Try a game, buddy?"

Balto held up a finger and shook it. "No, no, no. I know your game."

"If you know it, you're probably good at it!"

This shallow flattery had Balto's name all over it. He folded his arms, enormous in his Hoover High letterman jacket, and turned towards the hood of the '86 Firebird parked near the walk-up window.

"Now just watch, hot-shot, and if you think you can find it, then put money down. Red you win, black you lose…"

The crowd gathered around, eyeing Balto who looked so thoughtful and powerful as he carefully watched the cards fly around the hood of the car, occasionally being lifted to reveal the red queen. I had seen him dozens of times, and when the cards finally come to rest, it's really quite obvious where the queen is.

A child could pick it out, really. At least that would be the case if there was a Queen still on the table.

The cards came to a stand-still and the gambler said, "What do you say? Put some money down if you think you know where it is?"

All eyes turned to Balto. "How much you willing to bet?"

"Hey, as much as you want."

Balto pulled out a twenty and put it down on the middle card. The Monty lifted the middle card, revealing the Queen. "Hey, bud, how about that? You win!" He shoveled forty dollars over to Balto and the crowd cheered. Balto took pride in his win, taking all credit, as if there wasn't a single person in the parking lot with quick enough eyes and quick enough wit to have caught the Monty in action.

"Hey pal, you gotta give me a chance to win it back! Double or nothin'!"

Balto nodded his head. The card shuffling began anew. We were all told the rules again, about how red was the winner and black was the looser and that the name of the game had you as the chooser and all of that. Then the cards came to a halt and the Monty looked at Balto nervously, as if he had given his very best and was almost afraid of what Balto might do next.

Balto put the two bills down on the far right card. There was a silent pause, even the cashier at the walk-up window was watching now.

The Monty flipped the card over and, by God, it was Her Majesty again.

The crowd went wild. Balto jumped in the air, pumping his fist, like he had just repeated the touchdown at the final second he made against Roosevelt that previous night. He was 60 dollars up, and 60 dollars to a high schooler who doesn't work is a fortune. Especially at Taco Bell.

"How about that, folks. No way am I playing you again," the Monty said. "Anyone else want to try?"

Balto walked away victoriously and held the door to the Taco Bell open for us, his comrades. This was an unheard of gesture, suggesting that he was going to pay for a Taco Bell meal for us and that we would sit down to enjoy it. This could have been, incidentally, the very invention of the "fourth meal."

We sat inside with royal servings of nachos and enchiritos, eating like the very queen that Balto was so capable of finding. From where we sat, we could clearly see the other teenagers in the parking lot being duped out of their cash, the crowd now moaning with excited loss every few moments. I started to tell Balto what I thought; that he was the baited hook of the night, that the Monty used him as a participant that that we were so lucky to be in the right place at the right time.

This theory fell on deaf ears. Balto rarely listened to me, as I was the little brother of his friend, the inexperienced young lad who he believed looked up to him in every way. While this was, for the most part, true, it was also true that I was a watcher of people and rarely did anything myself. This allowed me to gather information and use it free of emotional attachment.

And I could see that the dude should walk away with his 60 dollars.

But Balto was already lost. As we conversed and enjoyed our meal, Balto sat with his eyes in sharp focus out the window. If only, he thought, there was a way to get that guy to play him again. If only there was a chance. His meal half-eaten, Balto stood up and headed for the door, smiling at our pleas to stop and sit the hell down.

I'm sure you know how things ended after that. The 60 dollars was lost. Another 60 was lost trying to get it back. Then, amazingly, another 60. Yes, Balto spent over $120 on our Taco Bell that night—perhaps the most expensive meal ever purchased at a Taco Bell, all said and done. The mighty Balto fell to the mightier Monty. But Carnahan, my brother, and I were treated to a hell of a meal.

Late Nights, Early Mornings

When I first started dating Charlotte, she worked fulltime at Starbucks. She preferred the early shift, getting there before the store opened at 5:30, that way she could get home and have the whole afternoon to herself. This didn't leave her with a lot of night, however, and when I showed up on the scene, without anything resembling a job, I had my nights open to do whatever I wanted. We'd be out and about or home and alone or whatever and suddenly, at 11 or 12, she'd start complaining about how tired she was. The complaint was always the same, "Holy shit, I'm so tired I feel like I'm going to throw up."

Now, this wasn't something that she worked up to. She didn't mention that she was tired at 10; she didn't say that she was going to bed early that night; she didn't sigh and stretch and unhook her bra. She just up and threatened vomit if she didn't get to sleep right away. It was something that I got used to, and I never once did see her puke. It was just a simple part of our day together—only avoidable if we were in a movie theater, where she would just fall asleep quietly. I came, at last, to find it somehow precious and charming. Even the "Holy shit" part.

I mention this because we stayed up late with Karl and Maggie playing cards in the basement. They had the pleasure to reintroduce me to Uno. We also played some gin and some poker. We made plans for the rest of the week and decided not to go to New York, but to go to an aquarium and Six Flags. We were having a great time and even started talking about how great it would be if we could find a job there near Groton and we could spend every weekend night like this. Then, all of a sudden, without any prior warning, "Holy shit. If I don't go to sleep I'm seriously going to fucking puke."

But these words were not emitted by Charlie. It was Maggie putting down her Uno cards and letting her face contort to a grimace of illness. "I'm serious, Karl, I have to go to bed." Karl laughed a little and put his arm around her and she rested her head on his shoulder. She couldn't be any more charming if her hair was shorter and if she seemed less mature. The strains of the *Patty Duke Show* theme song echoed in my head. How fetching.

The next morning we ran off to Mystic, Connecticut with Aunt Heather and Maybe-Uncle. There were a few too many mentions of the movie *Mystic Pizza* while we drove to Mystic Seaport, a little tourist destination that Charlie promised me was the highlight of her trip to Connecticut during her last trip there when she was 12.

Clearly, she remembered it differently.

The twin of Mystic Seaport lies in San Diego where it's called Seaport Village. In fact, there are almost certainly many more of these spots across the nation experienced through manufactured pseudo atmosphere. It's basically a collection of fake Victorian buildings filled with fudge shops, kite shops, flag shops, pepper shops, magic shops, tin sign shops, fairy figurine shops, funnel cake shops, and paid parking. There's nothing wrong with a place like this so long as walking and spending money is what you want to do.

Charlie accompanied Aunt Heather, roaming the shops looking for anything Betty Boop while Maybe-Uncle and I sat on benches talking about how women like to shop. I was really just sleepy, having stayed up too late, and I felt like I could puke.

Charlie remembered the place to be more compelling, and I totally understood. I once took her to San Diego's Seaport Village, touting it as a wondrous place to spend the day, based on my memories of it as a kid. We went there with friends of ours who lived in San Diego and had decent pizza while trying to find something to do around the village. There was a small waterfront area where a man was balancing rocks, and it was totally impressive. But just down the path was an even more amazing balancing act.

We were lured in by the loud ranting of an eastern-European behemoth, bragging about how great he was at amazing acts of balancing and feats of strength. In fact, the boast that was most audible through his thick Slavic accent was that he was going to, "Balance the stove on the face!"

We gathered along with an entertainment hungry crowd. And watched as he walked us through his routine. First, he was going balance a broomstick on his chin. He did that and we clapped. Next, he was going to balance a coke bottle on the top of the broom on his chin. He did that, too. His acts got bigger and grander, all the while, he repeatedly promised that we were going to see him, "Balance the Stove on the Face!" And all the while we could see it sitting behind him in all its intimidating glory: the stove.

We stood and clapped as various objects achieved equilibrium all on his face. We just couldn't wait. Finally, after a good 20 minutes, it was time. He walked over and hefted the massive stove onto his chest, then, finally, putting a single corner of the stove onto his face. The crowd was in silent awe and anticipation as his intense eyes showed his concentration. His hands came off of the sides of the stove and he straightened his spine. Indeed, the stove was suspended entirely by his face. He stood there for a while, the stove on his face, then he took it down.

We clapped, perhaps harder than we felt like. We dropped some money in his jar and walked on. I learned something then about showmanship. What do you do once you have the stove up on your face? Not much. In fact, some of his other acts were equally impressive, if not more so. The stove was hollow, you could see, and though I doubt my ability to balance it, I'm sure I could lift it to my face, for what that's worth. All this guy can do is build up anticipation, over and over boast and promise that he can indeed do this act. Then, once it's done, there's really not much left to do. The stove comes down and the show is over. The anticipation was everything. The boasting was more important than the follow through.

You'll notice this next time you watch a juggler. He'll brag about juggling seven things at once for the better part of an hour, then he'll do it and you'll feel a slight let-down. Or he'll talk about how he's totally going to extinguish this fire with his own mouth. He'll paint a searing picture of burning flesh and unkempt flames, but once the slightly fiery stick goes into his mouth and he pulls it out bare, the show is over and nothing was ever quite so great about it.

It gets one to think. Could one brag about anything and try and make it dramatic? Could one, for example, talk about how they were going to tie their shoes in an astonishingly interesting way for half an hour and get people to appreciate the tying of the shoe? Could you, perhaps, boast that you're going to wash dishes extremely well and get someone to think you're really good at this? I suppose in some fashion we've been doing this for years, but in reverse. Whenever someone talks about the huge fish that got away, they are simply impressing someone with a story and not with an action. Whenever someone pens a story about his own experiences with slight embellishment, he thrills us with a dramatic recounting and not with the actual happenings. I may as well write here that I balanced the stove on my face. But I didn't.

I can't remember now if Aunt Heather found anything Betty Boop or not, but I doubt that it matters. She may as well have, as her house and especially her bathroom would never register an added Boop item; they are already at critical mass.

Awkward Suggestions

Wal-Marts are everywhere. At the time, there were none in Maine, but that situation has been remedied by the corporation. In a few states, there are these stores called Meijer that are basically just like Wal-Marts, but they're a little bit more expensive and they have a little automated horsey ride that only costs a penny. In Connecticut, there is a store called the Big Y. For all I know, they're all over the east. They must be a little bit common because Karl and Maggie found it astonishing that we had never been in a Big Y. At first I didn't even know they were talking about a store. I imagined a Sesame Street style letter with smug little eyes on it awaiting our visit with a wise-cracking Brooklyn accent. This wasn't the case. It was just a normal store, at least from the outside, and I would not be astonished if you have never been to one. I'm not sure what the surprise was all about, unless our hosts were under the impression that every supermarket was called Big Y and that I was suggesting that I bought all my food farm-fresh or hunted or gathered it, depending on season and availability. I wasn't surprised they had never been in a Vons or a Savemart or a Kroger.

We stopped by the Big Y on our way out of town to get discount tickets for Six Flags New England. The name, Six Flags New England kind of makes me snicker a little. The original Six Flags was Six Flags Over Texas in the Dallas-Ft. Worth area. This was a clever title for the park because Texas had been under control of six different sovereign entities, not counting the natives, of course. Spain, France, Mexico, The Republic of Texas, the CSA, and the USA have all held the state at one time or another. It just felt a little silly to say the phrase in relation to some place as tri-corner-hatted as New England.

You'll note that this was the second rollercoaster park that we visited since discovering the Atlantic coast. It may come as some kind of shock or disappointment that my wife and I were looking for mindless gratuity rather than cultural enlightenment that day. It could have been the day that we finally went to New York, visiting the UN, the stock exchange, Ground Zero, MoMA, and Dave Letterman. Instead we opted to use the time and freedom to go to a combination rollercoaster and water ride park with Maggie and Karl. You will also note, I hope, that this was the superior of the rollercoaster parks that we visited, despite the lack of the heavy hitters like The Volcano and The XRC.

The Superman ride was amazing and smooth. One of those steel coasters that begs to be ridden because you feel like you're flying over crowds of pitiful spectators. But the Batman ride was one of those twisty-loopy jobs that makes me a little sick in the head. The worst part of that ride was my poor wife and her fear of being splattered all over the cement down below.

Sometimes, after watching a horror movie or reading a scary story, I'll walk down a dark hall or a dark path in the woods and feel that slight thrill of being scared. I suppose that's what rollercoaster parks are really all about: making yourself scared. But in this instance, Charlie decided to one-up the situation—either consciously or otherwise—by being sure, absolutely sure, that her restraints weren't locked down. I tried to tell her that if it wasn't, the coaster wouldn't work, that there are safety measures for exactly that kind of thing. But she'd have none of my nonsense. She knew that it was going to let go and that she would go flying out, smashing herself to bits in front of vacationers. At some point, as we ascended the first hill, her fear took hold to the point that she started trying to squeeze out a brave goodbye to me.

"I love you, I just want you to know that," she cried.

"You're fine. Don't be silly, you're fine."

"I'm just so sorry that it has to end like this, right at the beginning of our lives together."

"Sweetheart, pull it together, you're fine. The coaster wouldn't—," and there I was cut off by the screaming drop that then twisted into knot after knot of uncomfortable seasickness. Charlie survived, thankfully.

The heat wave that had harried us since Tennessee was still with us that day. In fact, in many ways, this was the most uncomfortable day that I have spent outside of Houston in my whole life. It was hot and sticky and no one could talk about much else than the weather the whole of the day. We waited in line for the Blizzard River ride—one of those circular raft rides with an arctic theme—expecting that the wait would yield a ride that would cool us off. We saw a disturbing sight there.

It was hot in the winding line. The vain attempt to cool off the patrons was a bunch of mist that dissolved into humidity as it was sprayed from black tubes up above the line. The people all waiting in line were the hottest, most desperate patrons in the whole park. This included us, yes, but we weren't the worst off. A few twists ahead of us in line were a group of people who looked pale and pallid compared to the other fellow park-goers. One of them in particular.

This girl ahead of us was sporting a Tweety Bird shirt. One strike. Her friends sucked. That was strike two. The heat was unbearable. Strike three for the unfortunate stranger. This girl's already white face turned a bloodless pale and she fell straight to the ground, like a building made of sandbags being imploded. Her friends looked at her more perturbed than caring.

"You okay?" one girl said.

Her friends picked her up to her feet, her head swayed a little, and she said, "I'm fine. Jeez. Leave me alone."

Her friends let go.

The girl tumbled to the ground again. When she was brought up this time, she had blood streaming down her face from a gash on her scalp.

"Shit," her friend said. "You alright?"

This was too much. She had passed out twice and was bleeding and her friend asked her if she was alright. Amazingly, she attested that she was.

"I'm fine. God."

They let go. She fell.

"Don't pick her up!" someone finally yelled. "Leave her down there. Someone get medical help."

Phone calls were made and some kind of Six Flags medical staff showed up. They offered water, they blotted blood, and they finally took the poor girl away on a stretcher. The people in line clapped, supposedly to give moral support to our fellow wounded. But I felt that we cheered because this poor girl and her two shitty friends were out of line, scooting us forward to the cold-looking cave that loomed ahead of us.

The ride, as it turned out, wasn't cold. It looked like an ice cave and a ride through a melting Arctic wonderland, but it was hot water and hot sun and there was no real relief. It was only after we were soaking wet that we decided to shift gears and head over to the water park side of things.

It's somewhat brilliant to combine the rollercoaster park with the water park. From a customer point of view, it really helps manage the crowds better. I don't know if it does what they would like it to do—bring in twice as many people—but it seems to absorb a crowd on a hot day. The disgusting part about it is all the people in their swimsuits.

Nothing is more distasteful than being in line for a rollercoaster and having the fat dude in front of you sporting nothing but his swim trunks. Then there are some skanky teenagers in their bikini tops, their shorts soaked through showing the underlying bikini bottoms. You take your seat in a rollercoaster unable to tell if the seat has been wetted by a weak-bladdered idiot fool enough to ride a rollercoaster in full knowledge of his condition or if they had just ridden the lazy river all morning.

We vowed to fight this problem by first visiting the rollercoaster park, then changing into suits for the rest of the day and enjoying the water park. Then, at the conclusion of things, we would change back again into street clothes, dried and tidy, no one the wiser. Luckily, the park even provided ample changing rooms, allowing you the humanity to avoid changing clothes in a bathroom stall. And yet, still, there are people running around half dressed and soaking wet all over the dry part of the park.

Karl and I were dressed first and waiting outside the dressing rooms, no doubt discussing either how long it takes girls to do things or how magical the girl's dressing room must be. When the womenfolk emerged, Maggie made a point to humiliate her husband.

"See?" she said pointing at my swim suit. "His shorts go down to his knees. You look like Magnum P.I. over there with your short shorts." And she was right. While I didn't see any real reason to bring it up to everyone present, but Karl was wearing the kind of super-short swim suits that one assumes was popular in 1950s clambakes. For a little too long, the collective thought lingered on Karl's legs, and therefore his nudity. This was not at all pleasant and how I wished that the two of them had traveled to the Big Y to get a more spacious swim suit for the man the day before, or even had taken a bit longer that morning while buying the discount tickets. It was okay, we lived, but still.

The next complication to switching to a water park in the middle of the day is the lengthy application of sun block. Coconut scented lotions were produced and handed around, with generous smearing and spreading about. Maggie turned to Charlie and said, "Hey, would you mind getting my back?" And Charlie began what to her was a perfunctory and pragmatic act, but which registered for Karl and me as a sacred ritual of sexuality.

Karl and I paused what we were doing and watched our wives touch skins. When Maggie was protected from the sun, she returned the favor to Charlie, generously lathering her back. Finally, we could take it no more and Karl and I started cat calling.

"Oh hell yeah."

"Maybe you should do her boobs?"

"Let's find some bushes or something to hide behind."

"You missed a spot, do it again, slower."

"And smile more!"

"Or pout."

"Kissing is allowed." We both nodded. Maybe we high-fived.

We probably didn't get that far before the girls turned on us with wrinkled brows. "We *are* cousins, you know," Charlie said.

"You guys are being disgusting," Maggie added.

This incestuous thought registered strongly enough for Karl and I to feel bad for a moment, before we were able to disregard it and allow it as a necessary evil. That was in our heads of course, but we were forced to perform shame and display remorse.

We moved on and explored the offerings of the water park. Water rides tend to be a bit more frightening to me because of the very real possibility of drowning. If one isn't afraid of drowning, I think it's because they've never nearly done it. They've never experienced the initial stages of the drowning to death process and therefore remain blissfully ignorant of the terror. But trust me when I say that the terror stays with you for a good many years and water has the ability to turn into something totally other than a benign natural resource in the perceptions of the very nearly drown.

Yes, I'm just a little scared of water.

The rides were good and the lines weren't bad. The downfall of the water ride, of course, is that in order to go on one, you have to walk uphill or even take stairs before launching. This is troublesome. Rollercoasters have no problem taking you uphill all by themselves. They in fact relish the opportunity, using to build anticipation and dread and even, in the best cases, actual remorse.

My favorite water rides are ones that use inner tubes. I think most, if not all, water rides these days use inner tube technology, but there was a time when this wasn't nearly so common. The average water ride used to use little foam mats that you sat on. True, you got much wetter, but you also got bumped up and generally pissed off. The end of a water park day would come along and you felt like you had been in a 10 hour fist fight.

There was one ride in particular that I liked a great deal at Six Flags New England. It was because you got to use an awesome four-person inner tube, making the ride into a virtual party. The ride down is as social as a dinner double-date and at least a million times more social than an afternoon spent on a social network. Yes, the Big Kahuna is exciting and social and I didn't die. This was good.

The sun was low in the sky when we changed back into our regular clothes. It was time for Charlie and me to press on. We had reservations in Vermont that had to be attended to and we had already lingered a day longer than we had expected. It was hard to leave, in all honesty, because being with Maggie and Karl was like being with old friends who are comfortable to be around. This quality, however, backfired at the last possible second. We were in the middle of saying our goodbyes, making plans for next times, and thanking all and each for a good time, when something came out of the blue.

"Hey, you guys," Karl said. "The other day, I was driving on the freeway just south of here when I saw something awesome." I wondered what it was and finally settled on either a UFO or a Bigfoot, though I wasn't familiar with the frequency of such things in this neck of the woods. "It was in the back of this van, right? And a girl and a guy were sitting next to each other in the back seat. They were making out, right?" We walked along towards the exit, wondering exactly where this story was headed. "So they stop kissing for a second, and the girl is messing with something with her hands. Then, without warning, the girl leans over, her head in his lap. The guy looked at me and gave a thumbs-up." Then he added triumphantly, "He was getting a blowjob."

The rest of the three of us were somewhat stunned. "Gross, Karl," Maggie said, obviously embarrassed by the direction the visit turned in the last possible second.

After thinking about it for much longer than I'd rather, I've come to an hypothesis. I think that, perhaps, Karl had indeed seen this incident of roadway debauchery; he had intruded upon this couple's intimate designs. This made an impression on him and he wanted to bring it up. Talking about sex stuff with couple friends is a tricky thing and jockeying for position with a story like this is a lot of work. He had probably damned himself for his missed opportunities at the Mohegan Sun. He was probably just about to broach the subject in some normal, and perhaps even debonair, way when his wife got sick from being tired during Uno a few nights earlier Very good.

I find it astonishing that I've not talked to them even once since the trip. I often wonder if it has anything to do with that exchange. I wonder if he caught hell from Maggie moments later for being so awkward, and this after the suggestion that she get it on with her cousin.

Probably, though, like a normal person, they just forgot about it.

A Pretentious Ass in the Green Mountains

Vermont is the shit. It's easy to mistake Vermont for just a regular New England state—they're all so small and indistinguishable to someone who's spent most of his life in Texas and California—but it's not. Vermont was not one of the original 13 colonies. Vermont was state number 14. This distinction—the fact that they waited and considered their options before uniting in statehood—shows that this place is a little different. Different is probably the best word, in fact, to describe Vermont.

You may be well acquainted with Vermont's beauty: the green mountains, the vast valleys, and the astonishing changing of the seasons. But the social structure is also different. I've found, in my wanderings of the state over the years, that Vermont communities are strange mixes of the supremely conservative and the superbly liberal. While the state is traditionally Republican in voting, it also holds some of the most liberal laws, including the inclusion of same-sex marriage. Occasionally there are rumors that the US will give Vermont up to Canada because they're so different. But these rumors hold less water than the rumors that Texas is going to split off and become its own nation. The US doesn't normally go around giving extra states to lesser countries just because people think or vote differently than what is considered mainstream. In fact, there are occasional rumors that suggest that the USA is into inclusion, and prides itself on the mosaic of cultures and peoples that make the country so unique. This rumor, however, could stand some substantiation once in a while.

Our purpose in Vermont was the clearest and most focused of any other place that we visited during our trip. We were there at that time because I was graduating from graduate school there. I was in a low-residency writing program, a school that I attended full time, but that I only physically went to twice a year for a couple weeks at a time. This is a highly efficient way to deal with a writing program, giving you plenty of time to work on your writing and little time dealing with bullshit. The financial aid and the low living costs of renting a room from a 100 year-old woman in Fresno made it possible for me to exist primarily without a job for the duration of the program. Yes, I have a lot of good things to say about it.

The school was founded with an educational model based on the idea of educational democracy—narrative transcripts instead of grades, learner-designed curricula, and an intense focus on the personal relationship with the education that is trying to be attained. The pedagogy is idealistic and not ideal for everyone, but in all the years of schooling that I've undergone, I would rate my time at Goddard as the most beneficial I have ever experienced.

There were only a couple more hurdles to jump through and I would be considered a person educated enough to reliably teach at college. Counting this as a foregone conclusion had enabled me to start handing out resumes and offering interviews as we traveled across country. But still I had to bind my thesis, get it signed off by all my readers, attend a few meetings and give a reading.

Goddard College is built on beautiful grounds. It was a farm from the 18th century, and was an estate since well before that. Many of the classrooms are in buildings that were modified from the farm or in a huge mansion with wandering hallways and beautifully carved moldings and fixtures. There are easily believable rumors that the whole thing is built over sacred Indian burial grounds.

It stands to reason that the place is generously haunted. Most of my fellow students had ghost stories of some sort. It is always the downfall of a haunting rumor, to me, that there is usually a mix of haunting-style experiences, such as apparitions and sounds, and poltergeist experiences, with things moving around and windows and doors closing abruptly. While I never didn't believe what a fellow student had to say or anything like that, I think that a place has to make up its mind: are you going to be haunted or are you going to have a poltergeist? I don't think these two mix very often, because, considering the nature of a poltergeist, it wouldn't want to share territory with something as tame as an apparition. But that's just me.

I actually did want to see something while I was there. It seems like the minute that you're actually looking for a ghostly experience, it never comes your way. Meanwhile, someone else who doesn't believe in ghosts is constantly harangued by every ghost in the country. It's not fair. So what I used to do is try and have such an experience. I would wander around the campus at night. I would sneak through the mansion. I would hang out inside the tea house—an old structure in the middle of a garden that was supposed to be made from the timbers of the gallows in Salem(!) But I never did see a single ghostly thing.

I did see a bear, though. Or something similar to a bear. But I never didn't believe in bears, so it doesn't really even out, in my mind.

I was walking back to my dorm one night from the library. Whenever I was in residence there, I had this intense urge to write. Things just came alive for me and, me being a poncy and pretentious ass, I had to start writing and write for as much time as I could. The library was the only place on campus where I could use a computer for typing, as only super rich people back then had their own laptops. The library is not centrally located at Goddard. No, the library is a half-mile walk through the woods, right past the old Indian burial grounds (if such a thing is to be believed).

It was raining this one night and I was the last person to leave the library. Now there are really two ways to get from the library to the main campus, one of them being to walk along the road for about a mile, or walking along the unpaved path for half as long. The half as long idea appealed to me, even on this dark night. I started walking while holding a newspaper over my head as some lame form of protection. I was about half way home when I noticed a sound behind me and in the trees.

My first thought was that there were a couple of students who had stolen off into the woods for some hanky-panky (an altogether common thing). I stopped and peered into the trees, calling out to the students that they were caught and may as well come walk on the path. There was no answer, but I could hear breathing. I took a step closer—like a total idiot—and made out a large black form. When it took a step forward, breaking small branches and twigs in front of it, I slowly turned around and kept walking. It mirrored my footsteps for about 20 yards or so. Every time I stopped walking, it would finish the step it was taking and stand still as well.

Now, I have no idea what this animal was doing watching me or why it was taking so damn long to eat me up. I really didn't want to know; I just wanted it to do something else. I thought for a moment about how I was going to get out of this mess. It was still standing there, it was still breathing, and it was so dark I couldn't see exactly what it was. Maybe it couldn't tell exactly what I was? If that was the case, I reasoned, it could work for or against me. So I decided that I would play off of that confusion, and start acting other-than-human. I figured that if I ran, it would chase. If I bored it long enough, it would pounce. My only choice was to weird it out until I got to the opening of the woods leading to the village of dormitories.

I'm not saying this was a brilliant idea, but I started singing and dancing. I sang little ditties based on circus music and flounced about like a moron. "This isn't how a scared person acts," it would think, "what the hell is this thing? I'll watch for a while and defer my dinner." It worked, at least to some degree, and when I got to the clearing in the trees and that beautiful, beautiful streetlight above the first building, I walked like a normal person, reasoning that it was better to be eaten alive than have another person see me acting like a fool.

I got back to my room, changed into dry clothes, and wrote the whole thing down. Writing it down seemed like the properly pretentious thing to do.

Temporary Home

We got to our hotel late, around two in the a.m. Our room was left opened for us with the keys on the bathroom counter. Now, this doesn't seem like a good idea to me. To this day, Vermont is the only state where hotel managers have just left my room open for me to occupy when I came in late. This happened a couple years earlier in Burlington, and now it was happening in Marshfield, the little tiny maple syrup town near Goddard. I went into the room first, hand on my pocket knife, making sure there were no psychos, hobos, or bears inside. It was clear and my bride was allowed entrance.

This hotel was the first place during all of our travels where we would stay five nights. It felt like we were moving in. We unpacked our bags and put our clothes in the closet and in the drawers. The decadence of lying down in a comfortable King bed where you will sleep for five days was unimaginable to us.

In the morning, we headed down to the complimentary breakfast. This was a small motel, like a motor lodge, with only ten or twelve rooms. The breakfast wasn't the regular bullshit you might expect from a discount Suites or anything, but an actual homemade situation with pancakes, oatmeal, eggs, bacon, and the best goddamn syrup you've ever had. The host was a jolly fellow, all smiles and back-slaps. He asked us if that was us coming in at two and we said yes. Then he engaged in his favorite hobby besides smiling: creating the conditions for an uncomfortable conversation.

"So, you guys are from California, is that right?" he asked us.

"Yeah, we're from California. I don't know for how long we're from there, but we're from there now," I replied.

"So are Joe and Amy here!" He points at the people sitting one table over. "Hey Joe, Amy, come here and meet Will and Charlotte!" The poor couple put down their pancake-laden forks and came over to shake our hands. The moment our hands touched, our host was out of sight, attending to something else entirely. This left Charlie and I actually holding hands with complete strangers with our only thread of relation being a single state that is 163,696 square miles.

"Hey," I said.

"Hi," said Joe. We were all standing now and our pancakes were getting cold and our orange juice was getting warm.

"Where in California?" I asked.

"Yreka."

"Eureka?"

"No. Yreka. It's closer to the middle."

There it was. That was the end of what we had in common. We nodded heads as politely as we could and all four of us went back to our seats to resume consumption while trying to avoid looking over at the next table.

Now, I understand why our host thought this was a good idea, but it clearly displayed his complete lack of understanding about Californians. Maybe something like this could have worked if you introduced two Vermonters in California; they might have a lot to say to each other. Or they might be polite enough to pretend like they do. But Californians are a completely different thing. We ignore each other as much as we can. The world can't stand Californians, and Californians are no exception. When we see each other on the streets, we look down, look away, or look at our watches. When Texans see each other, they greet, inquire how the other's doing, that kind of thing. For the most crowded state in the union, things can get awful lonely in California.

Charlie and I rushed through the rest of our breakfast as best we could and made a point to eat there at a different time for the rest of our stay in hopes that Joe and Amy were people of exact schedules. It worked, too.

On our first day in Vermont, I had no obligations to attend to at the college. We decided to make an excursion to the Ben and Jerry's Ice Cream Factory. We held in our minds intense visions of what this huge, Wonkaesque facility would have in store for us that day. Rivers of flowing chocolate ice cream, waterfalls of cookie dough, candy-coated pathways, marshmallow clouds, minty distances, and soft butterscotch sunsets. We talked about what we would eat, what we would admire, and the amazing kinds of ice cream that we would invent for the world to enjoy. We talked about how everyone would be robed in bleach-free hemp fabric, about how peace and justice would be strictly enjoyed on the campus of the factory, about how we would weave friendship bracelets for exchange with the employees.

We probably shouldn't have gone. Our expectations were much too high. And though they were somewhat tempered by the startlingly low ticket price — a buck-fifty for a tour — we were still disappointed.

The Ben and Jerry's Factory is not magical. It is boring. It's so boring that I thought about finding a soft place to go to sleep. On your tour, you begin by walking up step after step to a little hallway that goes right above the factory floor. The factory consists of a white floor, white walls, and huge stainless steel machines pumping out tiny containers of ice cream. There were no huge vats mixing the raw ingredients powered by little anthropomorphic mice on treadmills. There were no chocolate cows or strawberry raindrops. It was just a factory that made only two kinds of ice cream at a time each day.

We were led around by this slight little guy with a nametag. He showed us, in addition to the aforementioned lame room, a lame film about the founding of Ben and Jerry's and how it was evidently the most revolutionary thing in the world to put bits of things inside ice cream, even though it seems reasonably normal these days. The group we were with didn't seem terribly impressed either as cameras remained around necks unused and questions were absent, even when asked for. It was fine. Just fine.

At the end of the tour, there is a little room where you crowd in with a sampling of the day's ice creams in little paper cups that we were invited to enjoy. It was explained to us that this ice cream would be exceptionally soft, having not gone through the rigorous freezing process that refrigerated truck provides in shipment. I don't recall, for the life of me, what these flavors were, and I suspect it was because they left little impression. Which is much better than them leaving a bad one, right?

The last little bit of excitement was a simple question with a prize attached. The little tour guide asked us who had come the farthest to enjoy the B&J tour that day. The winner would be awarded a free ice cream treat that was at least 10 times bigger and grander than the free sampling. I knew we could score it. I patiently waited for each and every person to say where they were from first, so I could slam them with the westernmost state at the end. The first person spoke up; he was from Boston. Someone raised their hand and said he was from Philadelphia. Another one-upped him, being from Chicago. Ha! What fools they all were! Confident that I was safe to speak, I put my hand up and said, "California." Sounds of the slightly impressed people around me suggested my victory. Then one more joker put his hand up. "India?" he said, as if questioning. The treat was handed to him.

Now, I should point out that this was total bullshit right there. Why would this dude who was probably from India but like 30 years ago think he was entitled to my ice cream treat? His accent was as American as mine and his question-like phrasing of his answer seemed to suggest a "does it count if we were born there but just barely?" I could have produced my California driver's license and I'm sure he could have produced his Vermont ID.

I let it go. And yet I still carry it with me, evidently.

Outside we discovered the only really interesting part of the whole factory. A small wooden sign with a silhouetted crow stood nearby with a little arrow pointing to a path. On it was written, "This way to the Flavor Graveyard." Now, this was intriguing.

Charlie and I followed the path and arrived at a small clearing where headstones were erected. On each headstone was the name and description of an old ice cream flavor along with the years it was in production. We stood and paid our respects to old favorites like Georgia Peach, Peanut Butter and Jelly, Rainforest Crunch, and Ethan Almond. After reading and discussing the various flavors laid to rest before us, we were unable to derive any more fun.

We walked back down the path to the factory where we ordered a couple ice creams, sat down on a picnic table, and enjoyed the Vermont summer weather. It was at this point that we were farthest from home, we realized. Thousands of miles from home, sitting at the place where Ben and Jerry's is made, it's amazing to think that it travels this far to reach us every day. And to think that each little single-serving pint (for they are single serving, being so wonderful and indulgent) brings with it this pleasant summer weather to our old home in California where the sun is scorching the air; no wonder it's so welcome there.

Independence

Charlie and I had never spent a fourth of July together. Both years since we had known each other, I had been off at school in Vermont while she sat around Fresno doing God-knows-what. She wasn't out exploding any reasonable fireworks, that's for sure. One of the major flaws with California is their absolute intolerance for all things firework. I'm not joking when I say that sparklers are outlawed. In their stead is something that everyone calls sparklers but are really called "freedom torches." Let me tell you, if that small piss of colored fire is what freedom looks like, I'm going back to England.

California doesn't let you use any fireworks that send anything into the air. You can have fountains, sure, but their tiny shower of sparks, as many colored as they may be, doesn't inspire much patriotism. No. True patriotism only comes out in a man when he is able to wield flaming Roman candles, sending fireballs into the neighbor's windows. Your chest fills with pride for America when a perfectly aimed bottle rocket spins out of control, sending your friends and family running and hopping. If you happen to be near a lake and are able to aim an honest-to-God exploding firework deep into it, you see the fountain of water splash up and dead fish slowly and harmoniously float to the top of it, you truly understand what the Stars and Stripes mean.

This year, however, we were together and in the distant land of Ethan Allen and his Green Mountain boys. It was our third day in Vermont and there was a lull in the work that I had to do at the college. We hopped in our car, which felt so much like a comfortable home by now, and drove out to Burlington. We had heard that Lake Champlain was the location of one of the greatest firework displays in The New World. We consulted our Road Trip USA book to find a suitable place to eat in the city before finding a reasonable place to sit.

What food goes well with Independence Day? If you're surrounded by friends, family, and reasonable temperatures, an outdoor grill and a set of horseshoes is all you need. I had also discovered that Tex-Mex is about the most American one can get on a hot day, the spices and sauces creating a heavy mixture to balance out the humidity inside and out. But since we were in Vermont and weren't likely to crash anyone else's barbeque, neither of those options were available to us. I had had Vermont's Mexican food a couple years prior with a group of fellow students. I tried to urge them away from the prospect, but we paid the price anyway. Our food was unrecognizable as anything resembling Mexican. There were round things that looked sort of like tortillas, there was a mash of what were purportedly beans in a former life, and lettuce covered everything else in shredded opulence. When our meal was finished I gave a small I-told-you-so to my fellow diners and they looked at me puzzled. "That was really good," one of them said. Then I noted their states of origin: Upstate New York, New Hampshire, and Ohio. I can't imagine what it is like growing up without ever tasting actual Mexican food. It is a staple of life throughout Texas, the Southwest, and California. It is like someone from Ohio imagining life without sardines, or something like that.

Our guidebook suggested a diner and we were always ones for diner food. The book told us about some of their specialties and it sounded pretty awesome. We found the place easily enough, but were waited on about half an hour after sitting. That always sucks. The menu actually featured that revolting dish that our pastor had eaten days before our wedding: wet fries. We steered clear of them and thus have lived to this day without such sin gracing our lips.

All throughout our meal, we saw out the window droves of people and families headed towards the lake carrying folding canvas chairs and blankets, dragged along by dogs or dragging wagons full of kids behind them. Our meal was taking too long, we were afraid, and the whole of the waterfront would be occupied by Vermonters. We'd have to walk back to our car, heads hanging low, marching to the sounds of explosions in the distance and the collective sounds of an impressed audience.

Our meal was subpar, our waitress was snippy and dreadfully slow, and we considered, for at least the fourth time during our travels, not giving a tip. We tipped, though, and then scurried out towards the lake. It was crowded and we brought nothing to sit on at all, expecting, I suppose, that bleachers would be provided. Some distance from the lake was a building surrounded by watchers perching on every available space. There was a couple, about our age, sitting in a recessed window and we sat on the cement about 10 feet in front of them. The show was taking a long time to get going, the summer northern sun refusing to succumb to nightfall. The couple in the seat behind us started bickering.

I love listening in on conversations in public. I don't think that I'm alone in this, but it really is some sort of a compulsion. If I can't quite hear what the conversationalists are saying, I fill in the blanks with scandal and scintillation. But in this case, what they were talking about was quite clear. She was pissed at him and he was pissed that she hasn't gotten over it yet. What the "it" was, of course, was never mentioned. Listening in to a couple who argues about something and leaving that something absolutely unspoken, as Hemingway will tell you, is among the greatest pleasures in this world. Whatever it is that they were arguing about, it was too terrible and triggering to address directly. We speculated, as any good eavesdroppers would, about what exactly it was. An abortion? An act of indiscretion? A crime? It was all so enthralling. The two had hoped, I'm sure, that the fireworks would offer distraction from their issues together and that through the display of bursting colors in the air, the two would be able to forget their troubles and act like two people who enjoyed their own company for a single evening. And if that evening could transfer to sex quickly enough, maybe no issues would have to be resolved directly.

But the sun wouldn't go down, and they were stuck with each other.

Charlie and I, however, smelled blood. We knew that if the sun could outlast these two, their conversation would have to leave the public eye. This would leave the coveted window seat empty and we would have to be quick in order to usurp it. We listened intently as the conversation intermittently raised and lowered in volume. Any change in volume was a good sign in this case, and each fluctuation inspired giddiness in us.

Finally, the argument reached some sort of climax and the man went off on a monologue about how shitty it is to be with someone as shitty as she is. He ended his tirade in the only way he really could, by storming off and ruining the holiday for the both of them. He marched off in one direction leaving her alone in the window.

What the hell? Wasn't she going to go after him? Was she really going to sit in the window all by herself and celebrate Independence in the most depressing possible way? The sun was invisible now, the only trace left a blazing fire in the western sky. The time was drawing near, the music being played seemed like it was getting climactic, and yet this girl sat there, arms folded, face stolid, refusing to give up her comfort to a couple that was still in love.

Cheers erupted when the surrounding streetlights and parking lot lights shut off and the strains of "America the Beautiful" started over the speakers. The first rocket was sent streaming into the night's sky and exploded into an orgasm of color with the sound following a moment later. The sight was too much for the girl on the windowsill. She saw a beauty in that display, one supposes, that she used to see in her relationship until this unspoken trouble befell them. She stood up from her seat and walked away in the opposite direction that her beau went earlier.

The fireworks in Burlington that July 4th were the best I have ever seen. They went along with a musical presentation for a full hour and we sat like two enraptured in the comfort of the windowsill seat that lay absent like the love that had previously occupied the lives of the couple before us.

"This is another chapter without me," Charlie says. "Do you have trouble putting me on paper?"

"I guess?" I say. "I mean, you're probably going to read this...for real...and it's hard to render you fully present because it will be so weird for you to read."

"You're struggling with the writing process. I get that. Maybe change my name."

"I already did."

"Right. It's just that I remember that July Fourth so well. It was so wonderful and beautiful and meaningful. The fireworks show was the best I had ever seen and it was the first one that we spent married and the first one that we spent together. And then, in your story about it, I was hardly there. Just a prop."

"God, I feel terrible."

"Don't feel terrible. Just put in that one moment, when the explosions first started and the audience grew quiet and all those thousands of people got quieter and quieter until they faded away entirely and it was just you and me, holding hands in the windowsill, and the light reflected in our eyes and we soared together, in each other's arms. Okay?"

Graduation

There was a lot to do at the college before I graduated. I had finished my work, for the most part, but there was an avalanche of paperwork that needed to be attended to and no set time at the college to do it. I would look around for the various advisors and teachers whose signatures I needed, but they were often busy or teaching or unfindable. In the meantime, I showed Charlie around the campus that had before then seemed imaginary to her, as if it were a mental place to where I escaped twice a year since we had met.

We hiked through the woods, explored the old buildings, and used the computers in the library. It was very rewarding to finally be able to show someone around there and the mingling of worlds was at once exciting and confusing. It was sort of like seeing someone you know appearing in a cartoon: both are familiar to you, but it never occurred to you that they could coexist. I introduced my wife to many of the people whom I had worked with for years and was seeing, for the most part, for the last time.

The campus had been for me a liberating place. I got to get away from everything so that I could read, write, and explore my own abilities. This was all courtesy of financial aid money. Really, an MFA program when paid for by financial aid money, becomes a government sponsored artistic retreat. For two or three years, you can receive an easy-termed loan to study the arts in the way that you choose. I can't imagine why every grown man and woman don't go on to get an MFA, unless it is only that they look further into the future and become concerned about how, exactly, they are going to pay that loan back. I, for one, plan to fake my own death [once you've read that last part, black it out with a Sharpie. That way I will forever get away with it (if you read that on Kindle, it will erase itself.).]

When I wasn't obligated on campus, Charlie and I made excursions around the great state of Vermont, thinking that of all places we had been, this was the one where we could lead the most comfortable life, immersed in the woods and hills and away from the cities and congestion of daily life. The smallness of the state made it all the more appealing, but more difficult to find jobs. We made a list one night of the options for college teaching and found it a bit sparse compared to, say, Texas or California.

One night we had pizza at Plainfield's only pizza place, Positive Pie. The restaurant was comfortable and relaxing; it was like we lived in a cool old house and an awesome hippie made us a pizza for his own karma. Only we had to pay for it. Other than that one night, we found ourselves much too often dining at the local Friendly's. There is no meal that is more 'just fine' than Friendly's. Nothing special there at all, except that they actually give you an ice cream mess as part of a meal. Yes. This trip was doing wonders for my weight.

On our last morning in Vermont, we splurged on breakfast and ate at the New England Culinary Institute in Montpellier. The meal stands out as our best breakfast on the trip. It occurs to me as I think back on that meal that there are really two kinds of good cooking: the kind that is robust and dominating in flavor—like Texas barbeque or New Mexican food—and the kind that is delicate and balanced, creating a decoding sensation in your mouth as you try and isolate exactly what it is you're tasting and why it's so damn good. This was the second, more delicate, kind of good and definitely wonderful.

We got back to campus on time for my graduation. All of my paperwork was filed, I had given a reading the other day, and all that was left was to stand there with my classmates in the small tea garden, give a short speech about exactly what this graduation means to me, and then walk away from it all forever. And when I did walk away, I had a little piece of paper in my hand that certified my place in the academic community, allowing me to never have to work summers ever again, as long as I kept up my end of the bargain. It was an extraordinarily expensive piece of paper, and while I usually try not to give a lot of clout to the outside approval of institutions, I was proud and spent a bit too much time looking at it.

The sun was going down as Charlie and I left Goddard. We had checked out of our hotel and our car was once again loaded to the brim. Another paycheck had come into our account and we had the luxury of breathing a little easier for a few days. For the first time in weeks, we turned and headed west. It would be the primary direction from now on. West. We had made it to the Atlantic, we had seen what we had set out to see all the way along. Now it was time to turn back home, go to California, where we would regroup before figuring out where we would move our lives and start again.

The French

The "Bonjour" caught me completely off guard. I knew where we were going, but the realization that the border guard assumed that I spoke French first, then tried English was beyond off-putting. It was a sudden and shocking surprise on the scale of what God thought when one of his monkeys starting munching apples.

Look, I understand that we're talking about Québec and all those French-Canadians, but I kinda didn't know that, too. I mean, I heard that Frankenmuth, Michigan was a German town and that Solvang, California was a Swedish town, but both places are only so in an intricately tourist way; they borrow architecture and cooking, but everyone is as American as French fries. Hell, in every Chinatown I've ever been to, the predominate language was English, with a Cantonese sass thrown in. So I thought that Quebec was French-Canadian in that campy, touristy way. But here they are, right there at the border, with a guy asking me "Bonjour" in the middle of the night. I tell you, it's just plain un-American.

I explained my un-Frenchness by answering with a mighty "Howdy," and this gave his vocabulary a turn for the civilized[28]. He asked me in a more polite tongue what it was we were doing, where we were going, and

---

[28] This "Howdy" of mine echoed across the Canadian landscape, shaking the branches of every maple, molting the down of every goose, and scoring a touchdown in every hockey net.

all of that. We were driving through Canada; not exactly a short cut, but seeing a bit of the 51st state sounded slightly more interesting than just driving through more regular states. Our goal that night was Montreal where we had Pricelined a hotel.

We learned that night, while trying to find our way to the hotel with little luck, that everyone in Montreal prefers to address you in the French manner. This seems awful stubborn to me, as France is thousands of miles away from the middle of America, where people most often take to English. I'm not saying that English should be the official language of everywhere, because then I'd be just as bad as the French, but that there really is no reason to throw all sense of normalcy out the window just because you want to show off your snobbery.

What is it with the French, anyway? I'm not complaining about them in the normal "French are pussies" kind of way, nor the "French are rude" kind of way. What I want to know is why they are so damn prideful. That sounds a bit offensive, but let me illustrate exactly what I mean.

The French have a tendency to claim everything that they have respect for by putting a little French flag in front of the noun that has their attention. *French* toast. *French* fries. *French* kissing. This is snotty and uncalled for. There is no reason to claim these objects in such a way when other nouns would serve just as well. Besides, you can't tell me that the little fried potatoes being served at McDonald's have anything to do with the

French anymore. And French toast? It's not from France at all. And it's hardly enjoyed there. A simple hijacking, is what it is. The French kiss? They didn't come up with that. And in fact, there is a shameful admission of this found in the fact that in certain regions of France, it's actually called an *English* kiss. Folks, let us replace this form of Imperialism by changing the nouns to words more befitting.

French fries can be called "fries," "shoelaces," or "hunger sticks." French toast could be more apply named "egg toast," "sugar toast," or "Oxford Delight." The French kiss should be renamed "first base," "tongue wrestling," or "making-the-fuck-out."

Regardless of the language shock, Montreal was a breathtaking city. We had been through so many cities in such a short amount of time that it was hard to imagine a place feeling so new and exciting as Montreal did. It really did feel more like a European city than any of the other we had been through, and it wasn't just the language. People were riding bikes, for the sake of God, riding bikes! We happened to be there during some kind of big music festival. Judging by the looks of the crowd attending the festival—or, more specifically, walking to and from the festival and parking while disrupting the hell out of traffic—I would say that either Jimmy Buffet was in town, or there was a smooth jazz festival. That is to say, the streets were alive with baby boomers, each one sporting a more relaxed shirt than the last.

We had printed out directions for our hotel back at Goddard, but as things turned out, they were to the wrong hotel. I had a short and vaguely French exchange with the gentleman behind the desk at the wrong hotel and he gave me directions to the actual hotel. His directions were stripped down of all usefulness, not mentioning a single street by name. I remember them perfectly, after all of these years, because I concentrated so hard to retain the enigmatic clues that I was sure my wife could decode once I got back in the car.

He said, "Go straight for oh, three blocks. There's a light there and you turn left. Another left. Right at the second sign. Two more lefts just a little apart from each other in the next block. Now you're near the park. Turn towards the park but not all the way towards it. Like a clock, see, set to two o'clock or so, the park being at three. Then, two more lefts." I learned then that the French Canadians have the potential to be just as stubborn as the French when it comes to communicating with outsiders. There is the notion in their hearts that by distracting a cultural foreigner, you have defended your country to its fullest. This was, I suppose, the same strategy of resistance that the French used in every occasion that Germany took Paris by force. No doubt their blitzkrieg was fueled by the frustration they had in finding the closest bathroom based on the encoded directions of the cultural defender.

Without ourselves resorting to blitzkrieg or any other form of krieg, we wandered the streets, avoiding cyclists, until we found the proper hotel. I might add that the man behind the desk seemed strikingly similar to the first man behind the desk. That, in fact, the desk seemed very similar. But if, perchance, this were indeed the same gentleman, this time he found our room and sent us up. My poker face was as good as his, though, and when he asked if I had any trouble finding the place, I said, "No, of course not. I stay here every weekend."

Canadonian Nudists

Montreal was a fascinating place. It was the first time in our travels together that we had found ourselves in a foreign country. There is so much to explore in a foreign place, and the things that usually get to you are not the things that are outwardly different, but the things that are strikingly similar, but just a bit off. Like when you're staying in a hotel and the local channel has Jeopardy on at 7 instead of 7:30. Or when you find puzzling new forms of Sprite—*Sprite Remix* or *Sprite Citrus*, for example. One of our favorite finds in Canada was coffee flavored Dentine. Perhaps the most disturbing of all, though, is the different flavors of chips that one finds. Once, while in Europe, I bought a bag of Lay's Potato chips that were clearly BBQ flavored, but the cultural translation ended up being "Texas Paprika." Whoa. I'm a huge fan of Texas barbeque, but I have never once heard a pit boss refer to paprika in their restaurant. This surprising find was topped, however, in Canada where my wife and I found a new and more disturbing flavor of Lay's: ketchup.

I would like to know, as many of you probably would, what exactly is going on in the mind of the person who buys ketchup flavored potato chips. What desires drives one to do this? Does one crave a ketchup potato chip before purchasing, or is this a lousy substitute for a French fry?

Finds such as these let Charlie and I know that we were dealing with much more than just Canadians, and that this was much more than just Canada. Canada, as a word, was all too familiar for the place where we found ourselves. Canadian, as an ethnicity, was far too domestic a word for someone who enjoys or has the potential to enjoy ketchup flavored potato chips. Therefore we used our prerogative to modify the language a bit. From that point on, we were in Canadia and surrounded by Canadonians. It was really the only way that we felt right about things like coffee flavored gum or the queen being printed on coins.

Following the directive of our trip to discover and understand new places, we spent just a little time on our first night in Montreal trying to find a certain sex club. That's right, sex club. I had read about it in a weekly newspaper in Vermont and it seemed like the properly adventurous thing to do while visiting Canadia. The club was a place where singles and couples could go to have sex—with themselves or each other—in private or in the open. Now, this sounds like fun. But I expect that if we had found the place and had the balls to go in, we would have found the proposition to be less than fun. Dirty, for example, may be a better word.

We didn't find it, however, and it was probably for lack of trying. We weren't sure if we'd go in if we did find it and we weren't sure if we'd have sex in front of people if we did go in and we were positive that we weren't going to have sex with anyone else, if we did go in and did have sex, so things seemed a bit expensive, honestly, and off-putting. In fact, should I really take a realistic point of view, the place may as well have not existed.

But the next day, as we were seeing the country side of Canadia, we discovered on the map a little place that did seem like it was worth taking a look at.

We were driving across a good chunk of the country, headed over and around Lake Ontario, swinging by Toronto, and then hooking back over to the States to see Niagara Falls. We stopped at a McDonald's long enough to feel like aliens again, seeing on the menu that not only had the horrid McGriddle lasted these many weeks since our wedding day, but that it had made its way to Canadia. And in Canadonian, the McGriddle is called, quite disturbingly, the McCrepe. This painted a picture of a clown making fancy breakfasts in a stainless steel skillet, carefully sprinkling rosemary onto a gorgonzola and pear frittata of some sort. It was a disturbing image and one that could only come to life in the Canadoinian lands. It was an easy enough order to resist, however.

The main advantage of the McDonald's was that it had an ATM machine inside. There we were able to put in our card and draw out a bunch of little Canadonian play money. They're just like the little brother to our dollars!

It was a rather amazing thing, really, being able to take foreign currency from our own account with the simple push of some buttons. How far the world had come since I was a kid, driving back and forth between

Texas and California. I remember stopping in towns to get gas with my parents, driving around to all of the banks looking for an ATM machine that was compatible with our ATM service, not finding one, and praying that the next town would have one so that we could get gas and make it through the desert. Now you can use your debit card in the middle of Red Square to buy a McBorsch Burger or whatever.

In the lobby of the McDonalds was a pamphlet about local attractions, and that's when we learned about the nudist colony that was just a little off the path on the way to Niagara. A nudist colony (pardon me, naturalist club) seemed like the tame and semi-acceptable way to be naked around people and, possibly, experience an orgy. If an orgy breaks out at a naturalist club, it was merely as a result of all the awesome nakedness and not because a bunch of people set out to find a club and fuck that evening. There was even a campground there, so we could stay for cheap. This was a winning situation, and we knew it.

It wasn't because we were trying to get to the naked place before sunset that we bypassed Toronto, watching its outline on the horizon without experiencing the city, but it didn't hurt. We didn't know how much longer our money was going to last, after all, and staying in a city hotel was much more expensive than pitching a tent in the middle of a sea of human skin. So bypass it we did, with little promises on our minds of a return to experience New York and Toronto some other day.

We pulled off the Canodonian Interstate and followed the directions to get to the naturalist club. We drove into the gates and decided to take a lap around before stopping at the front office to make a commitment.

And damn, am I glad that we took that lap.

What did we see when we drove around the naturalist colony? I'll give you one guess. But first, before you let your imagination get carried away—maybe you thought of bunches of sexual adventures, or just a Garden of Eden with platonic ideals of nudity and harmony as far as the eye could see—let me remind you how things played out that first time that you ever walked onto a nude beach in college. Yes, that's right; what we saw in the nudist colony was nothing but penis.

The primary specimen at any nude beach or naturalist colony, so far as I can tell, is the Old Man Penis. This remarkable long object dangles without hope or style, attracting what we call "negative attention" from everyone around it. It's tragic really. We drove around the high trees, coming upon little cabins or trailers all surrounded by perfectly clothed women and naked old men. Old men wearing shirts walked down the road towards us, their junk hanging down above their bare chicken legs.

We averted our eyes as much as we could, acting like we were thoughtfully adjusting our radio or checking out the time on our watches. We were certain that at any minute, we'd be dragged out of the car, invited to a barbeque, and forced to watch as the naked penis men played a heated game of volleyball.

We had to get out of there. We had to get *the hell* out of there. With shaking hands, Charlie tried to point out the way we should turn at each fork in the road to make it back to the main road. But we took a wrong turn and ended up circling the endless goddamn resort again, for the sake of Christ and all that is holy. This time people stared with a little more concern. What was this filthy car with California plates doing amongst them? People stood and eyed us as we tried to give friendly nods of our heads without actually making eye-to-penis contact. If they were self-conscious about outsiders circling their territory and seeing their penises, they didn't show it by say, covering the penises or putting on shorts.

Now we were in for it. A guy in a golf cart was following us, waving his hand. He was, no doubt, from the front office and wishing us to register so that I could comfortably reveal my member. It was no trouble, really, to outrun the golf cart, but the problem was trying to look like we weren't trying to outrun the golf cart. This proved impossible once we saw the exit and I drove much too fast once the goal was in view. I floored it, hit the main road, and never looked back.

Niagara Falls

So you probably know this, but Niagara Falls used to be the number one destination in America for honeymoons. This started to be the case sometime after the Civil War, when the state of New York started pushing it as a honeymoon destination in print publications all over the country. It stayed the king of honeymoons until travel to Hawaii and other tropical islands became possible for people of moderate means. Promotion may have driven people to Niagara Falls for their honeymoon, but that doesn't actually explain why people followed through with this promotion.

Why honeymooners would want to visit the falls as part of the celebration of their marriage is a mystery to me. We were on the Canadian side, and it was delightfully touristy. It was one of those strips of tourist streets that had wax museums, haunted attractions, IMAX theaters, fudge shops, theme restaurants, and lame little places where they do old timey photography. Like a little Las Vegas, the tourist area was surrounded with hotels. Having given up on camping at the nudist resort, we started searching for a hotel that we could afford.

Our best option was called something like The Honeymoon Lodge, but probably not exactly that. It was under renovation, half the hotel covered in scaffolding. The parking lot was totally empty and we figured that we might have some leverage on pricing due to all of this. There was a lone proprietor who quoted us a price that we felt was way too high. Then she told us there was a Jacuzzi tub. Still, too high. We started to walk out the door and she dropped the price by a third. We were there.

Had we known how awesome the room was, we probably would have not bargained so heavily. By awesome, I mean tacky and amazing. The room was filled with mirrors. The walls were mirrored, the bed had a mirrored headboard, the dresser had *mirrored drawers*. Was there a mirror on the ceiling, you wonder? Some mysteries should stay unsolved.

The best part of the room, by far, was the red heart-shaped Jacuzzi tub surrounded by mirrors on three sides. Sure, it was no Champaign glass whirlpool bath for two, like the Poconos promised in all those bridal magazines so long ago, but it was close.

We left the hotel room and headed down the tourist strip towards the falls. Through a superhuman feat of willpower, we didn't go into the Ripley's Believe it or Not Wax Museum, the Haunted Castle, or the WWE Experience. We weren't so powerful when it came to eating, however, and we spent every dime that we had saved on the hotel room by stopping into the Rainforest Café and eating a small dinner and an obnoxious desert at the single worst table in the establishment.

By the time our themed dinner was over, the sun was going down and we rushed the hundred yards or so down the street to the railing above the falls, seeing them painted in the red light of the setting sun. And once the sun actually went down, they were painted in the red, blue, and green lights of the floodlights that shine on them for the first few hours of night time.

The falls were impressive. They're really big, but not all that tall. You always hear these stories of people going over the falls and miraculously surviving or tragically dying. But there are a bunch of falls that I've seen in my life that no one would dare to go over in a million years. If you tried to go over Bridalveil Falls in Yosemite, for example, your little barrel would be quite lonely when halfway down the 600 foot drop all the water from the falls floats away in a fine mist against the rock face. But it's not the height of Niagara Falls that people are impressed by, but the sheer volume of water that is constantly dropping over the sides.

They were pretty, sure. But honestly, they were no Grand Canyon. They were no Yellowstone, no Yosemite. They were fine. What was really remarkable was that Charlie and I constituted about a third of the entire population that stood in admiration of the falls that night, while there was a huge line outside the Haunted Castle and the IMAX theater had sold out their last show of the evening.

Niagara Falls is sort of the cautionary tale for natural wonders in our country. Niagara Falls was a huge tourist attraction before the National Parks system came into being, protecting many of the most naturally beautiful places in our country. It became clouded with activity, restaurants, and tourist traps before most people were able to come and see it free of distraction. The trains brought the crowds, the crowds attracted the businesses, and the Falls became a backdrop to a little slice of tourist consumerism.

It's really too bad. While standing on the cement walkway, staring across the suspension bridge to our native country, hearing the sounds of screams from a nearby rollercoaster, seeing the falls bathed in colorful floodlights, all we could think about was how gorgeous it would have been to be sitting quietly beneath tamarack trees with nothing but the moonlight on the water. Few people have ever seen that sight, and no one will ever again.

Coming to Amerika

We woke up early our last morning in Canadia since we had so far to go that day. On our way out of town we ran by Niagara Falls one more time and were the only people there looking at that flow of water. It was peaceful and quiet and we parked illegally so we weren't there very long.

Off we went, back across Canadia towards the border town of Detroit, Michigan. For the first time on our trip, it started raining, coming down so hard and fast that it was hard to see where we were headed at times. The drivers around us, at least, seemed adept in the rain. There's not much worse than being somewhere that it doesn't rain when a storm kicks up. In San Diego, for example, whenever there was a chance of rain, I stayed the hell away from the freeways. Every hour during a rainstorm in San Diego, there are an average of 200 accidents reported on the interstate. Luckily it only rains three or four hours a year there.

We were quickly hurtling towards the United States, ready to be freed once more of the tyranny and oppression of a monarchy, when we saw a sign that said, "Last Canadian Exit." We took this exit, deciding that it would be a great idea to stop and spend the rest of our Canadonian cash, rather than face harsh conversion charges. We had enough queen-faced cash to fill up on gas and then go inside for a few snacks.

Rest stops in Canadia are not like rest stops in the States. Rest stops vary greatly state to state, from the terribly dangerous ones in California (at least that's how we felt about them), to the Luxurious ones in Vermont. In Texas, rest stops went ahead and covered that whole spectrum and added a new one: picnic areas with tables, benches, trash cans, and shelters, but no restrooms. I had spent weeks and weeks seeing the rest stops of the nation, but nothing prepared me for the rest stops we enjoyed in Canadia.

Instead of being roadside buildings with technically functional restrooms housed within, Canadonian rest stops did it up, big time. There was a gas station, a convenience store, a food court, and a chapel all housed inside the spacious building. The bathrooms were well appointed, free of unpleasant odor, full coverage doors and sanitizer for the seats; a far cry from the door-less and horrid stainless steel commodes of some American rest stops.

But there was one more surprise that awaited us. We only had a few coins left and wanted to use them up. There were a series of vending machines near the exit and that seemed a fine place to spend. What sounds good? An ice cream treat, right? Totally.

This ice cream vending machine was a modern marvel of construction and function unlike I have ever seen. Machines in general fascinate me, I suppose, but I've always had a special place in my heart those old machines that border on the clockwork side of the spectrum. Old player pianos, for example, that do more than just self-tickle the ivories, but house drums, xylophones, whistles, and bells, just delight me to no end. This ice cream vending machine was not unlike that—a severely complex contraption that did whatever it took to vend you your ice cream.

You walk up to it and see the selection of treats. Ice cream sandwich, creamsicles, drumsticks, and whatever else Nestle makes. But smack dab in the front of the machine is a window so that one can see the inner workings. Inside, nothing special is happening, so it would seem. A closed freezer chest sits at the bottom of the window and some sort of black apparatus sits up above it. But once you'd paid your amount and made your selection, stand the fuck back and pay attention.

This machine bursts to life in an electrifying way. A mechanical arm opens the top of the freezer chest, revealing carefully catalogued rows of packaged goods. Then—to the delight of you and all of those around you—a tube reaches down and gingerly places itself upon the treat that is desired. Amazingly, a vacuum sound starts and it hits you what's about to happen: this tube is going to vacuum your treat into the air and deposit it in the receptacle. It does just this with mechanical efficiency and you hop up and down with joy.

I'm telling you, I would have been less surprised if the thing had anthropomorphized into a robotic butler and handed me my treat. What business did this vacuum contraption have moving things around with sucking power? How much could it lift with that thing?

Who dreamt this idea into being and, more amazingly, who gave them the green light? It was so fascinating to watch that Charlie and I downed our drumsticks as quickly as we could to get just one more and watch the machine go through its ritual.

The skies were clear when we left the building with our second treat and got into our newly filled car to head back to our home country. In honor of the first American city we would encounter, Charlie selected a Kid Rock CD[29], which just happens to be the most explicit and brutally censorable album I have ever heard in my life. The dude cannot stop cussing me out the entire time I'm listening to the music I've paid for. But it was Detroit, and we didn't have any Eminem and neither of us can stand any but the very best Motown music.

Charlie, in her exuberance to be back in the States, took out the video camera which we had only really used sporadically, and filmed our triumphant crossing of the bridge between the two nations as we listened to *Cocky* and saw the skyline of Detroit ahead of us. She kept filming as we got up to the border check point,

---

[29] Incidentally, I should really have mentioned our music situation in a little more detail. Charlotte hated beyond measure the fact that it was up to her to select music while driving. She would become enraged, or at least perturbed, when I asked her to change CDs if we had just been stopped at a gas station a few minutes before where I could have done it myself. The pressure was too much for her, she professed, and it was boring to reach down, find the case, and page through things anyway. She took to organizing a day-long playlist before we stopped for the morning, as this took the burden of choice far, far away from her. This particular day, she had planned for the Kid Rock album to play while entering Detroit and timed out the CDs accordingly. Because that's way easier than picking on the go.

where I was not expecting to be greeted in French this time.

The greeting I got, turns out, was much more rude than French. Even more rude than *the* French. Keep in mind that this was the first time I had done a post-9/11 crossing into our country and was expecting to be waved through once the gentleman saw my California plates. Instead, the border guard adopted his total-asshole voice, looped his thumbs over his belt, and said, "We're gonna have to take that camera."

"Why?"

"Your girlfriend there was filming us."

"We're excited to be home, bro. She was just filming our crossing."

He shook his head, as if he had heard this total bullshit excuse before. "Sorry bud."

"So what's so special about y'all that once filmed you get to keep the object that did the filming?" I was starting to miss Canadia about now.

"We're border guards. Some of us might work undercover and then people will know what we look like."

"Because this is totally going on CNN later tonight."

"You can just give me the tape."

"Dude, this is our honeymoon. It's our search for a new home. This tape is all the footage we have of the last 5,000 miles of our lives. I'd rather give you the camera."

He shook his head. Someone must have just tried this bullshit, I thought.

"Okay," I said, calmly. "How about I rewind it to where we got to the bridge and then I'll record the lens cap for a couple minutes."

He thought about this. He was softening. Maybe Charlie had flashed him her boobs, I couldn't be sure. "I'll have to watch you do it," he said.

I did as instructed, rewound the tape and started recording the darkness.

"That red light mean it's recording?"

"Yeah. I can show it to you after, if you'd like."

"Nah. That won't be a problem."

I kept filming for a couple more minutes. When you watch the footage now, you can hear the guard and I chit-chatting and defusing the tension over a black screen. Finally he sent us on his way and got back to much less important work. Just to think that I'm not allowed to film a guy from my own personal experience in this country. Like I'm going to sell his image to the drug dealers of Detroit. Is this not America?

Well, I don't have the footage, but I do have the memory of an elephant and the freedom of speech. So if you're a drug dealer in the Detroit area, listen up. If you're doing a deal with a dude who's about 38, 6'1" tall, 215lbs with a gray moustache and a mole on his left cheek, that's officer Polowski. Don't trust him.

So there.

McChicken

I'm writing this from Michigan[30]. It's a place I never thought that I would live. Do you realize that when you're in Michigan, you're never more than six miles from a lake or river? Do you realize that Michigan is the only state made up of two peninsulas? Do you realize that Michigan has more miles of coastline than any other state except for Alaska? And did you know that there is absolutely nothing to eat in Michigan?

I'm not really exaggerating that much, y'all. Sure, the metro areas of Detroit and Ann Arbor have some dining, but once you go north of there, your options get slight. Mainly, we're talking about bland American meat and potatoes. Don't get me wrong, now, there are steaks and pan fries in this world that send me for a spin, but the Michigander has not discovered seasoning. I have caught myself eating a hamburger in an establishment and actually having to salt it. Michigan still has Big Boy restaurants. Really, they do. Everywhere. In fact, Michigan seems to be the place that every dead restaurant chain lives on. Bennigan's, Big Boy, Damon's, Hot-n-Now, and other zombie restaurants pepper the streets.

There are two places that I've found to get a good burger in Michigan. The first is in a local fast food chain in the Flint area called Halo Burger. The sign features a

---

[30] I'm editing it in Huntington Beach, California, bitches!

happy cow with an angel halo hanging over its head. The other is a restaurant called Timber Charlie's in Newberry, a small town on the Upper Peninsula. If there is a single other restaurant with a good hamburger, I'd like to know about it. You can email me: willstronghold@hotmail.com, and I will try it out and give you my opinion. Chances are, I've tried it and rejected it, but go ahead, give it a shot. This utter lack of eating choices—in most cities, McDonald's is the only fast food option—has lead Charlie and me to call Michigan "McChicken" whenever referring to the state's cuisine.

There is one food, so far as I know, that is a McChicken original, and it is the pastie. It should be noted here and now that pastie rhymes with "nasty" not "tasty." It's basically a crust of some sort filled with ground burger, potatoes, and sometimes carrots or other root vegetables. They smother them with either gravy or ketchup, presumably, so one can taste it, as there is a distinct lack of seasoning in a pasty. They were popular in the iron mines of Northern Michigan because miners could construct them at home, cook them on a shovel over a candle, and then eat them while holding the very bottom crust only and tossing that crust out when they eat down to that point so as not to get heavy metals from their hands onto their food. But, perhaps the heavy metals would have flavored the pastie, making it worthy of the pallet, if eventually deadly.

Now I am probably being unfair. But there is reason for that. When one drives up north to the U.P., one sees about a million signs for the "Best Pasties in Michigan" at every single turn. So a good deal of anticipation begins to build up if these things are so popular that they are everywhere and best everywhere. In Texas, every single restaurant claims to have the "Best Chicken Fried Steak in Texas." And you know what? Any of these choices leads to a really fucking good chicken fried steak. But the two pasties that I've tried were totally undesirable. I may as well have been eating out of a dumpster.

My assumption is that it's a comfort food of some sort. I think that people probably grow up eating them, for whatever reason, and then are fondly reminded of childhood and Christmas, or something. My rule of thumb has always been, if you have to put ketchup on it, it's not worth eating. But I do really and truly suppose that there must be delicious ones out there, but I haven't bothered to try them. I will eat more in my life, seeking the meaning of them.

Just to flog a dead horse, I think that just about any other ethnic group could have made these better. Let's say that you described the basics of the pastie to a congress of cooks from around the world. Mexicans would have filled it with spicy barbacoa or picadillo or carne asada; Germans would have filled it with knockwurst. Czechs would have used spicy sausage. The Japanese could have used fish and wasabi. The French would have filled them with hasenpfeffer or escargot and I wouldn't have eaten them. The Chinese clearly would have used Kung Pao chicken and brown rice and would have thoughtfully skipped the crust altogether in favor of spring rolls or crab wantons. Even someone from another part of the States would have seasoned the meat before wrapping it in, for God's sake. Anyone would have done this better. I just don't understand.

While driving through for the first time, however, we did not have a pastie. We had—wait for it—White Castle.

White Castle was something that we had heard of for years. So far as I know, they invented the burger slider; at least I learned about sliders through a story about White Castle. They didn't have them in California, at any rate, but we had talked to people who came from the east who missed it so much that they could hardly believe they didn't have any White Castle on hand *right now*. California had In-n-Out Burger and Texas had Whataburger, and those regional favorites were always good choices. So my little wife and I mistakenly thought that White Castle would be of comparable quality.

White Castle burgers are small. They fit in your fingers without the possibility of getting anything on your palms. They have tiny grilled onions on them. They're basically served on dinner rolls. We ordered a reasonable amount of them, knowing their size. I think we ordered 6. You want to know how many we ate? I had one and Charlie had a half of one. Really. I almost never leave a burger unfinished, unless I'm suffering from the stomach flu, but I really couldn't put away any more than one tiny White Castle burger because it was so unbelievably unappealing.

I now think—correct me if I'm wrong—that people eat and jones for White Castle burgers by way of camp. It's bad enough that people like it for being bad, or something like that. You know, like Taco Bell.

Really, though, you don't go to Michigan for its food[31]. You go because of the shorelines, the wilderness, the camping, the wildlife (moose! Bear! Wolves!), and the relaxed pace of life. That said, the White Castle was enough to spur us out of the state during that first visit of ours. As bad as the food was, it wasn't so awful that we never came back.

---

[31] You go to McChicken for that.

Charlie's Childhood Dreams

Charlotte had always been a very independent woman. And before she was that, she was an independent girl. We can all trace our attributes to one traumatic event or another, and for Charlie, much of it goes back to her parents' divorce. Now, a lot of good came out of that divorce: a great stepmother, a couple stepfathers, three wonderful step sisters, and a step brother. She grew up with these mixed families and had a happy childhood doing so and has become the person she is through this process. The divorce is also responsible for how independent she is. This is all according to my expert opinion as a psychologist, which I am not.

When her parents announced their divorce when she was eight, she was, in essence, handed her own life. She didn't need anyone anymore. She could make her own decisions. She didn't need to trouble her parents with any of her childhood problems while they went through this tough time. She could take care of herself.

One of the ways that Charlie took care of herself was by performing nighttime patrols of the house, looking for burglars. She would wake up in the black of night, pick up her brother's baseball bat, and start a solemn march around the house, searching for the intruders she knew were there somewhere. On tip toes, she'd sneak into the bedrooms of the sleeping and slowly slide their closets open. When she was sure that no one was there, she'd move on to the next room. In all the nights she did this, as you can imagine, she never did find a burglar hiding in the darkness. But she did find something much more terrifying to her little self: spiders.

In the event that a spider was found, Charlie would have little choice but to tell her dad. It had to be destroyed and there was no way in hell she was going use her burglar bat for that end. So she'd wake her dad up with a trembling voice, tell him of the danger she had discovered, and wait for his response. Frustrated, he'd get out of bed, take a sandal to the arachnid in question, and go back to sleep.

Honestly, I find this tale from her childhood just a little hard to swallow. But only one part of it: in all the time I've known Charlie, I've noticed that once she sees a frightening bug of any kind, her eyes stay on it until it has been neutralized. I have a strict policy that I will not kill anything except an ant or a roach—vermin. And once I am alerted to the buggy danger of the day, I go and find my collection supplies and take my time of it while Charlie stands like a statue, eyes pinned open, yelling, "Quick! Quick! What is taking so goddamn long?" She just knows that the instant she looks away, the bug will get on her.

Aside from the spiders, though, Charlie felt fully independent in her own house; able to make her own grown-up decisions. She exercised her rights as an independent person by turning Hindu at the age of 12. She infuriated her parents by giving up meat, refusing to wear shoes indoors, and constantly talking about Vishnu, who they assumed was some guy from school she was trying to impress.

And, from a very young age, she decided that she would move to Chicago once she was out of high school.

When I met her, Charlie was living by herself, working as a Starbucks barista. To this day, she still speaks fondly about how wonderful it was to live by herself. I don't take offense to this, and don't think I should, as this never comes up when she is pissed or unhappy, but rather when she is in a good mood and enjoying life. Her apartment was only vaguely divided into three rooms in an old converted house. It was filled with nice furniture from the furniture store where her dad used to work. It was a cozy place, quaint, and full of character. I took a look around her place when I first got there and surveyed what I could find out about her. I went to the stack of books that she had in the corner and saw that they all shared a common theme: moving to Chicago.

"You moving to Chicago?"

"Oh, no. Not right now. I've always wanted to."

"What would you do there?"

"I don't know. Live there. Find some loft where I could live by myself and have a job."

"Sounds lonely."

"Sounds decadent."

That was just one of the things I had always known about her: she is as happy alone as she is with me and that's okay. She never moved to Chicago and we never really discussed doing it ourselves, though I guess it's not explicitly out of the question or anything. But when we drove into Chicago that day on our trip, it was the first time that she had ever been there. And it was the first time she had been there since not moving there, as well. Her face was lit up as we saw the skyline that had adorned the books that she had in her apartment.

"Just think of it," I said to her. "For the next few hours, you *are* living in Chicago."

She smiled, but kept her eyes on the city ahead of us.

Really, we did the city a disservice. I did Charlie a disservice. Because money was tight and when you're on the road long enough you start to rush even if there's nowhere you're rushing to; we weren't even going to spend the night in Chicago. We were going in for dinner, to drive around, see the sights that we were missing by hurrying so. This was more my decision than hers and I had been pushing going on through The Windy City without stopping because of the ungodly expense of hotel rooms at the time. And I'm sure I was rightly justified, considering our financial situation. But I tell you, if I had one thing to do over back then, it would be Chicago. I would have set the money aside earlier, skipped something else, and let the girl stay in the city that used to represent freedom and independence to her. I know it wouldn't have been the same, since she wasn't by herself and she didn't have to forge her way without support of any kind, as she would have liked it. But, hell, we could have stayed in a hotel.

There was one little financial glimmer of hope in Chicago. For the first time since Texas, we saw a Wells Fargo ATM. Charlie's mom had given us a check on the outset of our trip and asked us to kindly not cash it until July. This little windfall of money would have made it possible, or at least more possible, to stay the night there. Instead, as is often the case with me, I thought it a better idea to use it to eat.

We wanted to try Chicago style pizza. Our guidebook suggested two places and we opted for the original Pizzeria Uno on Ohio St. Uno, along with at least two other establishments, claims to have invented the pizza. I know that it is true that pizza is an American invention, as is much of our American ethnic food. Moo goo gai pan, for example, is from New York. And don't get me started on French fries.

The restaurant was crowded. Exceedingly so. We waited among the crowd packed into the breezeway of the restaurant. We got there just in time, as it started raining lightly at the same instant. A woman was leaving the restaurant with her friends, saw the rain, and proceeded to bitch her friends for all they were worth.

"It's raining. Great, just great. The rain is going to ruin every single day of our vacation. This is really the worst vacation *ever* and I don't know how you guys talked me into this. Really, if I had this week to do over, I would have stayed as far away from this place as possible!" She zipped up her windbreaker and slapped at her friend's hand who was just trying to hand her a purse. Her friends had a look of severe shame on their faces, unable to come to grips with their incompetence themselves. I wondered what the big deal was, why someone would go so bothered by a little rain that they would make their friends feel not only responsible for, but downright damned because of, the weather.

Later that night, I learned why. On our walk back to the car, we came upon what I first had assumed was a piece of public art, but then saw as I got closer that it was none other than this very lady. She had rusted in the rain and stood there like a giant tin woodsman, unable to move. Her friends—clearly more human than she was—were nowhere to be seen. I'd have ditched her, too. Or erased her hard drive or something. Terrible woman.

The pizza was good. Almost worth the wait. Charlie wasn't a big fan, when it comes down to it, as she much prefers the New York style or even, dare I say, the California style, which has a more substantial crust than the New York but not so deep as the Chicago. The crust to her was too biscuit-like, a reference that I honestly just didn't get.

As was often the case, though, the pizza was not really the main course of our meal. Instead, it was the floor show. In this instance, the floor show happened at a booth directly next to our table[32]. There was a man, his teenage daughter, and the daughter's friend. Charlie and I love speculating on the relationships of those around

---

[32] We were packed like sardines. I imagine that most nights are that way, the restaurant being small and dark and the people crowding in by the dozens. I really don't know what would happen if there were a fire, but I'd load up on pizza in all the chaos.

us, especially when they are just too damn close to ignore. In this case, there was some real unfortunate shit going down at that booth. The man, it became clear, was flirting with the daughter's friend. The daughter was aware of this and noticeably irritated. The friend knew this and was flattered. The man didn't know that either of them knew, but he could tell his daughter was irritable and he interpreted the friend's awareness as flirtation. It was a real embarrassment, folks, and something that I could hardly tolerate. At one point, the daughter spilled some water. Not all the water in the world and not even all the water in her cup at the time, but some water. A little ice as well. But the dad lost his shit on her.

"Carrie, goddamn it!" he yelled.

"Sorry," the daughter said, feeling shamed by her accident.

"Well?" the dad said, indignantly.

"What?"

"Are you going to go to the restroom and get me some paper towels, or what?"

The daughter left the table and the man's face went from a contort of anger to a shiny smile directed at the friend, who sat demurely. "So, Andi, what colleges are you looking at?"

"Oh, you know, Mr. B, all the usual ones around here," the girl played with her hair. "And some real long-shots, you know, because it's good to dream and all."

It went on and on like that and I just felt terrible for the three of them. The daughter must have been more embarrassed than I've ever been doing anything; the friend had no idea what she was playing with and should have been more sensitive to her friend; and the man was making a right ass of himself and deserved to baked into his own pizza.

On the way out of town, we drove through some of the more desirable neighborhoods near downtown. The row houses were picturesque and charming. Charlie imagined herself, no doubt, coming home from work to her house full of cats and an answering machine with a little number two flashing—the perfect amount of messages at the end of a day of work. She'd kick off her shoes, turn the TV on just in time for *ER* or *Friends*, and pour herself a bowl of Lucky Charms for a quiet dinner. She was 19 or 20 in her imagination, and she waited for the show to be over before checking the messages. This solitary life that she dreamed of never did come to pass, and I always hope that she's just as happy now. I guess, really, it depends on the day.

Cheese and Bad Manners: This is the Midwest

We pressed on for a long time that night, still in that imaginary rush. It had been a really long and grueling day and all we wanted was to stop. But I made us keep going, aimed at some imaginary point that we had to make it to for some unknown reason. We stopped at a truck stop just moments before the midnight closing of a Wendy's housed within to order that bastard son of a milkshake and a sundae, the Wendy's Frostie. The restrooms were down a long and dank hallway right between the Wendy's section and a little area of modern conveniences that included a payphone and a pay computer for Internet use.

How long has it been since you've seen a payphone? They really and truly hardly exist anymore. A long lost relic of the past that reigned for years and years. At one point in time, my parents actually set up an 800 number for their house that any of the kids could call from a payphone without having to worry about change or making a collect call. They were everywhere. And what I miss most about pay phones is that you had to stand in one semi-private place to make a call. Hell, some of them were even ensconced in their own little closet, giving you a nice, quiet place to talk. These days, the cell phone has made every conversation a public one. There is nowhere to stand and talk and be away from everyone else. And who else misses the wonderful phenomena of walking by a payphone and have it ring? Magical, I tell you, magical.

The brother of this payphone was a pay internet terminal. Think about how short lived these were compared to the mighty and wizened payphone. While never nearly as widespread, they did exist in many places (most commonly the Internet Café) and were just as useful as a payphone. But they have gone the way of their great-grandfather without ever living so long and honorable a life. So sad.

A man was waxing the tile floor of the Wendy's with a large, noisy machine that drowned out all but the most stern voices and sounds. I had had to speak up to order our Frosties and was pretty annoyed with the dude in general.

While Charlie used the little ladies room, I popped a couple dollars into the pay computer to check my email. Standing at the little computer stand, using a dirty trackball mouse, I wrote down the directions to a friend's house in Portland who had emailed me. I also learned that I had a job offer: one of the places in Texas where I had interviewed was willing to take me on as a part-time professor for the following fall, if I was willing to come. This was exciting news, as we could stop wandering and head straight south to set up shop, if we wanted, or we could press on and see if there were other offers, other opportunities, or other ideas that we wanted to explore. I stood there, staring at the screen thinking, when Charlie came out of the hallway.

"Hey, how much time you have left on that thing?"

"Couple minutes."

"Can I check mine?"

"Sure."

I closed the window with my email and let her log in. The little timer on the upper corner of the computer screen told us that she had about 150 seconds left. Just as she logged in, the man waxing the floor pushed his huge machine right up to Charlie.

"Excuse me," he said.

Charlie looked at him in disbelief; was he really talking to her?

"I said, excuse me!" the man gave my wife a look of indignation. She stepped back from the computer and the dude waxed the floor in front of the computer vigorously. Charlie looked at me with a confused expression and then started laughing as hard as she could. The man walked on, satisfied with his polishing, leaving Charlie about a minute to check her email. A minute that she could hardly control herself, she was laughing so hard.

The Waxman kept at that floor as hard as he could, leaving behind him a trail of muddy water. I don't think that the guy had ever used such a piece of machinery before, as he seemed to be doing more damage than good and there was a half an inch of water covering everything.

Charlie was nearly through with the time allotted to her. The Waxman was on the far end of the little room, trying his hardest to remove a stubborn stain near the exit door. He pushed his machine a little too hard, and it came unplugged from the wall. The outlet was the same one the computer terminal was plugged into.

"Hey," the Waxman yelled. "Hey." He was looking at me.

I did the sheepishly point-to-myself thing in disbelief that he would call me "Hey" twice.

"Yeah. You."

Now I was "You."

"Plug that in for me."

"Really?"

"Plug it in. C'mon!"

Charlie was buckled over in laughter. I bent down and took a look at the soaking wet plug. It was one of those big suckers with the thick black cord and a yellow cylinder that the prongs come out of. No doubt about a million volts wanted to run through that cord to power the Waxman's toy.

I moved the cord closer to the wall socket, hardly able to believe that I was going to plug it in for this jackass. I consoled myself with the thought of the large monetary reward Charlie would get for my death. As the plug made contact with the socket, a huge blue spark came to life and a puff of smoke went up into the air. For a moment, I couldn't tell if I was shocked or not. But, miraculously, I was fine. The floor cleaner came back to life and the Waxman kept pushing away at that stain.

Charlie tried and tried to get a hold of herself. She was hysterical. Finally, she was able to formulate words. "Do you have any more bills?"

"What?"

"For the computer. I didn't get to check anything."

"No, sorry. That was it."

We grabbed our Frosties and headed towards the door. It was blocked by the jackass Waxman.

"Hey!" I yelled. He didn't hear me. "Hey!"

He looked at me, noticeably irritated.

"Do you mind?"

He moved the behemoth and let us make our escape.

For the next hour, we kept driving. We were in Wisconsin; this fact was obvious, thanks to myriad signs for cheese. We couldn't stop wondering: Do people in Wisconsin always drive around looking for the proper cheese? Were these signs meant to attract tourists for cheese buying? Do people actually sit around craving curds? Can you say the word "curd" without grossing yourself out? Growing up in California, we had both become tools of the California Cheese advertising campaigns. We knew that happy cows came from California and that all the cows in Wisconsin were sick to death of the cold weather. California cows enjoyed warmth and earthquakes and liked nothing better than donating milk for the mild and pleasant cheeses that you buy in California.

It had never occurred to us that the entire California Cheese ad campaign was just compensating for how dominate Wisconsin really was. We just logically assumed that California had become the dominate cheese state. But I didn't know a single person in all of my childhood that ever said, "Yeah, I really love curds. I'd drive all over just looking for the best curds." The win goes to Wisconsin on this one. They may not have an ocean, or Disneyland, or the Sierras, but goddamn it, they have curds at every roadside stand. This is good enough for me.

We finally could stay awake no longer. It was clearly too late to camp, so we looked for the cheapest hotel that we could find. Across the street from the three millionth "Cheese House" that we had seen since entering the state was a Super 8 motel. We pulled in and I headed to the counter to bargain for a room.

Bargaining had been our way for quite some time. Why pay full price when you can whine your way to saving a couple dollars? You'd be shocked how many motels will grant you a discount if you say, "We're on our honeymoon." Especially if it's after midnight. But all the bargaining in the world couldn't make them have a room left that was nonsmoking.

"Well," the lady behind the counter said, "we do have one nonsmoking room. But I doubt you'll want it."

"Why? Is it the conference room? I totally play that game."

"Conference room?"

"Forget it."

"It's above the nightclub. Does that bother you?"

"Should it bother me?"

She shrugged her shoulders. Then she named a price that I could live with.

When Charlie and I got to our room, we realized why being above the nightclub might bother us. I reasoned that it couldn't possibly bother anyone because no one would ever go to a Super 8 nightclub. But, evidently, this was the only location in the entire Midwest that anyone would want to visit on this particular night. Music, laughter, noise, and shouting from below kept us awake until at least three in the morning. At three, the party just moved into the parking lot. Looking back now, I can hardly imagine why we didn't just go and join the goddamn gala.

If you spend much time with Charlie, she's bound to mention what to her is the worst habit that I have: I start important conversations right after she starts to drift off to sleep. To me, it just seems like a good time to talk. It's quiet, it's dark, and the words just kind of hang out in space for us to ponder together. To her, it's annoying as fuck.

"Hey," I said.

"What is it?" She's always a bit alarmed once this starts, as if there's an urgent matter concerning burglars or spiders.

"I forgot to tell you back where the floor waxing was going on. I got an email. There's a job offer in Texas."

"There is? Full time?"

"No, part time."

"Will, you could probably get a part time job anywhere," Charlie said.

"Maybe. Maybe not. I'm not exactly overflowing with experience. The part time gigs can lead to full time."

"Do we have to talk about this right now?"

"No. We're not. I was just telling you."

"It's just that...what the hell are we doing?"

"Sleeping."

"No. Not that. What the hell are we doing out here? We're above some dirty nightclub on the ass-end of Wisconsin doing what? We're rushing along, not doing a lot of anything, and I thought we'd be talking to people. Exploring towns. Looking at cities. Building a life."

For a few moments, there was only darkness. The party in the parking lot was beginning to dissipate. Quiet was the overwhelming noise.

"Aren't we?" I said, breaking the silence.

"Aren't we what?"

"Doing that. I mean, I know that in the beginning, when there was money and time we did a lot more of that. We found out what the cities were all about, what jobs there were, what kind of culture there was. But now."

"Now," Charlie said. "We're just headed back to our parent's houses in California, right?"

"You know, we need to regroup. Get our presents back from your folks. See what furniture we can get from them."

"I just don't even know if we should go back," she said. "Listen to me. This isn't how it's supposed to go. We are rushing and not staying in places that I've always wanted to see, and it's like we're going to sleepwalk through our lives together this way, Sol!"

"What did you call me?"

"I'm trying to get your attention, Sol. Your name is Sol. Mine is Randi. Randi Sue. We are married in real life and you're writing a story about it that is mostly true and helping you to ignore the direction that we have taken in our lives."

There was that name again. The same name the guy used at that conference room hotel. That lousy little deskman. The same name that is on the front of this very book. For a moment, I was awake again. My wife—my actual wife, Randi Sue Smith—was sitting next to me while I type these very words. The dark room faded and I see a mandala that my wife is concentrating on. It's 11 years later. And while we haven't sleepwalked through our lives, we have wandered. And gotten lost. And missed the directions and ended up just about everywhere and never felt like we were in control of it.

I'm dizzy. The room fades and the words fail me because they are only words and words aren't real and everything in our lives is real and slowly the mandala fades and the computer keyboard fades and I'm back in the dark of the room 11 years ago, back in the Midwest, back in the fabric of the cheap hotel bed.

"We're like 2,000 miles away, Charlie. There's still a lot of time left."

"Why are we rushing?"

"Have you seen our bank account lately? We're going to have to break into the credit cards soon."

Charlie sat up straight. "You brought the credit cards? I thought we agreed not to use them."

"We did. But I brought them in case."

"Hmm. I don't know if I should be pissed or relieved."

We had racked up a lot of credit card debt living on the California coast. But we still had a lot of credit card space on a couple of the high interest cards that we kept around to not use. These were seen as last resorts and we really, really didn't want to mortgage our future while trying to discover it.

"I wish we stayed in Chicago," she said, lying back down.

"I'm sorry."

"No. It's okay. Will?"

"Yeah?"

"Can you do me a favor?"

"Sure."

"Can you wait until the morning to talk about this? I'm really fucking tired."

The next morning came and when we opened the curtains, we saw a huge grey mouse holding a piece of Swiss cheese sitting atop the building across the parking lot. How the hell did we miss that the night before? The mouse was funny, silly even. Something about just how silly that mouse was stopped the conversation from the night before. Things were easy, they were silly, there were mouses eating cheeses on the tops of buildings in Wisconsin and this made things better.

Honest to God, when I'm stressed out about a project, or a meeting, or our terrible, terrible debt, I think about that mouse. It's a Godly thing, that mouse. Full of hope and forgiveness.

America, in a Mall

When I was 12, I saw a show on a cable network about the Mall of America. It was in far off and exotic Minnesota. This mall was huge. It had all the stores you could find in any mall, and it had stores that no other mall had. It even had a theme park in the middle of it. It was the shit, and I just knew that I would never go there. It just seemed so damned exciting, but not so amazing as to make a trip just to see it. I would have to be in the middle of a business trip, I reasoned, or be visiting someone who lived in Minneapolis in order to see this amazing work of shopping artistry. That's why when initial planning started for our honeymoon, I was quick to suggest—insist—on visiting the Mall of America.

Do you realize that in the winter, the mall is not heated? It uses the heat of the people inside the mall and circulates it around. As a matter of fact, it often gets too warm in the mall and they have to siphon air from the cold winter outdoors and bring it in to keep people from baking. This is somewhat revolting a notion, that the bodies of a bunch of mall-goers is keeping you warm. It's sort of like being in a huge hot tub full of people with no chlorine.

We pulled in to the mall while it was still early. Parking in the huge parking structure was plentiful and the line for the rollercoaster inside was short. There were over four million square feet of mall just waiting for our participation.

But we didn't get around much.

Charlie was sick. A headache, sinus pain, and a worn out disposition. There wasn't much walking in her and she was afraid that she was going to ruin my time. We spent a good deal of the time sitting and looking at maps. If we could only see a few corners of the mall, which ones did we want them to be? We looked at the General Mills Cereal Land, or whatever it was called, because Charlie had a thing for Lucky Charms, and they had a huge Lucky Charms Leprechaun standing triumphantly outside the area. There was a cereal bar there, where you could buy Lucky Charms, marshmallows only.

When lunch came around, we skipped the fancy restaurants and the huge Hooters in favor of cheap food court fare. When we felt like we had been there long enough, we left.

It was a lame time, but honestly, what did I expect? Even if Charlie had felt like a million bucks, what would we do? We didn't have a lot of money to spend, we didn't have all day to walk the halls of such a place, and there was nothing in particular that we were looking for. It was a monument to consumerism that people come from all over the world to visit. You can buy stuff anywhere, you can buy stuff online, you don't need to roll out to one big location to buy stuff. Shopping as entertainment, shopping as therapy, shopping as meaning for life; that's what Mall of

America is selling. The ritual of buying, the religion of money.

People didn't always get their self-worth through their ability to spend. Really. I recently saw an old Donald Duck cartoon that was made during WWII that pushes people to save their money and be thrifty. These days, people on TV—from our news commentators to our president—are telling us that we're bad people if we're not out spending. Spending is patriotic. Spending will save your fellow man. Spending will show your worth. And this consumer driven society takes a lot of you as a person. Just read *Fight Club*. Or talk to your grandma. Or start your own fight club with your grandma.

I have always taken some sort of comfort in malls. I enjoy watching people, especially during holiday shopping season. But there was just something so flat about being in a place that had built consumerism up to the logical and morbid conclusion. My wife was worried that her illness would ruin my time, but it probably saved my soul.

Robots, Pornography, and Prostitution[33]

It was time for some new reading material. We had been listening to audio books that we picked up at Cracker Barrels. There you could buy an audio book and then turn it in at the next Cracker Barrel minus a three dollar a week fee. This was an immense discovery. But it had been a while since we had stopped in at a Barrel and we were all out of tabloids to read while driving. Somewhere in western Minnesota, we stopped at a gas station and picked up a *Penthouse Letters*.

Back in the days of the Great Depression, movies were still a new and rare experience. A movie house would play one movie at a time, and with money scarce, in order to get people to come out to the movie, it had to appeal to everyone. A movie had to be a comedy, a drama, a love story, a musical, and, occasionally, a tragedy all in one. This led to some amazing Marx Brothers and Buster Keaton pictures that are really hard to challenge as far as entertainment value is concerned. On that summer afternoon, I stumbled on an amazing modern equivalent.

Charlie read the entirety of the *Penthouse* to me, from cover to cover, during the course of the drive that day. We discovered a few things about the universe that

---

[33] Best chapter title ever.

we had never known before that may still come in handy some day. 1) Everyone has a more exciting sex life than we do; 2) The average number of sexual partners is 3.2 every night; and 3) Most people have a penis measuring nine to twelve inches; girls like this.

For those have never experienced it, there is little more pleasant than listening to your wife laugh her way through hard-core pornography. It's a strong two-pronged sort of entertainment, a slight turn on mixed with large doses of humor. Under those conditions, one could drive for hours without ever feeling the faintest hints of boredom. Whoever started installing TVs into cars has it all wrong, they ought to instead get a bunch of mainstream women to read *Penthouse Letters*, letting them laugh as much as they need to, put it on CD, and make a million dollars a second.

Our goal that night was to make it to Sioux Falls. We knew we'd stay in a hotel, as there didn't seem to be anywhere close by to do any kind of satisfying camping. But we were sick to death of the prices. You see a sign along the freeway advertising a hotel up the road—a Super 8 or a Motel 6 or a Microtel—and they announce a price that sounds perfectly reasonable. $39, or $35, or $55, or something. But when you walk in to claim your room, the price is almost always double that. Why? Because there are two people. It doesn't matter to them that the two of you sleep in the same bed, use the same shower, and occupy the same space. They want you to pay for two, anyway.

It would make sense to me to pay for two if you were getting, say, two of something. If you and your wife are going to travel by air across country, you have to buy two seats. That's fine. I get it. If you and your wife want to eat at a buffet, even though you are all sharing the same trough, you will clearly eat twice as much; so that's fine, pay twice. But in a hotel? Are they afraid that we'll use so much water or breathe so much air that we really need to pay for two? We were sick of it. We'd do it no longer. We had decided that we would, from then on, sneak Charlie into the room and just pay for one.

This was tried out at the Cloud Nine Hotel in Sioux Falls. I parked a short distance from the front office and told Charlie to act like she's not there. I walked in, rang the bell, and waited a few minutes before an older lady named Madge whose nametag labeled her the owner/manager of the Cloud Nine.

"I'd like a room."

"How many?"

"Just the one."

"How many *people*, I mean."

"Just me."

"Oh, okay," she said.

Oh, this was easy. No problem. She asked for my driver's license and I handed it over.

"California?"

"Yeah."

She looked at me suspiciously. She compared my face to the picture, so I tried to adopt the stupid smile my ID has me sporting. "What are you doing here?"

"Pardon?"

"In Sioux Falls?"

"Just passing through."

"Long way from home."

"I don't have much of a home right now. Except the room tonight."

"Huh." She looked away and kept dealing with the paperwork. "All by yourself?"

"Yeah. Driving through. Headed west."

"Look, sonny," she put down her pen and looked at me. "There will be no partying here, do you understand?"

"Partying?"

"You know what I mean, young man. No women of the night allowed in my hotel. You got me?"

I was flabbergasted. She thought I was making a country-wide prostitute tour?

"I don't party that way, ma'am."

"I'll find out."

"Don't worry. None of that."

I paid my price for a single room and was delighted to save the money. But I decided it was better for us to find somewhere to eat before we went into the room, as she would no doubt be watching me.

We drove around the little town of Sioux Falls, somewhat amazed at how big the letters were on the map compared to how large the city is. The town was dead, no one was out and there didn't seem to be a lot of places open. Then, we saw it.

A sign hung in the air with a picture of some kind of little raccoon/rabbit guy sticking out his tongue and riding a tricycle. Gigglebees, was the name of the restaurant. Gigglebees. And the sign promised three things, in this order:

1. Robots
2. Pizza
3. Games

I don't know if you know exactly what this sign is saying. This sign is telling you that this establishment has—first and foremost—robots inside of it. In addition to having robots, they will serve you pizza. And, once you are through with pizza, or, perhaps, while you are still indulging, you can play games. I don't know about y'all, but any one of these three things would have me coming by itself. And here it was, a Mecca of triple proportions. If they had mainstream wives reading erotica, it would be the center of the entertainment universe.

And what is with the raccoon/bunny riding the trike? What, exactly, does this piece of visual rhetoric have to say? Does this creature enjoy this establishment? Do you, perhaps, feel much like this guy does when you're there? Or, is this an actual robot? Playing a game? Digesting pizza? Was this the elusive and mythical Gigglebee himself?

We did not take a picture of this; we were too stunned.

We hopped out of the car and *ran* to the door.

It was closed.

Forever closed.

There is currently a Facebook page called "We Miss Gigglebees." I suggest that you "like" it. We can connect this way. Through connection, we may find strength.

The next morning, I packed the car and checked out of the hotel room. I was sitting in the car, engine running, when Charlie ran out of the room and hopped into the passenger seat. At that very instant, Madge came around the corner, watched my frolicking wife, and then made eye contact with me. Her disapproving glare was something that I will never forget.

"Charlie," I said, "Blow this woman a kiss."

She did, seductively.

I read the woman's lips as we pulled out of the parking space. You're going to Hell, is what she was saying to us. Yes, she thought my wife was, literally, a whore.

Where the Heck Are We?

South Dakota is a strange place by any measure. I can't tell you that there isn't a certain charm, because there is, but that charm only lasts for about fifteen minutes and the state lasts for days. Grass, grass, grass: that's what you see. It's hard to imagine the settlers coming through there and being anything but surprised. In a time when one could walk from the Atlantic Ocean to the Mississippi River on the tops of trees—if one were an elf—just imagine the shock at seeing so many miles of grass, lying flat like a blanket over the scorched Earth. You would have to wonder where all the trees went.

I think the whole of South Dakota would look better with a sprinkling of wigwams and an ocean of American Bison roaming everywhere. But, for whatever historical reason, that is just not the case.

The empty view is rarely broken up with very much. The occasional bunny-shaped cloud is like a splash of shape and imagination when you can catch it. There was a period of a solid two hours where I hoped for nuclear war just so that I could see the Minutemen missiles launching in distant North Dakota; the trail of smoke and the thought of total destruction would comfort the weary eyes and even more weary mind. Damn *Glastnost* and *perestroika* for boring me so.

Luckily, there was one other distraction: a single, solitary billboard. It said, "Where The Heck is Wall

Drug?" I had no idea what it was referring to, but with the exceedingly stimulating billboard against the extensively empty scenery, I was sold.

A similar thing had happened to me before. When I was younger, and then again for every few years up until now, I have been suckered into paying a dollar or two to see "The Thing" in southern New Mexico. Driving through west Texas is a trying experience. When you're traveling back east, the next major town or city is usually an hour away, at most. In California, it seems like wherever you're going is 90 miles away. But in west Texas, the standard unit of measurement for time in a car is six hours. No joke. If you've driven extensively in west Texas, you know exactly what I'm talking about. The minute that something is three hours away, you're practically there.

You cross this grand amount of space with little sense of accomplishment because you eventually resolve to just let everything slide; you're never going to get there and you know it. In fact, a logical argument could be made that you never do get to where you're going because you've changed into an entirely different person en route. Somewhere along the way, you are actually standing in El Paso or Pecos or Odessa, or wherever you were headed and the overwhelming sense is that you've always been there; you don't even remember who that person was in the car, they have little to do with you. That's how dormant your mind goes when traversing distances such as these.

A few hundred miles before getting out of Texas, you see a sign that reads, simply, "The Thing! What is it?" You see the splash of yellow and the gross-out font that "Thing!" is written in, and you can't help but think, "Why, that's the greatest question ever posed!"

There's just miles and miles of build up. Each sign tells you a little more about where The Thing! is housed, but nothing more about what it is. There's burgers, there's moccasins, there's saddle blankets, curios, petrified wood, knives, and an antique gallery. Each of these would totally fail to elicit your attention without the headlining act of this wonderful, wonderful place.

Finally, you're there. You can't believe your luck. You park your car next to the corrugated metal façade on the side of the building, rainbow striped with large letters spelling "T-H-I-N-G-!" and you know that for the next hour or so, you're home. You walk in and, at first glance, you're in every other little gift shop in the state of New Mexico. You browse the topaz, you check out the Indian dolls, you consider three-wolf-moon paintings, and you keep an eye on the back door that leads to The Thing! Eventually, you ask for tickets for you and your family. Two dollars apiece. And you walk back.

You follow large painted monster footprints on the ground, as you go through building after building of antiques. There's quite a collection of cars, uniforms, old guns, and much more, each with a hand painted sign telling you how awesome an artifact you are looking at. One car is supposed to be Hitler's car, and for a brief moment, you're frightened that this is The Thing! you've been waiting for. You press on, walking along the sidewalk in the desert air in between the huddled metal structures. And at last, you're there.

A sign above a long box points down saying "Here it is! The Thing!" You walk forward slowly and peek in to the glass top of the six and a half foot long box.

The first people I ever knew who had seen The Thing! were my father and brother. They went through together one afternoon during a trip while I was sick with a stomach bug and didn't want to walk around. When they came back, I grilled them. What was it? Was it awesome? Was it cool?

They both kind of shrugged, but not in a disinterested way. I could tell that their hesitation to talk up the experience was based solely on their expectations of the other's evaluation. Was it cool? They looked at each other.

"It was interesting."

"Yeah, interesting. It was interesting."

"I mean, pretty cool."

A pause.

"Probably a fake."

"Yeah probably. But if it's not, kind of creepy."

"Really creepy, even if it was, really."

"Yeah, but part of it was fake. I mean, part of Lenin is fake, right?"

"Well, sure. Part fake, that's for sure. But maybe all."

Honest to God, they did not answer my question. They did not tell me what The Thing! was and I had to wait *years* before we traveled along I-10 again to see it for myself.

You peek in and see what appears to be a mummy. Not just a wrapped up nice and tidy mummy, but an actual decomposing face, partially covered in rags. You can see the occasional spot of dried flesh and the occasional rib bone sticking out of it. In its arms is either a baby mummy or a doll of some sort. In either case, it's this baby mummy or baby mummy doll that really stays with you when you're trying to sleep that night.

Is it real? It may as well be. The story is that years and years ago, a woman ran a little gift shop in the Mojave Desert half way between LA and Las Vegas. She was approached one day by a man who was selling three objects. When she was taken to his refrigerated car, she was shown three separate mummies. He had a price for all three of them, and she wouldn't meet the offer. Eventually, he took what she was willing to pay and gave her just one of the mummies. Then the man left and neither he nor the mummies were seen again.

The Thing! however, was put on display and was quite a hit. They later relocated to the deep southwest and started advertising for hundreds of miles in either direction. The only show in town.

Wall Drug was not The Thing!, but their advertising campaign is quite similar. There are vague hints of the coolness you will find in this roadside attraction, but nothing explicit. Nothing except the promise of "Free Ice Water." And this allure, this free ice water, and these signs reaching all over the plains make you think that nothing could be quite so joyous as stopping in at Wall Drug.

Their signs go on forever, actually. People set up signs in their yard saying "Where the Heck Is Wall Drug?" They give you free bumper stickers with the phrase. I've even heard of a billboard in Denmark and a sign on the very South Pole itself. This is an ambitious campaign for such an isolated destination. We couldn't resist, so we stopped in Wall, South Dakota to see what all the hubbub was about.

Wall Drug is a pretty awesome place. It's especially perfect if you want to buy something like a little tornado in a jar, a paperweight with a piece of dung in it labeled "South Dakota Bullshit," or a whoopee cushion. There's more to it than that, but those are what you'll spend most of your time looking at.

It's a sprawling bunch of rooms, all maze like, and each room specializing in a different kind of tacky gift shop ambiance. In one room, you'll find slews of bumper stickers and postcards, in another, stuffed animals and toys, and so on. In a couple of locations within the main gift shop, you'll find animatronic cowboys that will sing songs on occasion. They're kind of creepy, though, predating Disneyland and not refurbished nearly as often as the Pirates of the Caribbean.

Your fun doesn't have to end inside, though. There's a courtyard behind the main building and if you follow the path, you'll find a series of little rooms, each with a coin operated display of one kind or another. We had one quarter between us, so Charlie and I opted, at last, to put it into a machine that allowed us to watch a mechanical gorilla play the piano and sing. I can honestly say that as much as I've sat around thinking about gorillas in my life, I have never envisioned such a dapperly dressed anthropomorphized ape playing quite so zippy a ragtime song. It was well worth our quarter and I would say that I spent a little too long searching the grounds for lost quarter seeking a good home once it was over.

A room on the far end of the courtyard, near the bathrooms, housed what must be Wall Drug's newest robot, the T-Rex. It was clearly built during the *Jurassic Park* hype of the early '90s, as the dinosaur would reach his head over a steel wall covered in barbed wire and red sirens would go off as it roared. This robot was not coin operated but seemed to go off by itself every few minutes, first growling from behind the wall, then reaching up and giving it everything it had. It was impressively loud and I saw more than my fair share of screaming toddlers around it that afternoon.

While getting our free water—served in little yellow cups that say "Free Water" on them—Charlie and I had a bit of a fight. I wanted to eat. Not really because I was hungry, but because eating had once again become a hobby of mine during our travels. She, however, insisted that the food in the restaurant looked nasty and cost way too much. We should just find a grocery store, she said, and buy some bagels or something. She was right and more because she was right than because I thought I was, I started pouting. When would we be back here, I reasoned, and who doesn't want to try the cuisine at a place like this?

Charlie pulled the money card, "We didn't stay in Chicago because money was tight. I don't see any reason we should go wasting it now when this water is perfectly free."

I kicked imaginary cans on the floor. I didn't want to argue about it, but I had become addicted to eating at new places and didn't want to let the opportunity pass for a bunch of Lender's.

We walked out, thirst quenched, and nothing more. What I have learned since then has been pretty hard to take: My wife and I could have settled our dispute for free. Had we but known—had the ads let us know—we would have taken full advantage of the generosity of Wall Drug. You see, Wall Drug, I have come to learn, will give honeymooners free coffee and doughnuts. Free. It was another opportunity missed for lack of advertising.

Statues in the Mountains

Driving up to Mt. Rushmore is not unlike if you were to meet Bugs Bunny in real life. It is such a familiar sight but of something that your brain won't let you fully believe can exist. The four presidents carved high on the mountain is so perfectly seeable, that your jaw drops in full realization of where you are.

The Black Hills are a mystical place. The Native Americans thought them holy, and it is easy to see why. The hills jut up in tremendous bursts, refusing to ease their summits to the air, they form pyramids of rock and trees that surround you while you drive through the passes. Each one of these hills could have housed the presidents; they are all so dramatic and decorative.

It's free to see Mt. Rushmore, but you do have to pay for parking. You're already in full view of the celebrity before you lock your doors, but you walk on, seeking a closer look. Above you are the flags of the fifty states and then the flags of those other strange American places that are not states. All the while, you just can't take your gaze away from that amazing piece of construction, that magnificent example of hubris, that thrilling monument of human sculpture.

There's a lot of controversy surrounding the mountain. It is well worth looking into the reasons to protest such a landmark. But while we were there, I was too in awe of it. It is an image that had been etched in my mind since I can remember, and coming face to face with it was provoking. We stood and looked and took pictures. We read about its construction. We lamented that it was finished while half completed—it was originally intended to be a sculpture of the four presidents from their heads to their belts. It is an accomplishment that is hard to imagine, carving a sculpture out of a mountain. It seems very much like something out of your imagination that has just escaped into the real world and attracted a bunch of tourists.

We left the monument and sought a place to stay for the night. Our KOA directory pointed us towards the Mt. Rushmore KOA and we visited it. It was a crowded theme park of a campground. It was hysteric with activity. RVs were parked everywhere, and there were lines reaching out from the restrooms. Yuck. That was what we felt there, yuck.

We drove back towards the town when we came across the Black Forest State Park. We drove in and found the 10 camp sites absolutely unoccupied. The place was a miracle of trees and solitude compared to the KOA campground. The sun was quickly descending and we had just a little time to pitch our tent and get a fire going to make supper in the twilight. The night was warm, compared to many nights we had spent camping, so we took the rain fly off so that we could see the carpet of stars framed by tree tops through our mesh roof. The sounds that filled the night were of animals; coyotes howling in the distance, raccoons searching our site, mountain goats bleating on the hillsides.

We held each other through the night and soaked it all in. As the fire outside died down, the stars grew brighter and a thick strip of the Milky Way glowed behind everything. I felt infinitesimally small and wondered why the immense universe could afford happiness to one so insignificant. Before falling asleep, with my wife drifting off next to me, I saw four shooting stars and made the same wish each time.

Striking camp is only doable after you've had a mountain breakfast and coffee cooked out of doors. Without those luxuries, I would never be able to bring myself to wrap up the mess I make and suffer through endless efforts of getting a tent back in its original bag. These things would be impossible if not balanced out with the kind of gratitude one feels for such a simple breakfast made so utterly tolerable through circumstance.

We drove for about 20 miles to what will, for a very long time, be known as the other mountain sculpture. That is, until it is much nearer completion, it will always be the second place that people visit in the Black Hills. Someday, when it is finished, it will eclipse Mt. Rushmore in almost every way.

The Crazy Horse Monument, quite simply, will one day be among the greatest creations of mankind. Not from an ecological standpoint, I'm sure, but in the sense of creation and accomplishment it will stand among walking on the moon, sailing across the oceans, erecting pyramids, and anything else that man has ever dreamt into reality. It will be the largest and grandest sculpture ever made and the most impressive sight one can take in, save Grand Canyon itself. Of this, I am quite sure.

Since the inception of Mt. Rushmore, there has been considerable controversy. The mountain was a holy place to the Sioux and Lakota nations. The great writer and medicine man John Fire Lame Deer took great exception to the creation of Mt. Rushmore and led several protests against it. The name that the Native Americans gave for Mt. Rushmore was Mt. Crazy Horse.

Chief Standing Bear approached Korczak Ziolkowski, one of the Rushmore sculptors, with the idea of creating a monument to the great warrior Crazy Horse and the project was started in 1948, three years before the end of the Rushmore project. The sculpture of Crazy Horse is at least 900 times as ambitious as Rushmore; the plan is to have a sculpture in the round— that is an entire mountain turned into one great statue. The faces of all four presidents on Rushmore could fit into the face of Crazy Horse, with room to spare. Crazy Horse is depicted riding atop a stallion and pointing his outreached arm forward as the horse rears up. My god, it will be something amazing.

While Charlie and I were there, the face was completed and there was a hole going through the rock that will eventually be the space between the warrior's arm and his horse's main. The scale is enormous. All over the visitor's center there are reproductions of the statue and histories written out. Crazy Horse never allowed a picture to be taken of him, so the sculpture itself is an artistic representation of a man who lives as much in legend as he does in history.

The entire project is being done without the support of the taxpayer. At some point, the federal government offered to step in and complete the project, but the offer was rejected; it was to be an accomplishment of the people who support the project. It was the vision of the founders that it would be completed by the generous offerings of those who believed in it only. And man, did Ziolkowski ever believe in this project. On that first day of sculpting, he walked up the hill, a solitary artist, dug a few feet down and planted a stick of dynamite. He started this project as one man, transforming a mountain of Nature's creation into a vision of artistry, courage, and honor. It's hard not to be very, very impressed with that kind of dedication.

Ziolkowski died in 1982, but encouraged others to take on the project. He had a slew of children, seven of whom are still working on the project today. He didn't mind the slow pace of work, advising others to let it take as long as it must, just so that the work is done right.

The ambition just doesn't stop with the project. Eventually, a college will grow up around the base of the mountain, focusing on Native American studies and will serve to help in the education of Native American citizens.

It's expensive to visit the Crazy Horse Memorial right now. Much more so than seeing Rushmore. But it's worth it because you know that you are seeing something that will only happen once in the whole world. And you know that your money is going to help complete the project. There are other ways to give, and if you donate enough, you can go home with a small replica of the sculpture. We gave a few dollars for the privilege of taking home some of the rock that was blown off of the mountain in the sculpting. Surely there's enough of it to go around, but of everything we brought away from that trip, nothing is more valuable than a piece of the Black Hills.

Atonement

We ran out of food to cook on the last night camping in the Black Hills. The issue was easily solved by just heading out to eat; something we were absolutely sick of doing. One reason that we were so sick of eating out was because of the terrible, terrible service that had become so common to us. It wasn't just the trip, actually, but Charlie had been somewhat of a living legend in her family for eliciting bad customer service for some years by then. The prevailing theory was that since, as a customer service worker, she was quite rabid about giving friendly and helpful service. Her efforts didn't always go appreciated, though.

Charlotte worked at a Starbucks in downtown Fresno that she just loved. Her customers were regulars; business men and women who enjoyed their coffee at regular, predictable times. They were friendly and courteous—these are the traits of successful business people, they are people persons. It was easy giving good customer service to her customers downtown; they welcomed good service and were outwardly appreciative of it. All was well until she transferred.

Charlie moved to a Starbucks in a rich area of town in the position of assistant manager. At this new store most customers were rich kids, douche bag lawyers, and kept women. Life at this coffee shop was a living hell, a good deal of the time. Business was almost always booming and booming with total and complete dickheads who couldn't be less self-aware if they were rocks. On one absolutely typical day, there was a line going out the door and it was a line of impatient snobs, ordering with their mouths and using their ears to listen to their cell phones. Activity behind the bar was bustling; Charlie was training two new hires and filling in for a girl who called in sick and the orders kept pouring in. In the middle of this activity, a woman dressed to the nines while out shopping for the day, walked up to my wife and spoke up over the noise of steaming milk and Frappuccino blenders.

"Excuse me," the woman called out.

Charlie recognized the woman as a daily customer who often brought her drinks back to be remade. She would usually try and avoid actually getting her drink made by telling them how, despite how disappointed she is in her drink, she doesn't have time to wait for another one to be made. This was a familiar play that rich customers pull at Starbucks—it's a play to get a free drink coupon. Charlie saw that the woman had her drink in her hand and was sure that was the angle she was playing.

"Can I help you?" my wife called out.

"Yes. I dropped my gum over by the door. I thought I should tell you so that someone can pick it up before it gets stepped on."

Charlie's face registered disbelief and her mouth dropped open; no sounds would come out.

"Don't worry," the woman said, maybe noticing there was concern. "I'll put a napkin over it so that it won't get on anyone's shoe before you can come and clean it."

It was a daily struggle for Charlie to keep her cool with such customers, but she did everything she could to uphold her employer's ideas for customer service. It seemed like if Charlie could find it in her heart to be nice to these terrible scourges of mankind, that she might be able to get good service herself, being a nice and kindly customer. Alas, this was the opposite of true.

We decided to eat at a Chili's in Rapid City. It took over half an hour for the waiter to pay any attention to us. Then we ordered our drinks and waited another solid fifteen minutes to get the drinks. Finally, right as we had decided to leave, the waiter came back to get our order. Charlie was hoping to get soup and salad for a light dinner while I was, most likely, ordering the chicken fried steak.

"We're out of the chicken enchilada soup," the waiter said when she finished ordering.

"Oh, darn. What other soup do you have?"

"The green chili soup is pretty good. Most people like it better than the chicken enchilada. I think it's better."

"Okay, I'll give that a shot," Charlie said.

The waiter walked away without making eye contact once. He was a young guy, early 20s, with a totally hip white-guy afro. He seemed like he'd be pretty cool, but he just didn't want to be there.

The food finally came. Charlie's soup was bad. She hated it.

"I'm sorry," she said to the waiter, "I really don't like this soup."

"Is it cold?" the waiter asked.

"As a matter of fact, it is cold."

"Yeah, that stuff is pretty bad when it's cold. Actually, it's not my favorite soup. Funny, they made up more of the chicken enchilada after you ordered."

"Can I switch to that?"

"Sorry, I already typed your order into the system."

The waiter must not have had any idea why I was laughing as he walked away. Charlie was perturbed, but I shared my meal with her.

"That soup better not be on the bill," she said.

But of course, when the bill came, the soup was on it. It sat untouched in her bowl—a soup that she had ordered on his recommendation, that she complained about, and that the waiter admitted was bad, especially when cold, despite his previous endorsement. It was really outrageous.

Money had been tight for a long time. It wasn't getting any better any time soon. We reviewed in our minds all the bad service we had received all over the country, all the times we had considered not leaving a tip.

"This time, we're doing it," Charlie said.

It's the cardinal sin of someone who has worked in the service industry. Those who have had such a job know the pressures and troubles of waiting tables and they know that anyone can be over worked, any establishment can be understaffed, and any waiter can have a bad day. They depend on that tip money, not as extra walking around money, but as part of their income. In many places, waiters make salaries of under three dollars an hour from the restaurant. You just don't walk out of a place without leaving a tip if you have any compassion.

But we did it.

We put all courtesy and reason behind us. We paid our bill, because we didn't want to break any laws, but we drew a little line in the place where you write your tip. A little black line signifying our discontent and disrespect for the lad who had served us.

Even though we felt perfectly justified in not tipping, we skedaddled. We got the hell out of there the instant after signing the receipt. We prayed the guy hadn't written down our debit card number.

Marching to the End

"You were always so melancholy about the trip," Charlie says, looking at the title to this chapter. "I was always so excited. Everything was so new and thrilling and open and we were there together. That's how I felt and how I feel now a lot of our days together. But there was something in you that was actually in a rush to finish things."

"It was the money, more than anything," I say.

"No," she says. "It was being uprooted. That was new for you, somehow, even though you had lived in so many different places. Me, I never had my roots in. I didn't wander like you, but my roots never took hold. You were on edge."

"I'm telling you, it was the money."

"It was the future. Heck, it was the present."

I think about this. "It was so new. It was exciting, but it was new. Maybe I was scared, not of the trip, like the actual driving, but of...I don't know."

"Of our lives? Of what our lives were going to be now? Was that it?"

"Maybe. It's not that I didn't want it. It's just...for the first time, I felt like it was on me. Like I had to grow up. And it was there in the Black Hills when that really became obvious. That's what this chapter is about."

"Suddenly, it was like Sunday afternoon," she says. "The weekend had passed and you knew something else was coming up."

As we left South Dakota, our trip ended. We had a long way to go to get back to what possessions we had left, to load up, to drive again, find a house, start a job, form a life. But through myriad late night discussions, we decided to accept the first job offer I got and, for the moment, try and forget everything else we had seen. It wasn't an easy decision, especially for two adults who have a really hard time seeing themselves as adults.

I used to think, when I was a kid, that adults just had their shit together. They knew what they were doing. They were grownups, that great and powerful brand of being, brandishing adulthood at every child in the world, showing them what wonders and pleasures await the well-balanced person. Every kid wanted to be a grownup. I was constantly asked what I was going to be when I grew up, because that's where all the action was. That's what childhood was for, learning to be a thoughtful and efficient grownup. I thought they just knew things, that they were guided by their knowledge. I used to think that world peace wasn't a pipe dream, so long as there were enough grownups to decide to accomplish it. There were all these little things that you wanted to do and you were always told, "Wait until you grow up."

It's a sham. Grownups don't have their shit together any more than a four year-old does. They save these great and wonderful things for adulthood, but as it turns out, they are mostly childish, petty things. Dating, smoking, porn, drunkenness—these are not the marks of what I used to think of as an adult. They are children run wild. Grownups are children whose parents left for the day. Grownups are children who are no longer afraid of spankings or consequences. Grownups are spoiled brats who can't keep their hands to themselves. Every kid who ever caused trouble in your class, every kid who always had to sit in the corner because he was disturbing everyone else, every one of those kids grew up and learned nothing. They run everything. They dominate your life with their bullying and peer pressure and absolute horseshit.

It's the great deception. You work and work and hope and dream because you are told about the lofty position you must attain if you are to grow up properly, and it's just not there. Meanwhile, you missed everything about being a kid. So you act like one. Forever.

Charlie and I weren't grownups, but we weren't really kids either. We were somewhere in between, and I think that's how so much of our generation is: locked in arrested development, treading water and waiting for something to come along and save them. What else was our little foray into the world but an instance of treading water? Why else would it have been so painful to actually make a decision and live somewhere, work some job, be responsible? For the years that we had known each other, we had never actually given any serious thought to that moment. We had never seen anything beyond this trip. It was the goal. It was the destination. It was our future.

Only it was ending right there before our eyes. We had miles of nothing to see for a few days, and then we'd have to move on. It was unbearable. Driving, stopping, driving, stopping, all the while knowing that what we were driving towards was the end of everything we had ever planned for ourselves.

In Billings, Montana, we made love six times in a KOA Kabin. It would be our celebration for the end of it all. It was our goodbye to everything. It was the last instance of vacation that we really felt.

In just a couple days, we covered more terrain and more miles than we had in the previous week. We burned the road behind us. We drove late into the nights. We listened to only one, short audio book by Steve Martin. We turned it in at the last Cracker Barrel on our route. It was like a burial.

Late at night in northern Oregon, the tire finally gave way. I had been watching it intently since Arizona, hoping that it would last the whole trip. But it was past midnight and we were stuck on the side of the road, sitting by our car with a blow out and a broken tire iron. I don't know how it broke, but it did. Right then and there. Snapped in two.

The stars spread out above us and our cell phone showed no reception. It was my fault that we got into this mess. My fault we didn't stop and fix the tires ages ago. I just thought that maybe if we could make it back to our folks' houses, we'd be fine. We'd cross that finish line and we'd be fine. Another example of how we gave no thought whatsoever to whatever it was waiting for us after the trip.

A tow truck spotted us and helped us get back on the road. We checked into the dirtiest hotel of our trip and slept above the blankets. The next day we spent in a Wal-Mart, waiting for the new tires to be put on. We paid with a credit card that we swore we'd never touch. And with that simple movement, it felt like our whole future had just been mortgaged.

Even now, years later, those tires have not been paid for. Not by us, at any rate. And the feeling of disapproval is palpable. Another little sign that we didn't make it into the coveted club of adulthood, whatever that may be.

We waited on a bench swing that was set up in the garden section of the store. I started to doze off. Charlie scooted up close to me and I put my head on her shoulder. She held my hand and squeezed it.

Old Friends, New Pressures

Growing up in Fresno, everyone always talks about leaving. It's a shit town, everyone reasons, with no authentic character and no artistic sensibilities. While that may be true, what we didn't know the entire time we lived there, was just how awesome the city is. Maybe it's only true of Fresno, or maybe it's because if you scratch the surface of any city, you find shit. We didn't know about how diverse it is in cultures. We didn't know how great the food was. We didn't know what a wonder it was to be so close to the ocean, so close to the mountains, and so close to the big, cosmopolitan cities. Most of all, we didn't know how extraordinarily big Fresno was.

When I moved to Fresno at the age of six, the city had around 300,000 people living in it. In the 15 years I lived there, it had grown to half a million. And we still felt stifled, like we were in the ass-end of nowhere.

Between Minneapolis and Seattle, there are no cities with a population greater than 50,000. That's a 10th of Fresno's size. We really and truly learned what an enormous city we grew up in during those last days. We had crossed the point during the last few days that is the farthest you can ever be from a McDonald's in the lower 48 states[34]. We learned that there was no reason to

---

[34] Depressingly, it is 107 miles from a McD's as the crow flies. That's as far as you can get. What the hell makes them so successful?

complain about where we were, that we could have made it into whatever we wanted it to be.

There was a mass exodus from Fresno among my friends at about the time that Charlie and I got married. About a dozen people that I knew all up and decided to move to Portland, Oregon. They didn't have any particular job prospects, no roots in the place, just a little experience as visitors and that was all. But they linked arms like army ants deep within the mighty bivouac and moved to Portland.

We got into Portland late at night and found my friend Justus' house unlocked. He and his wife, Amelia, were out for the night with some important people, but they welcomed our presence even in their absence. We helped ourselves in and before thirty minutes were up, Charlie was asleep on the futon in our designated guest room. I stayed up and sat on Justus' couch, drinking a glass of water and reading the last book that I had brought on the trip. When Justus and Amelia got home, Amelia disappeared into her bedroom and Justus and I went into the backyard where he smoked a thousand or so cigarettes.

"You guys should move here, you know?"

I nodded.

"You can work part time at the college where I work. It's not too far from here."

I nodded.

"You know that Amanda and her boyfriend are coming into town tomorrow? They're looking for an apartment. Hell, if Ryan moves up here, there will be no one left in Fresno."

"We're not moving to Fresno."

"I know. But that place has a way of sucking you back."

It is probably true of most people's hometowns that they become somewhat of a vacuum once left. The black hole effect had brought countless people back to Fresno's waiting arms. It was long theorized by Fresnan youth that the only effective way of actually leaving the place was to move with a bunch of people and set up a Fresno-Minor of sorts in some other town. I had done it with many others when I moved to San Diego out of high school. But one by one, we had failed. One by one, we had been brought back. But this Portland project of theirs had potential.

"I don't know, man. I just have a feeling, you know?"

"Suit yourself," Justus said.

We sat outside and caught up. Under the stars, with a smattering of lightning bugs, and the sound of crickets, we talked like we used to back home. And as far as I can remember, that's the last time I ever saw him.

Charlie and I looked for a place for breakfast. We had heard from our friends that Portland was the greatest breakfast place known to man. We discovered that to be true, without the slightest sense of sarcasm, when we stopped in at a diner and found a certain menu item.

"French toast cinnamon rolls?" Charlie started in disbelief. "That can't be what it says it is."

"Oh yeah," the waitress said. "We take our homemade cinnamon rolls, dip them in egg and cream, and fry them up."

"Powdered sugar?"

"Powdered sugar, butter, syrup, the whole thing."

It had been a trip full of eating, so what was one more meal? Memorable, is what it was. That French toast cinnamon roll was a device powerful enough to stop time. Each and every bite hung in the cosmos for what seemed like forever. The quiet chewing was best done with your eyes closed. There was nothing to talk about, as we were sharing an experience of extraordinary proportions. When our plates were at last cleaned, we put our forks down and smiled at each other.

French. Toast. Cinnamon. Rolls.

I granted a short and heartfelt era of peace between me and the French. They had done good. Very good.

When I went up to pay my bill, I handed my card and the receipt to a guy who looked more like a hippy than a cashier.

"French toast cinnamon rolls, huh?"

I smiled.

"Those are the shit, aren't they?"

"Yeah," I said. "They are, indeed, the shit."

My first card was declined. My second was declined. Charlie still had one that worked.

The Last Chapter

South was the last direction of our trip; a direction we had not used in any significant way so far. We would head straight south down I-5 into the depths of California. We would pass through mountains and cities and into and out of the lives of a thousand other people for a brief instant. Outside of Lake Almanor, we saw over 100 deer one night. We drove at 20 miles an hour, hoping not to hit one. In a Hometown Buffet near Sacramento, we heard a boy regaling his family with how much fun he was having on their summer vacation. "The ocean, the movies, all you can eat, how much more fun can you have? How much money do we have, anyway?"

If it seems like I'm rushing to an ending, I assure you that I am not. All that was left on the road was hiding from the future. It was like that time, Sunday afternoon, when you know that the weekend is going to end. All you can do is wish the next day away, but it doesn't leave. It looms over you, all the more powerful the more you wish it away until it eventually dominates the horizon and bleeds into the Sunday, tainting everything.

The sun was going down when we rolled off of Highway 99 and onto Herndon Avenue in Fresno. Fresno's warm and dry summer night was in full swing; warm and comfortable. The billboards were the same that were hanging when we left five weeks before. The radio station was playing the same Kenny Chesney song. The gas prices were only three cents higher.

"Good to be home," I said with indifference. "Long trip."

Charlotte nodded her head. And then there were tears in her eyes. "This is stupid," Charlie said. "Let's just keep going."

"Keep going?"

"Keep going. Don't let it end. Don't ever let it end. Let's never settle down. Let's never be in one place for more than we can stand. Let's burn it all down behind us and move on, every single day."

About the Author:

Sol Smith is author of eight published novels, in all. Some of them might interest you and some of them likely won't. When not writing—which is most of the time, if we're perfectly honest with each other—and we should be because, look where we are—he is often found at work, where he teaches writing and life lessons to college students. When he's not there and not writing—which, again, is a significant portion of the time—he's at home with his wife and four daughters. It is worth noting that since the writing of this book, the author and his wife have crossed the country a good 20 times more by car, mostly with kids and dogs and a cat inside that car.

www.ingramcontent.com/pod-product-compliance
Lightning Source LLC
Chambersburg PA
CBHW031818110426
42743CB00057B/632